Tensions and Triumphs in the Early Years of Teaching

Tensions and Triumphs in the Early Years of Teaching

Real-World Findings and Advice for Supporting New Teachers

Susi Long
University of South Carolina

Ami Abramson
Brennen Elementary School, Columbia, South Carolina

April Boone
Frances Mack Primary School, Gaston, South Carolina

Carly Borchelt
Red Oak Elementary School, Stockbridge, Georgia

Robbie Kalish
Shandon United Methodist Preschool, Columbia, South Carolina

Erin Miller
University of South Carolina and Horrell Hill Elementary School, Columbia, South Carolina

Julie Parks
Lonnie B. Nelson Elementary School, Columbia, South Carolina

Carmen Tisdale
Parkside Elementary School, Fredericksburg, Virginia

National Council of Teachers of English
1111 W. Kenyon Road, Urbana, Illinois 61801-1096

Staff Editor: Bonny Graham

Interior Design: Doug Burnett

Cover Design: Pat Mayer

NCTE Stock Number: 02909

It is the policy of NCTE in its journals and other publications to provide a forum for the open discussion of ideas concerning the content and the teaching of English and the language arts. Publicity accorded to any particular point of view does not imply endorsement by the Executive Committee, the Board of Directors, or the membership at large, except in announcements of policy, where such endorsement is clearly specified.

Every effort has been made to provide current URLs and email addresses, but because of the rapidly changing nature of the Web, some sites and addresses may no longer be accessible.

Library of Congress Cataloging-in-Publication Data

Tensions and triumphs in the early years of teaching: real-world findings and advice for supporting new teachers / Susi Long . . . [et al].
      p. cm.
   Includes bibliographical references.
   ISBN-13: 978-0-8141-0290-9 ((pbk))
   1. First year teachers—United States—Case studies. 2. Elementary school teachers—United States—Case studies. 3. Elementary school teaching—United States—Case studies. I. Long, Susi, 1952–   II. National Council of Teachers of English.
   LB2844.1.N4T46 2006
   371.1—dc22

                                                                2006024660

To our families with love and gratitude.

Contents

Acknowledgments ix

Introduction xi

1. That September Evening 1

2. Becoming Us: Eight Teacher-Researchers 19

3. The Teachers We Hoped We Would Be 36

4. We Were Going to Be Teachers *for Real* 57

5. Living Up to a Vision: The Being Perfect Disease 87

6. Administrators and Colleagues, We Need You 120

7. Being Political: New Teachers, You *Do* Have a Voice 159

8. How Can You Help? 188

9. Our Visions Today 229

Epilogue 245

A Selection of Books That Help Us Understand More About . . . 247

References 249

Acknowledgments

In Appreciation

Eight educators involved in a seven-year study and writing a book owe a huge debt of gratitude to many people. Even when our family, friends, and colleagues wondered if this book would ever become a reality, they understood the importance of the experience to us. We are grateful for the use of their homes and schools as places to meet; for their lovingly critical eyes, ideas, and inspiration; and for their patience and faith.

We can never adequately thank the many teachers and administrators in universities and public schools who took so much time from their busy lives to read entire drafts of our manuscript and provide feedback that helped us think in new ways about ideas and issues, commas and semicolons—Ginnie Abramson, Jennifer Boone, Shaela Brittingham, Floyd Dinkins, Amy Donnelly, Curt Dudley-Marling, Sandra Euster, Belinda Flohr, Brooke Fonder, Donna Goodwin, Marilyn Johnston-Parsons, Morgan Jones, Kendrick Kerr, Melissa Klosterman, Jan Long, Heidi Mills, Lyn Mueller, Sonia Nieto, Tim O'Keefe, Bob Shannon, Franki Sibberson, Irma VanScoy, Susan Till, Julie Waugh, David and Phyllis Whitin, and Cheri Williams. We send very special thanks to Sonia Nieto and Curt Dudley-Marling, whose reading of our manuscripts pushed us in ways that significantly transformed our thinking and our text. We are particularly grateful to Heidi Mills, who spent untold hours helping us work through important issues and ideas right up to the last iteration of the final draft. Kurt Austin, senior editor at NCTE, thank you for believing that we had something worthwhile to say. And to Bonny Graham, a remarkable copyeditor—thank you for expertly (and gently) smoothing the rough edges.

Hearty thank yous to David and Phyllis Whitin, Julie Waugh, and Dinah Volk, who came to almost every one of our presentations. Long before we began to write, you made us feel that our work had value. Your friendly faces in the audience meant more than you know. To Carol Flake, Teri Kuhs, and Ed Dickey at the University of South Carolina and to our local parent teacher organizations and school districts, thank you for making funding possible that allowed us to share our work at national professional conferences. Warm thanks to Donna Bell and Donna Jarvis, kindergarten teachers extraordinaire; thank you for rooting for us from our internship days through these seven years.

We are endlessly grateful to friends and family who provided places of peaceful respite where we could focus on our work. Susan and John Till, your beautiful beach house allowed us to enjoy the perfect mix of work, play, and relaxation. Who can beat authors' circles at the surf's edge? The Spruill family home at Murrell's Inlet gave us a place to think and write *and* enjoy great seafood and peaceful nights. David and Katherine Kalish, how lucky we were to spend time in your spacious mountain home. Our weekend there gave the nature lovers among us the tranquility we love, while those new to the mountain experience learned to skip stones across the Nantahala River and brave the possibility of snakes and bears.

We have all depended on the love and generosity of our extended families, whose pride in our work boosted our spirits as they supported us in many ways: Susan and John Till, Shannon and Chad Poteat, John and Kristi Till, Ashley Till; Duvy and Jody Spruill; Ginnie, Ben, Brian, and Ian Abramson; Edwin and Beverly Free; Deryl Williams; Kathy and Ray Borchelt; Charlie and Jannie Ervin; Darlene Schneider; and Bob Shannon. A special thanks to Robbie's mom, Jody, who helped us hunt down references and for financing aspects of this journey that we probably don't even know about. And, of course, to Susi's husband, Jan, who shared their home with eight women on a mission week after week—thank you for cooking for us, cleaning up after us, smiling at our silliness, and loving your wife so much that you always welcomed us.

Most of all, we thank our loving husbands and children: Terry and Abby; Jeff, Jessica, Joanna, and Jacob; Taylor; Jan and Kelli; Page and Josie; Kenneth; Dutton, Ella, Livie, and Max; Nathan, Karis, and Caleb. We cannot begin to count the ways that you provided us with the time, energy, and inspiration to push forward. You believed in us, even when we almost lost faith (again and again).

Finally, to colleagues and administrators who always went the extra mile to make us feel supported and welcomed in our schools and districts during our early years of teaching, thank *you*. You did, indeed, make a difference in the lives of new teachers.

Introduction

Susi Long

> It was Monday or Tuesday that I left for work feeling so apathetic. It was one of those beautiful fall mornings. I wanted to be excited about where I was going and what I was doing, but I wasn't. I didn't dread going to work; I simply wasn't excited or enthusiastic. How sad. I've wanted to teach since I was a little girl. Not because it was an appropriate thing for a little girl to grow up and do, not because I wanted a job compatible with raising a family, and certainly not because it was "easy" or "nondemanding." I described my desire to teach in my essays for job interviews as a passion. Until this year, it was a passion. Now, it's not.

These are the words of a first-year teacher. She is one of seven teachers who tell their stories in this book. Ami, April, Carly, Carmen, Erin, Julie, and Robbie graduated with master's degrees from an initial certification program.[1] Excited and full of energy, they set out to look for teaching jobs. They shared specific beliefs about teaching and learning, and a real vigor for bringing those beliefs to life. They were knowledgeable, confident, and had an overwhelming desire to make a difference in the lives of children and in the field of education. Knowing that university study was just the beginning of their education, they looked forward to learning from and with passionate colleagues and administrators. At the same time, they were aware of a pedagogical status quo in public schools that was increasingly defined by fears related to high-stakes testing. They worried about the narrowing of curricula as more and more schools addressed testing pressures by focusing on discrete skills, often at the expense of in-depth, intellectual explorations of ideas. Having experienced opportunities to learn through inquiry-based collaboration with other learners and having observed public school settings that valued the same depth of teaching and learning, they felt strongly about bringing those kinds of experiences into their own classrooms. They believed it could happen. They were positive and hopeful.

Then realities hit. While most of them were encouraged by their first days in the classroom, it didn't take long for them to encounter barriers as they worked to bring visions of great teaching to life. For some, the challenges seemed almost insurmountable. After only weeks in the classroom, excitement, confidence, energy, and enthusiasm were replaced by self-doubt, feelings of isolation, and disappointment. They said things like: "I had such hopes and dreams for how my classroom would be. It seems so far from that"; "There is too much to even write about. The problems run so deep that no matter what I do, I can never seem to get to the heart of it"; and "I felt horrible all day long. I came home and cried harder and longer than I have all year." Some of them were so disillusioned they began to question their own competence: "What if I just don't have what it takes?"; "My biggest fear is that I'm not talented enough to pull this teaching thing off." Most disturbing was the deep disappointment experienced by some as they felt the heart and soul of the teachers they hoped to be slipping away. One new teacher wrote, "I'm losing a sense of who I am. I don't even know the person who graduated less than a year ago. If I leave now, maybe I can find her again. If I don't leave, I think I'll soon be unrecognizable to us all."

What happened to these amazing young teachers? Why did some lose their self-confidence and passion for teaching so quickly? Why did they begin to second-guess their knowledge and convictions? Was it merely inexperience? Did they simply need to mature as teachers? Or were there other barriers that made teaching so difficult? For those who did not experience such disappointment, what made the difference?

This book draws from data collected over seven years—retrospective data from the preservice year and data collected during their first six years in the classroom—as these teachers negotiated their way in the teaching profession. The intent of the study was to better understand barriers and support in the early years of teaching: What challenges cause new teachers to question their ability to teach and their desire to remain in the profession? What kind of support sustains and exhilarates them? As a university instructor in their graduate program, I initiated the study, but, as described in Chapter 2, we soon became collaborators in a joint endeavor. By the end of the first year, the work was no longer defined as professor-studying-teachers; we were full partners in the study. As co-researchers, we made research decisions and collected, organized, analyzed, and wrote about data together. Our collaboration meant that parallels to my experiences also became a part of the data. And it meant that we became co-authors as dreams of this book became a reality.

The findings shared in this book build from the preservice days, the job hunt, and the first days of teaching, through the next six years. We share stories of success, but we also illuminate tensions and challenges. We describe struggles, not to dwell on the negative but to address a national dilemma—the fact that we lose almost a third of all new teachers within the first year of teaching and almost half of them by the end of their fifth year (Ingersoll, 2002). Through our analysis of seven years of data, we offer insights about conditions that drive new teachers out of the profession or that allow them to slip toward the very status quo they set out to change. We hope that our work provides a foundation for asking hard questions about the responsibility of every educator to prevent struggles and to provide support as new teachers work to bring visions of great teaching to life.

This Book: What You Will Find as You Read

Before completing the final manuscript of this book, we sent drafts to twenty-seven outside readers representing a range of educators—preservice teachers, new and experienced teachers, school and district administrators, and university faculty. We discussed their responses at length and used them to deepen our analyses of data. Responses from outside readers also helped us address interests and concerns from the broad audience we hoped to reach. University faculty, for example, often looked for our ability to build strong arguments based on solid analyses of data that included anomalies as well as consistencies. Classroom teachers affirmed our conviction that stories from our personal lives, while not typically found in professional books, were integral to our teaching stories. They wanted to know us as human beings who bring personal histories and family realities to our work as teachers. They helped us see that many of the challenges new teachers face are not unlike those that experienced teachers face every day. Administrators helped us see that there are many sides to every story, which led to deeper convictions about the importance of working together to promote open conversations that encourage real communication. Teacher-researchers pointed out that descriptions of methodology—how we planned and carried out our study—help others see possibilities for collecting and analyzing data in their own work. And new teachers urged us to validate their concerns and frustrations, but also to provide suggestions they could use in negotiating their own early years of teaching.

Feedback also helped us see that the book can be read in different ways. As one reader said, "it can be read from front to back or a chapter as needed." While that is true, the text is, at its heart, the story of eight educators seeking to understand what happens to new teachers. As such, we think readers will have a greater appreciation for and understanding of important issues and implications if the text is read as the story unfolds. Groundwork is laid in the early chapters that brings deeper meaning to stories told later in the book.

Chapter 1, "That September Evening," opens as our group met at Erin's house in September of their first year of teaching. The chapter describes the excitement with which we came together and the rapid deterioration of the façade that all was well—the exposure of realities behind the happy talk. We use the events of the evening to introduce issues explored in detail throughout the rest of the book. The chapter moves from the collective voice of the seven teachers to my voice, explaining how and why I initiated the study, and then into autobiographical narratives that allow each of us to shake hands with readers—to share who we are, how we became teachers, and what led us to this project.

Chapter 2, "Becoming Us: Eight Teacher Researchers," describes the evolution of our group from our first days together through the last days of writing the manuscript that became this book—how we grew as researchers, writers, and friends through the process of collecting, analyzing, and writing about data. It is an important process to follow. To appreciate the impact of issues described in later chapters, it is helpful to know what we did to capture and understand early teaching experiences. This chapter communicates the depth, breadth, and rigor of our research while helping readers see possibilities for examining teaching and learning in their own contexts.

Chapter 3, "The Teachers We Hoped We Would Be," uses stories from the preservice year to describe these teachers' beliefs as they left the university. To appreciate the triumphs as well as tensions expressed later in the book, it is important to know the beliefs they held entering the profession. This chapter also provides a basis from which implications for university preservice experiences are considered in Chapter 8, as well as a foundation for drawing comparisons and contrasts to convictions expressed seven years later, described in Chapter 9.

Chapter 4, "We Were Going to Be Teachers *for Real*," moves from the end of the preservice year into the job hunt and the first weeks of school. Ideas embedded throughout the chapter will be helpful for new and prospective teachers as they look for jobs, set up classrooms, and meet their students for the first time. In this chapter, triumphs are shared, but the first tensions also begin to appear as new teachers work to put their beliefs into practice.

Chapter 5, "Living Up to a Vision: The Being Perfect Disease," is an exploration of issues faced as these teachers tried to live up to their visions of great teaching. They share stories that illuminate their disappointment in slipping toward the status quo, what happens when visions and mandates collide, frustrations in trying to pin down and implement ideas from graduate school, their love-hate relationship with professional books, the struggle to engage every child, the sense of being overwhelmed with *stuff* that teachers have to do every day, and the challenges of trying to juggle work and life.

Chapter 6, "Administrators and Colleagues, We Need You," focuses on the critical roles of administrators and colleagues in the lives of new teachers. The stories in the first half of this chapter describe ways that administrators can set the tone for schools that foster collaboration, joy in teaching, and professional growth, or, conversely, how their actions can contribute to teachers' loss of confidence, passion, and delight in the profession. In the second half of the chapter, we discuss collegial relationships, mentors, and induction programs. Stories from our data contrast the feeling of being alone in a school to that of being in the company of kind, supportive colleagues who are fellow learners.

Chapter 7, "Being Political: New Teachers, You *Do* Have a Voice," shares ways in which these teachers effected change even when they felt the least successful. We wrote this chapter to show how easy it is for new teachers to overlook the strong and wonderful things they do—the actions they take that make a difference in their own lives, in the lives of children, and in the profession at large. We raise questions about how institutional policies, high-stakes testing in particular, are often at the core of barriers that new teachers may perceive as merely personal challenges.

Chapter 8, "How Can You Help?," is divided into separate sections, each speaking directly to specific educational stakeholders: administrators, directors of induction and mentorship programs, colleagues of new teachers, university faculty and internship coordinators, job seekers, and new teachers. The chapter provides suggestions in answer to the question: What might every educator, including the new teacher, do to support the energy, fragility, knowledge, and drive that new teachers bring to the profession?

Chapter 9, "Our Visions Today," returns to individual narratives to ask: Where are we now? What are our current beliefs? What triumphs and tensions do we experience today, seven years after graduation from our teaching certification program? What questions remain? Although this chapter ends the book, it does not provide "I've-come-full-circle" stories or happy endings in a traditional sense. We describe convictions and beliefs that are stronger than ever, but also challenges that remain.

Voice

This book is written as one voice, reflecting our mutual passion for examining every issue. The text shifts from *we* to *I* and back again as we move between collectively written narratives and quotes from data. This allows us to honor our individual voices and experiences while co-authoring every paragraph. No chapter is written by any one group member. As in any group, however, some of us are heard more through our actions than our words. That is why, at times, you may see more representations of one group member than another.

Our writing style is to draw heavily on data quotes—our own words from reflective journals, email messages, and transcribed conversations—to illustrate points we hope to make and to enrich explanations of issues and ideas. In many places, data quotes *are* the explanations. Because many of our quotes provide analytical commentary, more of them are embedded in the text than would be the case when strictly following style guides.

When we share the words of a group member, we usually name that person. Sometimes we do not. When speakers are not named, it is because we want to give voice to a critical issue while recognizing the importance of protecting ourselves and others. Pseudonyms are used for all children except our own offspring. To honor colleagues, principals, and university faculty who have supported and inspired us, we use their real names.

Subheadings in this book are usually quotes drawn from data chosen to guide the reader through the text by reflecting key ideas we hope to convey. When a quote is used as a subheading, it is usually found again embedded in that section of the text and attributed to the speaker. Quotes are printed verbatim except where excessive repetition of words and phrases does not further the meaning of the message and where simplification of grammatical structures allows a smoother translation from spoken to written genre.

Perspective

In this book, we share eight perspectives on issues and events in the early years of teaching. Others may interpret the same events differently, but the point of this text is to provide an opportunity for educators to read "this-is-how-it-feels-in-the-moment" stories that are sometimes difficult for new teachers to share and therefore go unheard. It is a perspective often dismissed as others sometimes focus on new teachers' inexperience rather than the serious nature of the issues they bring to the conversation. Reading about events and issues described as they occurred, however, we gain insights into possible reasons why so many leave the profession or compromise their vision to such an extent that they lose passion for teaching. While the teachers in this book don't profess to speak for all new teachers, we predict that their stories will resonate with many.

Shouting from the Rooftops

The teachers who share their stories in this book demonstrate that it was far more than inexperience that created barriers to living the teaching lives they envisioned. They began their careers wanting to make a difference in the lives of children. They realize now that an important part of that process is working to make a difference in the profession at large. Presenting issues they faced, they hope to prompt others to take action. They want people to *do* something. As the facilitator of the study in which these teachers and I collaborated, I join their voices. This book is, as Carly put it, our way of "shouting from the rooftops." Working with them and paying attention to other stories locally and nationally, it is easy to see the need to shout.

In many situations, barriers exist that push the knowledge, drive, and excitement of new teachers far underground. Their struggles continue while too little is done to change school and district cultures, university structures, and mentorship and induction programs so that new teachers are embraced and nurtured in lasting ways. Rather than sustain and build on the energy that new teachers bring, we lose many to mediocrity or to other professions. It is time to look carefully and honestly at their experiences and put real solutions into place. For these reasons, we write teacher-to-teacher, but also teacher-to-administrator, university professor, and experienced colleague. We hope that our stories will encourage you to look beyond the rhetoric that too often dominates programs and practices to create environments that truly welcome and care for the energy and innovation as well as the inexperience and self-consciousness that new teachers bring. We invite you to read, consider, and go out and make a difference for every new teacher who leaves your university, enters your school district, walks across the threshold of your school, or moves into the classroom next door. New teachers, we hope our stories will give courage and provide hope. We write to tell you that you do indeed have a voice and you can use it to work with colleagues and administrators to contribute to education as a profession that consistently and reflectively moves forward. Most important, we write to let you know that you are not alone.

Note

1. At that time, the teaching certification degree available from their university was a Master of Arts in Teaching (MAT), a fifteen-month program designed for students who held bachelor's degrees in other fields, sometimes with an education minor. Since then, an undergraduate certification program (BA) has been implemented in addition to the MAT.

1 That September Evening

We still wanted to be exuberant clones of teachers in professional books and in classrooms we visited. To us, those classrooms represented the ideal. But many of us felt we were not living up to those ideals and we could not figure out why it was so hard.

Seven New Teachers Begin the Story

Figure 1.1. Toasting the first days of teaching. Our smiles don't tell the whole story. (Two teachers in this photo were not able to continue with the group, Carmen had not yet joined us, and Susi is taking the photo.)

It is difficult to remember exactly how we felt that September evening when we met as a group of brand new teachers (Figure 1.1). We look back and try to remember details—how hot or cool it was or what we ate and drank—but those details do not come easily to mind. We were at Erin's house. Photographs remind us that Susi brought champagne to toast our first weeks in the classroom. The rest of us brought potluck dishes. It seems strange that, for an evening that became so important in our lives, we cannot remember more details. Maybe that's because it was much more than a meeting or a gathering of friends. We had grown to know and care for one another through our preservice teacher education program. We had developed a special bond through experiences within and beyond the university classroom: an inquiry project about Gullah culture on St. Helena Island, driving a university van from South

Carolina to The Ohio State University's Children's Literature Conference, a holiday party at Robbie's house, all-night authors' circles at Julie's house, and completing our comprehensive exams. Since graduation, we had been meeting all summer to discuss the job search and the excitement of setting up our first classrooms. But this evening was different. It was the first meeting after the school year started. And it was the first time that we truly let our vulnerabilities show. The photograph of our champagne toast reveals only the surface. Soon after the photo was taken, façades began to crumble and raw emotions surfaced. The struggle to live up to the teaching lives we envisioned was already more difficult than we had expected. Tears, anger, and disappointment began to break through the pretense that all was well.

We left our graduate program with such high hopes.

At that point, we still wanted to be what Carly called "exuberant clones" of teachers in the professional books we read and the classrooms we visited during the Master of Arts in Teaching (MAT) program. To us, those classrooms represented the ideal. Vivid descriptions of fabulously organized, smoothly running centers of learning left an enormous impact. We wanted to emulate the teachers who created those classrooms. Our convictions were strong. We believed that the pursuit of meaningful inquiry and engagement in purposeful interaction were foundational to learning. We knew that instruction should be informed by getting to know children in many different ways. We were insulted by scripted programs that tell teachers what to say and do, and believed that skills taught in isolation contributed little to children's learning. Our classrooms would not be driven by worksheets and basal reading programs. We understood literacy learning as a strategic, meaning-making process that is supported when children have opportunities to learn about reading and writing by using it for real purposes. But many of us felt that we were not living up to those ideals, and we could not figure out why it was so hard. We had left our graduate program with such high hopes. For some of us, it felt like we were already failing miserably. Unexpectedly, that September evening became the moment when we first took risks to voice our disappointments and fears.

I never imagined it would be this way.

The night began with food and some "I love my class" kinds of sharing—happy talk. Then Erin began to talk about the teaching situation in which she found herself. Her school rigidly mandated a scripted reading program that told teachers what to do and say while emphasizing "worksheet after worksheet" used to teach skills in isolation. From our graduate school experiences, we knew enough to be on the lookout for mandates that were merely myths—"*They* say you have to"—but these directives seemed very real. Feeling that she could not use her "hard-earned knowledge" about teaching and learning, and terrified at what she was beginning to see in herself, Erin said, "I'm at the point where I understand why my elementary school teachers were always so mean. I feel like I'm turning into that kind of a person. I hate what I have to teach, and the kids hate it. And that doesn't make me like what I do as a teacher. I never imagined it would be this way." She continued:

> Yesterday, the second-grade teachers planned. You would cry if you saw my lesson plan book. From 9:00 to 9:30, I literally have to read word-by-word instructions from a phonics card. That includes dictating meaningless sentences and meaningless vowel sounds that my students have to write. I was told that, no matter what, I should not finish phonics early. Teachers even gave me hints on how to drag out phonics because the principal would be in my room to be sure I was implementing it just that way.

We were all shocked at the absence of autonomy Erin experienced and saddened by the disillusionment she felt (Figure 1.2). Her honest articulation of deep disappointment opened the door for others to share difficult experiences. Although April's teaching was not governed by strict mandates, she described the sense of aloneness that comes with teaching differently from colleagues. Like many of us, she felt isolated by her beliefs and practices:

Figure 1.2. Our faces reflect the shock and sadness we felt as Erin told us about her teaching situation.

All of the other kindergarten teachers do letter-of-the-week. I'm proud that I'm holding my own and teaching letters and sounds in more meaningful ways, but I really feel like a loner. Sometimes I lose confidence and worry that, if everyone else is teaching one letter a week, then my children might be missing out. I do my own thing, but I'm not as bold as some to step out and share my ideas.

We passed the tape recorder around the living room, establishing a habit we continued for the next six years—recording our monthly meetings. Transcripts of those conversations, along with weekly email reflections that we posted on our group's listserv, became the heart of our study, the data we eventually analyzed to better understand the early years of teaching. As Julie held the tape recorder that night, she began to talk about how discouraged she felt trying to find a balance between home and school. Describing her attempts to be a good mother to her two-year-old while creating the classroom she envisioned, she said, "How am I going to balance all of this? I'm responsible for educating kids at school, but then I've got my own child who misses me. I don't want to miss out on her life, so sometimes I give worksheets to my students 'cause I can't find the time to plan in other ways. But I feel so guilty for doing that or for using the textbook." She continued in tears:

> It has been overwhelming trying to figure everything out, just sorting out all the paper they've given me. I can only deal with so much at a time, so the kids just might get some worksheets. I want to be doing other things, but it's probably gonna take a year or two to get where I'd like to be. I can't do anything more.

An atmosphere of unhappiness and guilt began to grow as those of us who were also experiencing rocky beginnings took risks to share what was *really* happening in our classrooms. Even those who experienced less despair were concerned that they were falling into the habit of using worksheets, textbooks, and "basals with boring stories" just a little too easily. We look back now and recognize the courage and trust it took to admit our fears and disappointment. Erin, having landed in a school with a very different perspective on learning and teaching from the one with which she left the preservice program, said, "I would have fainted before I would have let anyone see my classroom in the state it was in with phonics cards adorning the wall." Robbie and Carly, although their school was more welcoming of diverse practices, also felt tensions. On their way to the meeting that evening, they had discussed whether they felt comfortable admitting to what they called their failures: "Should we tell them we use the textbook? Do we admit to this?"

Sharing the admission that we were not the teachers we hoped to be was particularly difficult because Susi was there. She had been our instructor in several courses. She had supervised some of us during our internships. It was hard to tell her that we weren't always teaching according to the beliefs we'd developed in the MAT program. We didn't want to let her down. We had a vision of the *perfect teacher* and that's what we wanted to be—for Susi, for the MAT program, and for our students.

The talk that Erin initiated was difficult, but it led to a real sense of relief when we realized that, with this group, it was safe to risk exposure. Later, Carly wrote:

> At the beginning of the meeting, I was too ashamed to admit that I'd been using worksheets. It was like the 8th deadly sin. When everyone finally broke down and began confessing that their worst nightmares were coming true, I confessed too to using the dreaded worksheets. Finding out that I was not the only one was like having the Pope forgive my vilest sins.

That evening we did have happy moments to share, but, as Ami said, "no one wanted to flaunt good situations in light of friends' pain." In spite of their worksheet and textbook disappointments, for example, Robbie and Carly "couldn't wait to share the exciting things that were happening." Ami and April also had positive stories to tell. Later, Robbie wrote, "We felt really bad sharing any of the good stuff because it was so difficult for everyone else," and Carly said, "I resisted telling more about my successes because I felt it was more important for the others to find some peace in their fears."

It didn't take long, however, to see that everyone was facing a challenge of one kind or another and needed a place to voice frustration and disappointment. Some of us were frustrated with the worksheet-driven, textbook-oriented curricula that dominated our schools. Others had quickly become disillusioned trying to be perfect at everything at once. All of us longed for colleagues who embraced the kind of pedagogy we were eager to make our own. Some had even experienced ridicule from colleagues about teaching ideas. A few of us felt wronged by the MAT program: How could they have led us to believe it would be so easy? Teaching was not what we expected it to be.

Most demoralizing was the feeling that we were not living up to our own expectations. Erin voiced a frightening possibility that, for her, felt very real: "When you leave a university excited about changing the world through education and find yourself in a school that hates the very meaning of change, it becomes easier and easier to give in to the pressure to conform to what is going on around you. Before you know it, the person you once were, full of hope and energy, slowly disappears." Susi had seen this kind of disappointment and disillusionment before. It is what had led her to initiate our research group just four months earlier.

Susi's Turn

> I heard comments from our graduates like, "I find myself becoming just like the boring, old-fashioned teachers I said I would never be."

When I came to the University of South Carolina as a beginning professor, it was immediately clear to me that many students graduated with master's degrees from the initial certification program with an impressive foundation for a career in education. They had a strong theoretical and practical knowledge base, confidence, and a desire to make a difference. Visiting local schools, however, I found little evidence that their learning had become a part of school and district cultures. The Center for Inquiry (Mills & Donnelly, 2001) was a stunning exception, and there were pockets of innovation in schools here and there; but on the whole, graduates' energy and enthusiasm for new ideas seemed to disappear as they found themselves sucked into the world of high-stakes testing and programmatic mandates. I heard comments like, "I find myself becoming just like the boring, old-fashioned teachers I said I would never be"; "My new colleagues tell me, 'Forget what you learned in the MAT program. It's crap. It's not the real world'"; and "What happened to me? Somehow, the teacher I was going to be got buried when I started teaching."

Certainly, this suppression of innovation is not intentional on the part of administrators, university faculty, and experienced teachers in schools. Administrators and school district personnel are frantic given the challenges of high-stakes testing, competition for federal funding, and school report cards in a culture that "mistakes measuring schools for fixing them" (Darling-Hammond, 2004, p. 9). Experienced teachers struggle to find their way in the midst of mandates to implement programs that tell them what to do and when to do it, feeling the pressure to teach to the test when "a good school is one that either has very high test scores or is moving toward them at a prescribed rate of improvement" (Meier, 2004, p. 67). In a society of what Karp (2004) calls "counterfeit accountability" (p. 58), it is easy to see why administrators begin to believe the rhetoric of publishing companies who promise high test scores and why teachers succumb to the same kinds of pressures. For university faculty, opportunities to focus on sustainable support of graduates are rare. Professional collaboration between universities and schools is something that gets crammed into already overloaded schedules in both institutions.

This problem is not exclusive to South Carolina, nor is it a recent phenomenon. It is a pattern repeated across the country as many new teachers abandon ideas from their preservice programs and draw instead from the local status quo or from memories of their own public school experiences (Hayes, 1998). Instead of infusing the profession with new ideas and energy while learning from the wisdom of experienced teachers, a frightening number of new teachers conform or leave the profession altogether. Almost a third of teachers in the United States leave the field sometime during their first three years, and nearly half leave after five years (Ingersoll, 2002). In low-income communities and rural areas, rates of attrition are even higher (National Commission on Teaching and America's Future, 2002). This attrition rate has been a point of concern and discussion for decades. New teachers "leave the profession in such numbers and so rapidly that newcomers do not stay around long enough to fill the vacancies for the long haul" (McCann, Johannessen, & Ricca, 2005, p. 3).

There are, of course, exceptions. Sonia Nieto (2003) writes that "when teachers are treated as professionals and intellectuals who care deeply about their students and their craft, they will be enticed to remain in the profession" (p. 128). We see this with the implementation of long-term professional study groups like those evolving from the work of Kathy Short and her colleagues in Tucson, Arizona (Birchak et al., 1998); the National Council of Teachers of English (NCTE) Reading Initiative (Smith & Hudelson, 2001); and in our state, the South Carolina Reading Initiative (Donnelly et al., 2005; Morgan et al., 2003). Teachers and administrators developing intellectual professional communities are also described in the work of small schools such as the Central Park East Schools in New York (Meier, 1995), the Mission Hill School in Boston (Meier, 2002), and South Carolina's Center for Inquiry, where teachers nurture one another through regular curricular conversations (Mills et al., 2001). When these kinds of opportunities do not exist, new teachers can find themselves alone. The struggle to sustain their knowledge and continue to grow is enormous. Pressure to teach to the test becomes overwhelming and confusing as they try to justify their practices. Without recognizing subtle shifts in their practice, new teachers find their dreams of innovation beginning to slip away. Before they know it, they find themselves conforming to school norms that may or may not reflect the most recent understandings in the field.

While I suspected that these issues were at the root of new teachers' struggle to hold on to understandings from their preservice programs, I wanted to know more. What happens to them day to day? What are their stories moment to moment? What incidents, issues, and attitudes cause so many new teachers to struggle not only to hold on to their knowledge and convictions but also to deepen and expand their understandings? What barriers do they find to living the professional lives they envisioned? What support sustains them? How might universities, school systems, and local schools work together to create cultures that celebrate and nurture the energy, knowledge, and passion for learning and teaching that characterize many new graduates? These questions led me to ask my first cohort of preservice teachers if I could follow them through their first year of teaching. Eight students expressed interest and, two weeks after graduation, we began meeting regularly. Within a few months, for various reasons, two group members decided they could not continue, and another MAT graduate joined us. By January of the first year of teaching, we had become the group of eight—seven classroom teachers and a university professor—that continues today.

Teacher Research Is More Than Just Data: Getting to Know Eight Women

> Bound by common convictions about many things, we also represent diverse backgrounds and experiences.

From our first days in the MAT program, we watched one another grow and change. We have developed an even stronger affection and admiration for one another that allows us to share fears, failures, confusions, and successes with trust and gratitude. We support one another not only as teachers but also through joyous as well as difficult personal times. We care deeply about our stories and are committed to telling them.

Bound by common convictions about many things, we also represent diverse backgrounds and experiences. Our worldviews range from conservative to liberal and everything in between. We vary in our religious beliefs and cultural histories. We were raised in large and small families and come from a range of economic backgrounds. Some of us were born in South Carolina, but we also come from Florida, Georgia, and New York. These aspects of our lives—what we value, who we cherish, what worries us, what cheers us, what motivates us—are critical to telling our professional stories. They are embedded in our work as teachers and as researchers.

Because of our belief that teaching is much more than day-to-day life in classrooms and that research is more than methodology, we introduce ourselves through the following personal narratives. They lay a foundation for weaving connections to our personal lives throughout the book and provide a touchstone to which readers can return as our teaching stories unfold. And so we begin the story of our early years of teaching by introducing ourselves as teachers, yes, but also as daughters, mothers, wives, sisters, and friends.

Ami

I am a fourth-generation teacher. I grew up surrounded by fabulous teachers who gave me lots of hands-on experience in classrooms from a very early age. My great-grandma, grandmother, brother, and both my parents are teachers. My dad worked with children in special education programs in New York for thirty-four years. I grew up learning beside my mom, who implemented best practices before they were called best practices. My mom's classrooms were safe havens for children to love learning. She created learning communities that made all children feel important and loved. She always filled her classrooms with literature; I cannot count the books— thousands and thousands. She is a natural teacher and my greatest role model.

I was raised in Westchester, New York, just a few miles north of New York City. My family's house resembled a huge school. Our bedroom walls were painted with chalkboard paint, and my two brothers and I were given creative reign to paint, stencil, draw, and create. It was a hippie household with educational toys everywhere, many of which ultimately became treasures in my own classroom. My family spent summers traveling across the country. From my parents, I inherited a passion for exploring new places.

After high school, I ventured south to the University of South Carolina, where I completed undergraduate and graduate degrees. I began my teaching career in a first-grade classroom. The next year, I looped with my students to second grade. Then I piloted a multiage class of six-, seven-, and eight-year-olds. This was an exciting change. I loved the family atmosphere and endless possibilities for teaching and learning that the multiage classroom held.

I joined our research group after graduate school when Susi asked if she could follow us through our first year of teaching. At first I was excited to stay in touch with my friends. Within a few months, I couldn't imagine teaching without the support of such amazing people.

April

Ever since I can remember, I wanted to be a teacher. When I was in elementary school, I always asked my teachers for leftover copies of worksheets so I could take them home and play school with my friends. I even had one of those old one-piece student desks with the little cubby on the bottom. I always imagined myself as a teacher.

I began teaching and still teach kindergarten in a small, rural primary school. It was always my dream to teach kindergarten. Even now, I have no desire to teach at a different level. Kindergarten children keep me motivated and on my toes with their enthusiasm for learning, their curiosity, and the comments they make about anything and everything.

I grew up in West Columbia, South Carolina. My husband Terry and I met in high school and married after college. We are very involved in our church. We teach Sunday school and work as members of the youth staff, and I sing in the choir. We have a daughter, Abigail, who just turned two years old. She steals our hearts every day with her smiles, giggles, songs, and squeals.

I got involved in this research project when Susi invited us to participate at the end of the MAT program. She wanted to see what our first year of teaching would be like, how schools would accept and support us, and what impact we would have in our classrooms. It sounded like an exciting project and I wanted to be a part of it. I thought it would be a great way to stay in contact with a professor I loved and with other members of my cohort. I felt as though I would still be connected and not alone in the teaching world.

Carly

If someone had told me when I was a teenager that I'd be a schoolteacher in a few years, I would have laughed my socks off. I was never the type of girl who dreamed of being just like my favorite teacher or forced my dolls and friends to play school with me. In fact, I was a bit of a rebel as a student. Many of my teachers would probably faint to know that I am one of them.

My first taste of teaching began during my undergraduate years when a sociology professor involved me in reviving a volunteer program. I tutored middle school students and adults. Later, I stumbled on City Year, an Americorps-based community service organization. Through opportunities with them, I worked as a teaching assistant in first-grade classrooms. I would never have become a teacher if it had not been for my City Year experience. Through it I learned so much about myself and the world around me. Soon after, I made the decision to enter the MAT program at USC.

I began teaching in a fourth-grade classroom. Two years later, I worked for a year as a Title I reading teacher with fourth and fifth graders. When my daughter Karis and later my son Caleb were born, there was no question whether I would stay at home with them. With my children, I found a sense of peace I'd never experienced before. At the same time, I missed the intellectual stimulation of being in a school and found myself becoming a little too complacent about important educational issues. I guess I realized that completeness doesn't happen through one person or one part of your life. It has to be the sum of all of these parts. After three years at home, I made the decision to go back to teaching part time in a fourth-grade job share.

Seven years ago, when Susi asked if she could follow us into our first year of teaching, I jumped at the chance to join. I knew it would provide me with invaluable support in that first year. Little did I know that I would need our group for many years to come.

Carmen

When I think about what made me want to teach, I have to think about *who* made me want to teach. I believe that my strong compassion for children began as I watched my mother work with autistic children. She was phenomenal. When I think about the way my heart loves, I think about my mother. Over the years, I watched as she gave unconditional love to all children. She and other wonderful teachers in my life—Mrs. Loftis, Mr. Dean, Mrs. Roberts, Mr. McInnis, and Susi Long—made me want to teach and contribute to others' lives as they contributed to mine.

I did not initially go into education when I entered college. Although I desired to teach, I listened to the comments of others who said that teaching didn't pay enough and that children had become too difficult to handle. After stints in retail and banking, however, I knew that my purpose was not being fulfilled. I quit my job, took a leap of faith, and entered the MAT program. It was one of the best things I could have done.

My first teaching job was in second grade in the South Carolina town where I grew up. This meant a lot to me because I could teach the children of people I knew and be close to my family. My grandmother has eighteen children, so you can imagine what a blessing they are to me. We share a lot of laughter. I'm told we are a unique bunch.

I took a year off from teaching after my fifth year. The reason for my sabbatical was marriage to my wonderful and funny husband Kenneth and our move to California and then to Virginia. Now I've settled into teaching again, this time in third grade.

As for this group, I wasn't there that September night at Erin's house; I joined a few months later. Once I heard about the meetings and the listserv, I asked to be a part of the group. Now I feel even closer to them, close enough to share my insecurities and inhibitions. They give me affirmation and understanding.

Erin

I was raised to believe I could do anything in this world and that I should choose to do something I absolutely loved. I always knew I wanted to be a teacher. My parents continue to be very driven by their careers, my mother's in education and my father's in science. Work has simply always been a fulfilling part of our lives. I grew up outside of Orangeburg, South Carolina, on a family farm. The farm has grounded me my whole life. No matter where I am, I feel pulled back there. Both of my sisters, my brother, my parents, and I live within an hour of one another, and our lives are incredibly intertwined. Our family get-togethers at the farm help us all remember that home and family are the two things that matter most in life.

When I was in graduate school, the seed for lifelong learning about teaching was planted and continues to thrive. I love learning about pedagogy. My first teaching job was in a second-grade classroom. After four years, I became a Reading Recovery teacher and worked one-to-one with struggling first graders.

Since I began teaching, I have married and had three children. Ella, Livie, and Max helped me see the need for balance in my life. After teaching for six years, I reached the point where I questioned whether I could continue to teach passionately while parenting my young children. I ultimately decided to scale back from the demands of teaching full time. I now work as a liaison between the University of South Carolina and a local professional development school. I supervise student teachers and teach undergraduate courses in literacy.

I became involved with this project after being asked by Susi if she could follow us into our first year of teaching. I didn't want to lose touch with my classmates and with the knowledge I gained in the MAT program.

Julie

I am a wife, a mother, and a teacher. I married my best friend and we have three children. Although I am in a profession that could become an obsession, my family keeps me grounded. I didn't always plan on being a teacher even though I went to college with every intention of going into education. Growing up with a mother who was a teacher, I was exposed to the profession through her experiences in the classroom, as well as through her after-school tutoring. But if working with children was a first love, art was a close second. In college, with encouragement from my art professors, I went into graphic design and then worked for a design firm in New York. But deep inside I knew my desire to work with children was unfulfilled. I decided to change careers when I was twenty-nine years old and began course work in the MAT program.

My first teaching jobs were in second- and first-grade classrooms. After three years of teaching, I gave birth to twins and stayed at home for a year with Joanna and Jacob and our daughter Jessica, who was then four years old. I've now been back in the classroom for four years teaching kindergarten. I absolutely love it! I enjoy my students' eagerness and passion for learning.

I joined our research group because I wanted to be able to share my experiences with like minds. I felt that this would keep alive my enthusiasm for trying new teaching strategies. We had all been such good support for one another in the MAT program, and I hoped that would continue. I soon realized that the emotional support was just as important as the teaching support.

Robbie

I have been a teacher since the day my parents installed an old chalkboard in our garage. I decided at an early age that I wanted to teach, but before that, I wanted to be a brain surgeon, a mechanic, and a beautician. I owe the decision to teach to my fourth-grade teacher, Bonnie Iseman. She believed in me when others did not. I wanted to be that kind of teacher. I am fortunate, however, that my undergraduate school didn't have a program in education, because those four years allowed me to study anthropology, experiences that I use every day in my classroom.

Neither of my parents is a teacher, but they raised three daughters who are involved in education. I think that is a pretty amazing commentary on the way they raised us to be compassionate and giving. I began teaching in a fifth-grade classroom in a rural school outside of Atlanta. I moved back to South Carolina two years later when my husband Page entered law school. I took a job teaching third grade. Now we have a beautiful daughter, Josie. Just before she was born, I moved to teaching half days in a preschool program. I love being a mom more than anything in my life.

I joined this group as soon as it was suggested. Susi was going to study our transition from being student teachers to being teachers in our own classrooms. She wanted to see if our ideals, dreams, wishes, and fears changed in that first year. When we met that first time at Susi's house, I remember thinking, "This will be sort of fun, to be in a professional study and have Susi write an article about us."

Susi

My father was the most significant influence in my decision to become a teacher. Everyone who comes in contact with him goes away touched by his excitement for life and for, as he says, "the world of ideas." He always sees possibilities where other people see barriers. I grew up hearing my father talk about great educators—John Dewey, Herbert Kohl,

Sylvia Ashton-Warner, and A. S. Neil. Once he even wrote to apply for a job at Neil's school, Summerhill. Dad was a professor in a college of education for thirty years, a vibrant leader and an innovative educator.

I began teaching—and met my husband Jan—in 1974 in a wonderfully progressive elementary school in Clearwater, Florida. I taught first grade and, later, combination first/second-grade classes, looping (back then, we just called it "moving up with the kids") as the children became second and third graders. In 1980, Jan and I took jobs as teachers in American schools overseas. We lived overseas for seventeen years. During that time, our daughter, Kelli, was born. She brought us into Dutch, Icelandic, and British worlds as she attended local schools. We moved back to the United States shortly after Kelli turned thirteen. Today, at twenty-two, she is off enjoying the adventures of becoming her own person. It brings us the greatest joy that she continues to involve us in her new worlds.

In 1997, I became a faculty member at the University of South Carolina, and the following year I initiated the study on which this book is based. From the time they were my MAT students, these teachers, now my research partners, have touched my life in incredible ways. The depth of their commitment to children, to me, to one another, and to our work is impossible to convey. They are treasured and irreplaceable in my life.

Moving Forward as One: Eight Voices Write as a Collective

> The evening marked a new beginning for us as a real community,
> a place where we could be honest and not perfect.

Our experiences together as teachers, researchers, writers, and friends began during the preservice year and continue today. The September evening at Erin's house was a first turning point in that journey. As Ami put it, the evening marked "a new beginning for us as a real community, a place where we could be honest and not perfect." But the evening was not simply a time to vent. Conversations filled with despair were also tempered with a sense of pride and optimism that would continue to reemerge even in our most difficult moments during the years to come. The next day our emails to one another revealed characteristics of the group that we were just coming to know—the ability to pick each other up, remind one another that we were not alone, and give each other hope. We wrote:

> *Robbie:* You know what the good part is? At least we know that we want to teach differently. At least we know there's something better. But we're still all learning. We learn a little bit and we take it and adjust it. And next year, we'll rely on worksheets and textbooks a little bit less.

> *Julie:* Even if we're not doing it all right now, we know that we *can* do it, and we have it inside of us and we know that it's possible. We're not going to let each other be like, "Oh well, we'll just give it up."

> *Ami:* I think we all need to take baby steps and celebrate each tiny step.

> *Erin:* The conversation last night was so necessary. I keep having this refreshing "ah-hah—I'm not alone." I was so afraid that everybody would completely surpass me and leave me behind in a sea of worksheets. But that's not so. I'm gaining experience like everybody, but I'm struggling like everybody.

> *Susi:* I know we all can make a difference in education, so don't beat yourselves up. Allow yourselves and me to be learners, and feel comfortable with that. You are all fabulous for kids. I see it in your smiles and your hugs and your commitment to always moving forward.

> *Carly:* I love you all to the moon and back. Don't ever give up. I say this as I plan another wonder worksheet for tomorrow's map skills lesson. But, hey, then we go to the library to research our cities, so maybe next year I can bypass that worksheet and think of a better way to teach latitude and longitude and scale and distance. But right now I've got a fiancé to go and see, and then I have a skate night and my kids would love to see me there. So I'm prioritizing.

In the next years, much took place that helped us get to the point at which we could look back and say, "Look how far we've come!" But we also looked back and said, "Did it really have to be so hard?" After carefully documenting our experiences for so many years, we have much to share about settings, structures, attitudes, and behaviors that support new teachers and those that sap us of the desire to make a difference. The following chapters describe our journey: the process of the research that became this book, the development of beliefs that shaped our visions of great teaching, issues met as we attempted to live up to those visions, the roles of administrators and colleagues in our lives, the voices we possessed but didn't recognize, thoughts about how educators might work to end the cycle of struggle and disillusionment for new teachers, and our current visions.

As experienced teachers today, we can see how easy it might be for other experienced teachers to read our words and say, "Well, of course the early years are difficult. Get a grip, this is teaching." We, too, wonder at the intensity of our younger selves. But because we have captured our early thoughts, fears, and concerns through data collected in-the-moment, we are able to give credence to the new teachers we once were. *We must listen to them as intently as we wanted to be heard then.* While some of our struggles were certainly due to inexperience, we know now that there is much more to the story. Learning to be a teacher is an intense journey that involves thoughtful and often difficult reflection, but the journey doesn't need to be filled with barriers that cause new teachers to lose confidence, vigor, and the desire to effect change.

We share our experiences as teachers and as teacher-researchers. For some of us, this means traveling back to places that are unpleasant to visit. For others, it means looking at current challenges that, as experienced teachers, we continue to face. For all of us, it is an opportunity to answer Susi's initial questions that have evolved to become our own: What happens to the enthusiasm, confidence, knowledge, and energy of new teachers as they enter the profession eager to make a difference? What barriers do they find? What is the support that sustains them?

2 Becoming Us: Eight Teacher-Researchers

If we hadn't all taken on more active roles and if we hadn't continued for as long as we have, we wouldn't hear so many voices speaking so strongly, and we certainly would not feel the same depth of connection to one another.

Why Write a Chapter about Becoming Us?

If Susi wrote about us by herself, it would only be an eighth of the story!

We laugh now as we look back at the differences in our initial perceptions of our group's purpose, articulated in our mini-biographies in Chapter 1. Susi, in a university sort of way, wrote that we came together "to better understand the barriers met by new teachers attempting to implement ideas learned in their preservice program." The rest of us nodded agreeably. We were intrigued with the idea of being involved in "Susi's little research project." At that time, we saw the group primarily as a support system and a way to keep in touch with friends from graduate school. We said things like: "I wanted to have like minds to share my experiences with"; "I needed support and just simply loved my friends"; "I felt like I would still be connected and not alone in the teaching world."

During our first year of teaching, the nature of our group began to change. Rather than defining ourselves as a *teacher support group* or *Susi's research project*, we grew to become a group of eight teacher-researchers working collaboratively to document and make sense of our experiences. The process of that change—the story of becoming us—is critical to understanding our teaching stories: how *did* we evolve from seven teachers studied by a professor to eight co-researchers who collected, transcribed, organized, analyzed, and wrote about data together?

The story of becoming us is also important because it helps to place our work in the realm of rigorous research. Whereas first-year teaching diaries (Codell, 1999); anecdotal accounts and retrospective reflections; shorter-term studies (Goodnough, 2004); self-studies by individual teachers (Foss, 1999; Hankins, 2003; Kane, 1991); interviews, surveys, and focus group studies (Gilbert, 2005; McCann et al., 2005); and research conducted by university faculty (Bullough, 1989; Harste, Leland, Schmidt, Vasquez, & Ociepka, 2004; Johnson, 2004) provide important windows into the early years of teaching, our work reflects a complex research process that involved eight perspectives in collaborative self-study over seven years. The amount of data and depth of analytical conversation involved in our research brought us to understandings that we never could have envisioned alone or in our first years together. As Ami wrote, "Can you imagine a piece that was written just about our first year or even our first two years and then using that to say, 'These are the problems and this is what you need to do about them?'" Over time our deepening relationships with one another allowed us to take more and more risks to share experiences, views, concerns, and fears and, ultimately, to analyze those experiences in open and honest ways. Our conversations in the seventh year about experiences in the first six years yielded deeper insights than did our earlier analyses of data. Erin said, "What we saw in the data when we first started coding is different from what we are able to see now. We didn't pick up on things that we are picking up on now. Our early stories provide a voice that even *we* couldn't understand at the time." Much of the power of our work comes also from the fact that it represents eight perspectives. Ami explained, "If Susi wrote about us by herself, it would only be an eighth of the story! We had eight sets of eyes looking at data."

For these reasons, we see this chapter as an important preface to stories about our lives in schools. It describes the process of our research grounded in our relationships with one another. It details critical incidents that led us deeper and deeper into a collaboration that allowed us to understand much more than we could have understood alone or over a shorter period of time. This chapter describes the evolution of our work—how we did what we did, who we continue to become, and how we came to understand critical issues in the lives of new teachers.

The Story of Us

Susi did not set out to support new teachers curricularly.

As we began sharing drafts of this book with friends and colleagues, Susi realized that some of them assumed that, for the past seven years, she had been meeting with a group of classroom teachers to provide curricular support. That's not the case. Susi wrote, "I just wanted to know what would happen to them." Frequently our meetings evolved into curricular conversations as group members posed questions and shared teaching ideas. Sometimes we engaged in the study and discussion of professional literature. But talk about curriculum evolved *through* our conversations, not as our primary reason for coming together.

I always wanted to be a part of us.

We began formally keeping track of our experiences in the last weeks of our MAT program when Susi audiotaped our oral comprehensive exams and we pulled together material from that year's MAT courses and internship experiences—papers, reflective journals, lesson plans, inquiry projects, and other assignments. Two weeks after graduation, we began meeting. Susi asked everyone to send weekly reflections via email. She kicked off our first reflections by asking us to describe our beliefs about teaching and learning and to identify key graduate school experiences that led to the development of those beliefs (described in Chapter 3). As the summer went on, we wrote about hunting for jobs, setting up classrooms, and meeting new colleagues (Chapter 4). When we began teaching, Susi sent new questions to guide our writing: What did you do this week that you really loved? What is hard for you? What is frustrating? What's working? What isn't working? What barriers do you find to being the teacher you hoped you would be? How do you negotiate those barriers? What support do you find (Chapters 5, 6, and 7)? Robbie created a listserv that allowed our weekly email reflections to become a part of an ongoing conversation. Initially, the listserv was a place to send data to Susi, but it quickly became a touchstone for sharing, reflecting, responding, and supporting. As we write this book, Yahoo! Groups tells us that we have logged 10,219 emails since graduation!

In addition to the listserv, we met one Saturday a month, usually for five or six hours at a time. Sometimes we met in one another's classrooms; more often we met in our homes. Each summer we planned weekend working retreats. It was important to get away from the responsibilities of home, family, and school to concentrate on our work together. Monthly meetings and summer retreats provided opportunities to talk at length about the barriers and the support we found when trying to live the teaching lives we envisioned (Figure 2.1). At each of these sessions, we captured our conversations by audiotaping them.

Sharing our successes was fun. Articulating our struggles through email reflections and in group meetings was not always easy. Even though we had been friends before the project began and had supported one another as graduate students, it took a lot of courage to put our frustrations out there for everyone to consider. It was hard to admit that we were sometimes disappointed in ourselves. Difficult moments in our teaching lives became all the more vivid when we voiced them or com-

Figure 2.1. A Saturday meeting at Robbie's parents' house.

mitted them to print. Carly said, "I always wanted to be a part of us. I believed that our stories were important and vital, too important to just give up. But there was a lot I didn't want to admit to myself. Talking and writing about it made the pain even more real."

There was a point at which Susi wondered if our stories were too hopeless to write. At the end of the second year, she was surprised and dismayed by the depth of our self-doubt and disillusionment. Would our stories discourage people from ever going into education? This became a motivating factor in the decision to continue our research beyond the first and second years. Susi wondered if the next years would bring a more hopeful outlook. If not, she wanted to know why. The rest of us agreed. Before we knew it, seven years had gone by since graduation and we were still trying to make sense of our experiences.

Robbie remembers the turn toward collaboration.

During the first year, we were all committed to the project, but it was still very much Susi's research. Basically, she called the shots and the rest of us were along for the ride, trusting her to know what she was doing. This lack of ownership meant that, for quite a while, we did not share a common sense of purpose in terms of the research. We shared our experiences in supportive, interested, and passionate ways, but we were not yet evolving as co-researchers with a common vision. Several critical incidents caused our roles to shift.

Robbie commented that the turn toward collaboration began "when Susi asked us to call her Susi instead of Dr. Long." During the MAT program, even though she always referred to herself as Susi, as April wrote, "We called you Dr. Long out of respect for you as one of our professors." This seemingly superficial change actually represented an early shift for us as a group. At first awkward, the growing ease in using *Susi* paralleled our deepening friendships. Carmen said, "I would call you 'Dr. Long' and then correct it with 'Susi,' but now you are my girl. It feels so natural now to call you 'Susi,' to pick up the phone just to say 'Hi.'"

The turn toward collaboration was nudged again when our weekly listserv entries moved beyond direct answers to Susi's questions. Those topics were embedded in further communication, but the rest of us quickly took control of the listerv for the things we needed to say. Robbie said, "We didn't really pay too much attention to your questions after a while. At first, you were leading us, imposing those question-naires and stuff. I don't mean imposing in a bad way; but almost from the beginning, we were already rebelling against those questionnaires and taking more of our own role in the work."

In the meantime, risks taken that September evening at Erin's house not only opened the door to honest sharing among new teach-ers, but also led to Susi's greater involvement as a participant in the group. She described going home that night irritated about feeling de-fensive when group members expressed anger at the preservice expe-rience: "Hadn't I told them to take it slowly and cautioned them not to expect to do it all overnight? Or had I? How had my demonstrations in class contradicted those messages?" The next day she wrote to the group about the "twinge of defensiveness" she felt the evening before: "In the same I-want-to-be-perfect mentality that you all were voicing, I thought, 'But I *did* stress that great teachers don't happen overnight!'" Once she backed away from a defensive reaction, Susi began to reconsider her role in the group and the impact of the study on her own teaching:

> The more honest I am with myself, the more I realize that I spent so much energy convincing you guys that you should be the most knowledgeable teachers around that I didn't think that, *of course*, that means you would want to be that way immediately. Did I even talk about how to deal with the feelings you're having now? As a result of Friday evening, if it's okay with you, I'd like to add my own journal entries to the weekly collection. I can see that this is becoming a story not only of your growth but of mine as well.

The group welcomed Susi as a participant who would share her own experiences as a professor and a classroom teacher. Erin wrote, "Putting yourself in this honestly will make a huge difference. It really opens the lines of communication." Susi was relieved to see this change taking place: "It feels *great* to no longer sit in some distant seat, but to look openly at my growth as well as yours."

These were, indeed, turning points in the group's relationship, but Susi still made decisions about the group's direction, organized the data, and posed the questions. It was not until a fourth event occurred that our work became more authentically collaborative and we gained mutual ownership of the research.

It was the first time we recognized the magnitude of the study and began to see ourselves as researchers.

At the end of the first year, we planned a weekend retreat to look back on that year of teaching. We met at Erin's family beach house near Charleston. On Saturday morning, in a moment that Susi will not easily forget, the rest of us handed her our collected cash—$200—to help with the purchase of toner, paper, notebooks, dividers, audiotapes, and batteries. But this was not just about money. Susi wrote later, "Incredibly, they handed me all of that money and then asked to extend their role beyond merely providing data for a professor's research. They wanted to be a part of data collection, planning, and organization." April explained, "Once we got started, we knew that it would be a lot of work, and we didn't want Susi to do it all on her own. It was a huge responsibility." The study had become, as Carmen put it, "*our study*, not just Susi's; we knew we had taken this on together and we had to support our baby."

This was the first time we recognized the magnitude of the study and began to see ourselves as researchers. With this shift, we joined a rich tradition of teacher researchers (Cochran-Smith & Lytle, 1993) intentionally negotiating the process and content of our work together. Susi continued to facilitate the group, but she was no longer the sole decision maker. As Ami explained, Susi's role was to help us stay "focused and responsible as far as collecting data, organizing, analyzing, and writing." Robbie suggested that "*guide* would be a good name for Susi."

Our growing relationship as fellow researchers was not just about our commitment to the work; it was directly connected to our friendships with one another. Figuratively and literally, "breaking bread together [was] a central aspect of writing, talking, and thinking" (Hubbard

& Power, 1999, p. 185) as we worked and played together. During the first beach retreat, for example, we spread out around the house with laptops and data while a huge pot of Julie's spaghetti sauce simmered in the kitchen. We stopped for walks on the beach and talked about our lives, our families, and our work. We lingered over dinner and, as Julie writes, "sat on the screened porch chatting, laughing, drinking, and relaxing." Moments like these led, in the months and years ahead, to greater trust and respect for one another. They allowed us to talk more openly about difficult issues, which, in turn, deepened what we were able to see in our data.

The only time I felt like not doing this anymore was when I transcribed my first set of tapes!

Our new roles as teacher-researchers meant that we became participant observers (Atkinson & Hammersley, 1998) studying our own lives as well as one another's. We were positioned to examine multiple perspectives individually and collectively (Cochran-Smith & Lytle, 1993). Our new roles also brought new responsibilities, such as transcribing audiotapes from all of those Saturdays and weekends! To be able to analyze our experiences, we needed to see our words in print. Even though transcribing was not everyone's favorite part of the process, we each took a turn. Julie wrote, "The only time I felt like not doing this anymore was when I transcribed my first set of tapes!" Several times along the way, we chipped in to hire transcribers, but we were never satisfied with that process. It was difficult for others to understand our overlapping talk, and we were not comfortable making our conversations public before we decided what to share with a wider audience. But we also knew it would be impossible to capture the intensity of our experiences if we could not retrieve our words as they had been spoken. So we transcribed.

It was time to begin making sense of data.

Soon, our data—weekly email reflections and transcripts from Saturdays and summer retreats—grew to fill twelve large three-ring binders (Figure 2.2). Although we continued to collect and transcribe data for the next four years, at the beginning of our third year we decided it was time to begin making sense of data accumulated to that point. We were excited about heading into the analysis process, but we were a little fuzzy on the details. Most of us had only a vague idea of where we were headed with all of the notebooks of data. We *did* know that important stories were embedded in those pages, and we wanted to make sense of them so they could be shared in clear and helpful ways.

Figure 2.2. Some of the data notebooks with weekly emails and audiotape transcripts from our first years.

Susi gave everyone a crash course in qualitative data analysis so that we could begin to gain deeper insights into the "dimensions and dynamics" (Dyson & Genishi, 2005, p. 81) of our early teaching experiences. We began by doing what Wolcott (1994) calls "processing data" (p. 24): we each took a couple of data notebooks and read through them page by page and line by line, scribbling key words and phrases in the margins to identify specific issues, incidents, or ideas that seemed to be important in our early years of teaching (Figure 2.3).

Coming together after the first reading of data, we compared margin scribbles and considered patterns we were beginning to see— ideas and issues that appeared again and again in the notebooks. We developed a list of those patterns, named them as categories, and created abbreviations or codes for each (Figure 2.4). For example, we repeatedly found data stories about the struggle to balance our educational beliefs with mandated practices in schools or districts, so we named that pattern *Balancing Beliefs and Mandates* and coded it as *BBM*. The codes made it easier to indicate and then find related data excerpts as we scribbled in notebooks during further readings.

Over the next few months, we traded notebooks back and forth until each one had been read by at least three group members. With multiple readings, we were able to rethink the significance of categories from different perspectives. Collectively, we could confirm, disconfirm, or add to patterns that individuals saw as important.

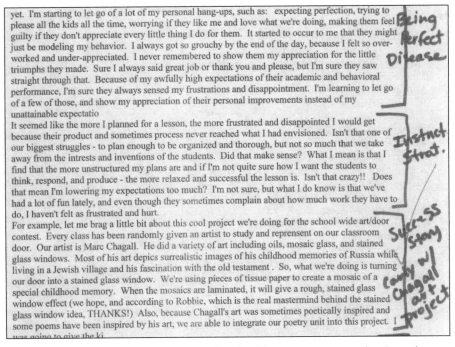

yet. I'm starting to let go of a lot of my personal hang-ups, such as: expecting perfection, trying to please all the kids all the time, worrying if they like me and love what we're doing, making them feel guilty if they don't appreciate every little thing I do for them. It started to occur to me that they might just be modeling my behavior. I always got so grouchy by the end of the day, because I felt so over-worked and under-appreciated. I never remembered to show them my appreciation for the little triumphs they made. Sure I always said great job or thank you and please, but I'm sure they saw straight through that. Because of my awfully high expectations of their academic and behavioral performance, I'm sure they always sensed my frustrations and disappointment. I'm learning to let go of a few of those, and show my appreciation of their personal improvements instead of my unattainable expectatio

It seemed like the more I planned for a lesson, the more frustrated and disappointed I would get because their product and sometimes process never reached what I had envisioned. Isn't that one of our biggest struggles - to plan enough to be organized and thorough, but not so much that we take away from the intrests and inventions of the students. Did that make sense? What I mean is that I find that the more unstructured my plans are and if I'm not quite sure how I want the students to think, respond, and produce - the more relaxed and successful the lesson is. Isn't that crazy!! Does that mean I'm lowering my expectations too much? I'm not sure, but what I do know is that we've had a lot of fun lately, and even though they sometimes complain about how much work they have to do, I haven't felt as frustrated and hurt.

For example, let me brag a little bit about this cool project we're doing for the school wide art/door contest. Every class has been randomly given an artist to study and reprensent on our classroom door. Our artist is Marc Chagall. He did a variety of art including oils, mosaic glass, and stained glass windows. Most of his art depics surrealistic images of his childhood memories of Russia while living in a Jewish village and his fascination with the old testament . So, what we're doing is turning our door into a stained glass window. We're using pieces of tissue paper to create a mosaic of a special childhood memory. When the mosaics are laminated, it will give a rough, stained glass window effect (we hope, and according to Robbie, which is the real mastermind behind the stained glass window idea, THANKS!) Also, because Chagall's art was sometimes poetically inspired and some poems have been inspired by his art, we are able to integrate our poetry unit into this project. I was going to give the ki

Figure 2.3. Excerpt from a data notebook with one group member's early margin scribbles—key words to identify potential insights.

We settled deeper into the analysis process.

From summer retreats and monthly meetings to a January weekend at Susi's house, we settled deeper into the analysis process while continuing to collect new data. In our personal lives, we celebrated four weddings, saw Susi through the first months of the empty nest, *and* shared excitement in Carly, Erin, and Julie's announcements that they were pregnant, Julie with twins!

During the January weekend, we met to tally data excerpts. With data notebooks in hand, we gathered around Susi's dining room table and called out the tallies we had recorded for each notebook: "There are nine examples of *Success Stories* in Notebook Five"; "I found three examples of *Second Year Changes* in Notebook Eight." As we called out numbers, Julie made tally marks on chart paper, allowing us to consider potential findings: Which categories seemed significant enough to write about? Which ones might be grouped together as related ideas? What were the anomalies and how would we write about them? In a moment characteristic of us as a group that constantly blurs the line between

Friendship Support (FS)
Professional Support (PS)
     - Questions and Answers
     - Noticing when someone needs help
Balance between Beliefs and Mandates (BBM)
Administrators (ADMIN)
     - Autonomy
     - Support
Colleagues (CoWork)
Mentors (MENT)
Positive Relationships with Students as Motivation (POS REL)
Shared Experiences as Support (SH EXP)
Susi's Growth (SUSI)
Taking Care of Yourself (TAKE CARE)
Support for Pedagogy (SUP PED)
Being Perfect Disease (PERFECT)
Standardized Testing (TEST)
Lack of Support for 1st Year Teachers (NO SUP)
Despair/Overwhelmed/Self-Doubt (DESPAIR)
Negotiating Group Organization (NEG GRP ORG)
2nd Year Changes (2nd YEAR)
1st Year Doubts (DOUBTS)
Reaching All Students (REACH ST)
Classroom Management/Community (COMM)
Parents (PAR)
Student Stories (SS)
Politics (POL)
Lessons from other Schools (OTH SCHLS)
Lessons that Flop (FLOP)
Assessment (ASS)
Instructional Strategies (INSTR STRAT)
Success Stories (SUCCESS)
Major Decision (DECISIONS)
Networking (NETWK)
Setting Goals (GOALS)
Professional Reading/Resources (RDG)

Figure 2.4. The list of categories and codes generated from our initial review of data.

work and life, as Julie tallied data excerpts she felt the first butterfly kicks of her twins (Figure 2.5)!

Sometimes our group is about buckling down and getting to work. Other times it's about being a friend. That makes for a nice mixture.

The next day we assigned one another two or three categories, read related data, and constructed "analytic narratives" (Dyson & Genishi, 2005, p. 84). For instance, one of Erin's categories was *Colleagues*, so she

Figure 2.5. Julie tallying frequency counts and feeling her twins kick for the first time.

used the coding in each notebook to find and reread every bit of data pertaining to colleagues. Then she constructed a narrative to describe initial thoughts about the role of colleagues in our early years. This helped us think a bit more about potential insights or findings that our study might offer.

Hubbard and Power (1999) describe a feeling of "murkiness" (p. 117) at this point in the analysis process. Murky is how many of us felt as we jumped into writing narratives with varying levels of comfort and clarity. Julie remembers watching Erin "typing away at her laptop" and wondering, "How does she know what she's supposed to be writing?" Robbie wrote that she and Carmen "were having the hardest time concentrating, sitting by the fireplace where there was a warm and toasty fire burning." Others found the cold day, the fire, and the quiet just right for writing. Erin was five months pregnant and, with her husband out of town, it was a perfect time for her to focus on our work. She wrote: "Susi made a fire and I sat close to it and indulged in a cup of hot chocolate. I remember feeling cozy and focused and didn't have a hard time writing that day. I felt the satisfaction of accomplishing a good deal of work and, seeing the narratives evolve, I began to visualize how the book might actually look."

Midday we stopped to celebrate Erin, Julie, and Carly's pregnancies. The baby shower once again represented the mix of work and play that had come to define our time together. We were always productive, but sometimes our productivity had little to do with the immediate tasks of data analysis and writing. As Robbie put it, "Sometimes our group is about buckling down and getting to work. Other times it's about being a friend. That makes for a nice mixture."

I'm a bit scared that words won't adequately capture our true message, feelings, experiences.

Over the next four years, we used the narratives begun that day as a basis from which further data collection, analysis, and writing were done. Then, after six years of meeting, sharing, considering, collecting, transcribing, scrutinizing, coding, and analyzing, we were ready to craft more comprehensive stories to share with the wider world. The task was exciting yet daunting. Carly wrote, "I'm excited about the possibilities, but I'm a bit scared that words won't adequately capture our true message, feelings, experiences." We wondered if we would be able to pull it off: How could we blend our voices in ways that would honor us as individuals and yet create a coherent whole? How could we fine-tune years of data to adequately yet concisely communicate the intensity of our lived experiences? How could we validate our feelings as new teachers while being sensitive to the perspectives of others? What aspects of our experience were we comfortable making public? How vulnerable were we willing to make ourselves?

As we began to consider what a book describing our study might look like, we reviewed a wide range of professional texts and paid attention to possible structures for telling our stories. We made a list of do's and don'ts—elements of other research accounts that we found engaging, as well as styles and formats we wanted to avoid. We talked about audience. We looked at existing publications and considered the gaps we might fill. We discussed finding a balance between telling compelling data stories and foregrounding the rigor of our research.

It was one of those times when we were jamming.

Once we began writing in earnest, we held regular authors' circles, each one lasting many hours. With the help of a speaker phone and Carmen's no-limit phone plan, Carly in Atlanta and Carmen in Virginia were with us for every meeting, even for the record-breaking authors' circle that

Figure 2.6. Erin (with Livie), April, and Julie reading drafts of our writing in preparation for authors' circles.

lasted eight hours! We began each session by reading the latest draft of a chapter and scribbling our thoughts in the margins (Figure 2.6). Our focus on the writing process during this time was intense. Robbie's description of her arrival at a weekend writing retreat communicates that spirit of concentration:

> When I got there at 8:30 Saturday morning, I expected everyone to be moseying around in their pajamas, sipping coffee and chatting. Instead everyone was reading the latest draft of Chapter 3. After a short pause to ask how my pregnant self was feeling, they got right back to work. It was one of those times when we were jamming. It felt so good to be a part of the group.

After reading on our own, our pattern was to sit together and discuss one page at a time: "Does anyone have thoughts about anything on page 156?" These discussions were about far more than just editing and revision. They allowed us to talk our way into deeper understandings and to rethink findings again and again. To borrow Ralph Fletcher's (1993) words, we "actually discover[ed] what [we had] to say in the process of writing" (p. 21). In the last months, these conversations revolved around feedback from university and public school colleagues who read and responded to our manuscript. Their thoughts pushed us in new ways and greatly enriched what we were able to see and express. Throughout this process, we restructured the book and rewrote each chapter many, many, *many* times (Figure 2.7).

Figure 2.7. The structure for the book changed many, many times.

The entire process was wonderful and excruciating at the same time.

The research and writing processes were invigorating and gratifying, but they were also simply hard work, much more so than any of us anticipated. Sharing in monthly meetings was one thing; reading lengthy transcripts of long-forgotten words and trying to communicate our experiences to others was quite another. There were certainly times when one or the other of us considered bowing out, but we kept going because of our commitment to the message we hoped to send, the personal and professional growth we experienced through our work, and our friendships. The entire process was wonderful and excruciating at the same time.

Some of our most exciting ah-hahs came from our most difficult conversations—group talk that was intensely reflective and sometimes personally disturbing. In our seventh summer, for example, the rest of the group talked for hours to help Susi see that, because she had crafted the book proposal from our individually written narratives, the rest of us needed to regain a vision of the bigger picture. Susi's guilt about taking too much control was a point of personal tension, but the rest of us jumped in with a plan to put the proposal aside and revisit data to see if the proposed book design still worked. Intensely reflective talk also emerged in the final stages of writing when we recognized silences in our data regarding issues of race. Through the years, we had shared stories about racial issues related to classroom experiences, but we rarely explored them deeply. As we wrote this book, we looked back and wondered why (this is discussed in greater detail in Chapter 7).

Just before the book was about to go to press, we engaged in what were probably our most difficult yet most generative conversations. We spent many hours discussing how to validate the feelings of new teachers while honoring the perspectives of educators whose beliefs were different from our own. In the process, we recognized the need to better channel the frustration, disappointment, and anger we felt as new teachers in ways that might open honest and productive dialogue in schools, school systems, and universities. It was difficult to find that balance. Seeking it led to discussions about how much of our own voice might be lost along the way.

Looking back, it's amazing that we all stayed with the project as long as we did, particularly in light of the added responsibilities of data collection and writing. Over the years, there were times when we all had to take a few steps back: Susi, the year before she went up for tenure and during her daughter's last year in high school; Robbie, the fall when she moved, bought a new house, got married, and started a new job; Carmen, when her plate was loaded with National Boards on one side and her wedding on the other; April, Julie, Carly, Erin, and Robbie as they juggled life as teachers and as mothers of young children; and each of us as we faced family tragedies at one time or another. Carly wrote, "it never seemed to matter who did more or less at any one time. No one ever made me feel guilty about not giving 100 percent at times. I did that enough on my own." We all felt that way. When one of us had to step back, someone else always stepped up to take on whatever needed to be done.

Becoming Us Is a Never-Ending Process

What happened to us isn't unique. Many books and articles describe the lives of new teachers. The issues we faced are issues that many teachers face every day. What makes us different is that we documented our experiences over a long period of time and analyzed them from the perspectives of eight educators. We moved from the blurry days of wondering where this would all lead to taking charge of our direction as teacher-researchers, a level of involvement that made all the difference. As Ami said, "If we hadn't taken more active roles and if we hadn't continued for as long as we have, we wouldn't hear so many voices speaking so strongly, and we certainly would not feel the same depth

Figure 2.8. All of us: April, Susi, Ami, Erin (front row); Carmen, Robbie, Julie, Carly (back row).

of connection to one another." As a result, we write with a unique combination of individuality and collectivity.

Becoming us (Figure 2.8) is a never-ending process. It continues as we grow in our ability to understand our experiences. Carmen wrote, "We don't remember everything, but because we wrote it all down and transcribed our spoken words from the very beginning, we can look back, gasp, cry, laugh, and be proud. People need to know how far we've come and how much we've learned." In the following chapters, we share what we've learned—our beliefs as new graduates leaving the preservice program and our stories as new teachers working to bring those beliefs to life.

Critical Insights from Chapter 2

- We began as a group of teachers studied by Susi. Within a year, we had become a group of *eight teacher-researchers*. Taking joint responsibility for a project carried out over seven years brought us to understandings we could never have envisioned alone or in our first years together.

- Sharing our successes was fun. However, even though we had been friends before the project, it was difficult to admit our struggles.

- Our trust in one another deepened as we shared our personal as well as professional selves. This allowed us to talk more openly about difficult issues, which led us to see more in the data.

- At first, data analysis seemed like a confusing process. We wondered where we were going with all those notebooks of data.

- Analyzing data, we experienced many ah-hah moments. The most exciting ah-hahs were usually the result of hard conversations that pushed us to go beyond ideas we were comfortable with.

- The research and writing processes were simultaneously wonderful and excruciating. Although invigorating, gratifying, and tremendous learning experiences, they were also simply hard work.

- Inviting twenty-seven teachers, administrators, and university faculty to read our manuscript at various stages was an incredibly important part of the process. Each response resulted in group conversations that deepened our analysis in new and important ways.

- Our thinking was pushed once again as we began to notice the silences in our data—what we chose not to talk or write about—as well as what we *did* say and do.

- As we began to consider what this book might look like, it was helpful to review a wide range of professional texts, paying attention to possible structures for telling our stories. We made a list of do's and don'ts.

- It's amazing we all stayed with the project for as long as we did. One reason is that our group embraces a balance—sometimes we are about buckling down and getting to work; other times we are about being a friend.

3 The Teachers We Hoped We Would Be

The tree. That was the first thing that commanded my attention when I walked into Dori Gilbert's first-grade classroom at the Center for Inquiry. It was an enormous tree that seemed to fill the room. Clearly, it was a way to bring the outdoors to life in this space. Once I stepped in further, I knew that scientists lived there. The work of inquiring scientists was everywhere. Soon the children began sharing their writing. Respect was clearly a priority as everyone listened intently and responded to each writer. I took notes until my hand hurt. I didn't want to miss a thing. This was the way I hoped that my classroom would look, feel, and be.

I will never ever forget walking into that third-grade classroom at Indianola. The first things I saw were giant ficus trees with twinkle lights that lit the room. Children sat at wicker tables. Chests of drawers housed books and other materials. Children were in all parts of the room working on different things. In another classroom, two children sitting in the loft were completely involved in the class discussion below. The atmosphere was relaxed, yet children were engaged as learners. Teachers really listened to children. You could tell that they respected one another. It was culture shock. I was in love.

The spirit at the Center for Inquiry in Columbia, South Carolina, and at Indianola Elementary School in Columbus, Ohio, embodied so many ideas and beliefs that defined our experiences as graduate students. We visited these schools during our preservice (MAT) program. These were the first opportunities for many of us to see classroom practices that we had read about in professional books. The visit to Indianola was part of a cohort road trip. Bumping along Interstate 77 in a university van, our cohort of preservice teachers made the journey from South Carolina to The Ohio State University's Children's Literature Conference. While in Ohio, we visited Indianola and Wickliffe Elementary Schools. At the conference, we met authors of favorite children's books, and we heard teacher after teacher talk about using children's books as the foundation for reading and writing in their classrooms. We had never seen so many teachers in one place who believed the kinds of things we were learning.

The Beliefs by Which We Measured Ourselves and Others

These experiences, in conjunction with other opportunities in our graduate program, were critical to the development of our beliefs about teaching and learning. Through course work, internships, school visits, a culminating synthesis paper, and oral exams, we explored the notion of classrooms as supportive communities for caring, inquiring, risk-taking learners and teachers. We read, talked, experienced, planned, implemented, and reflected. In the process, we developed strong beliefs that formed the lens through which we looked at schools, administrators, and potential colleagues during our search for jobs. Once we found jobs, the same convictions guided our construction of classrooms and curriculum and formed the foundation for our reactions to programmatic mandates. At times our beliefs led us to supportive colleagues and at other times to feeling alone in our schools. Our convictions could lead to a sense of accomplishment, but they were also the source of disappointment and self-doubt when we thought we were not living up to our visions of great teaching. As we left the university, our beliefs defined the teachers we hoped we would be.

This chapter describes these beliefs, providing an important preface to stories of our early teaching experiences. To understand the barriers we met and the joys we experienced as new teachers, it is important to understand the beliefs by which we measured ourselves and others.

What Did We Believe?

Looking back at reflective journals, synthesis papers, and oral comprehensive exams from our graduate school days, and at our responses to questionnaires that Susi asked us to complete the summer after graduation, we were able to identify beliefs we held as we interviewed for and began our first teaching jobs. We were also able to retrieve stories about people, school visits, internship experiences, and readings that led to the development of those beliefs. All of the stories told in this chapter come from some aspect of our fifteen-month preservice program, including the professional literature cited.

We entered the teaching profession believing that . . .

Classrooms should be warm, authentically inviting physical environments.

We wanted our classrooms to be welcoming and visually pleasing, yet authentically so. Through our graduate experiences, we began to see contrasts between classrooms that were merely cute or pretty and those that were authentically beautiful because they reflected the lives of the learners and teachers within them. During our language arts methods course, for example, we met onsite at a local elementary school where we arranged an empty classroom for and with first graders who spent time with us each week. When some of us brought in an It's-a-Small-World-styled bulletin board border and a manufactured Weather Bear, Susi's response left little doubt that the cute little bear and the borders, with their simplistic view of cultural difference, had little to do with an authentically inviting environment. Erin's email to Susi a year later captures our realization that the construction of inviting environments is about much more than putting up commercially made bulletin boards and cute classroom decorations:

> Remember last fall when Carly, Carmen, and I were doing the calendar/circle area? The first thing we did was buy that stupid weather bear. Can you imagine all the work we put into that cutesy stuff? It's so embarrassing! I'm sure you about flipped when we came with all of that awful stuff.

It didn't take long for us to begin noticing disparities everywhere between what Carly described as "perfectly beautiful, cookie-cutter classrooms and classrooms where life springs forth screaming beauty from deep within." Our understanding of beauty grew richer with each new experience: visits to Phyllis Whitin's kindergarten in South Carolina and reading texts such as Joanne Hindley's (1996) *In the Company of Children*, Bobbi Fisher's (1998) *Joyful Learning in Kindergarten*, and Jill Ostrow's (1995) *A Room with a Different View*. In each of these settings and texts, we learned that classroom beauty grows from the passions of the children and teachers who live there and from their mutual explorations as learners.

We learn more in communities where learners and teachers foster mutual respect; learn to know, value, and care for one another; and feel comfortable enough to take risks.

Joanne Hindley (1996) writes that "wonderful places . . . aren't really wonderful until the people who live in them care about one another" (p. 2). The first class that most of us took in the MAT program was with David Whitin, a professor who was truly gifted at creating an atmosphere in which people cared deeply about one another. He took time to really listen and to process our ideas during class conversations. He analyzed and considered our thoughts in ways that made us feel val-

Figure 3.1. We worked in small groups to pursue answers to our own questions.

ued and, in the process, encouraged us to value one another. He taught community-building strategies not through textbooks or lectures but through demonstrations: he arranged desks in a semicircle so that we were not isolated but encouraged to engage as full participants; we worked in small groups much of the time; he introduced daily rituals like poetry readings; and he made time for us to regularly share appreciations about one another. Carly wrote, "Like a magical force that connected us, he seemed to create a complete union of souls." We wanted our students to feel as valued as we felt.

In classes later that summer and throughout the next year, our understandings about building communities of learners continued to grow. An atmosphere was created that let each of us know we were valued members of the cohort. We felt a sense of connectedness through shared experience as one professor read aloud and made music a part of every class session, as we worked in small groups to pursue answers to our own questions (Figure 3.1), through class trips and related reflection, and as we participated in social occasions organized by instructors and on our own. We saw professors' delight in learning and interest in us as individuals as key to the connectedness we felt.

We also came to believe that a strong community grows when teachers allow their students to get to know them as people and as fellow learners. We recognized a sense of vulnerability and compassion displayed by some of our favorite teachers, those who allowed us to see what made them laugh, cry, worry, and wonder. We loved Ladson-Billings's (1994) description of classrooms where teachers' "relationships with students are fluid and equitable and extend beyond the classroom [and where] knowledge is continuously recreated, recycled, and shared by both teachers and students alike" (p. 25). We wanted to create the same atmosphere in our own classrooms.

During visits to the Center for Inquiry, we were introduced to the idea of building community based not on rules but on rights and responsibilities developed by teachers and children working together (Mills & Donnelly, 2001; Peterson, 1992). Ami experienced a similar view of community building during her internship in Stacie Mandrell's second/third-grade classroom. There Ami became a part of a community in which specific curricular structures and rituals—community circle time, playing soft music, singing, and sharing favorite books and stories—supported the celebration of individuals as valued learners and teachers. Rights and responsibilities were developed by and for everyone: rights to learn, share, wonder, trust, explore, play, and laugh; the responsibility to support one another as learners.

Like Bobbi Fisher (1995), we believed that "community is the entire orchestra playing in harmony, with each musician contributing his or her best to the piece" (p. 1). We wanted to create such orchestras. April wrote, "I want a classroom where children work together as a community of learners. I hope that my children will feel so comfortable that they will take risks in their learning. I also hope that I will be a good model of risk-taking." We left the MAT program wanting our students to feel loved and respected from the moment they walked into the classroom. Like Joanne Hindley (1996), we wanted to create classrooms where "children and adults live well, teach and learn respectfully and rigorously" (p. x).

Learners are supported when they have opportunities to inquire and reflect; respecting students' questions means that curriculum can be generated from their interests.

John Dewey's (1938) ideas about learning through experience provided the basis for our belief that school learning should be experientially active and meaningful and that we learn best when we have a stake in charting the direction of our learning. *Learning Together through Inquiry* (Short et al., 1996) was a critical text for us as we read about inquiry-based classrooms. The same book introduced us to the work of Paulo Freire, whose ideas helped us build a vision of inquirers as problem posers, not just problem solvers. We began to see the inquiry process as *how learners learn*, not as just a project or a time of the day. We developed a strong belief that learners seek deeper understandings when they have reason and support to do so. This was closely tied to our belief that education should not be about learning facts or figures for a test or completing worksheets. It would be our responsibility to provide students with strategies they could use as learners who pose questions and know how to seek answers for a lifetime.

We were first introduced to the notion of inquiry-based education in a summer course just before our fall methods courses. The idea was somewhat overwhelming at first because most of us had little or no experience with such philosophies from our own school days. Robbie explained, "I was being presented with a way of teaching that was really foreign to me. That course was the beginning of my knowledge that teaching wasn't going to be exactly what I expected it to be!"

Conducting our own investigations within the broad topic of Unity in Diversity in South Carolina, we learned structures for supporting students as inquirers. We engaged in small-group studies based on our own interests about everything from South Carolina Gullah culture, to the history of shag dancing at Myrtle Beach, to the inequities among schools in South Carolina. Initially, we were confused by the process. Gradually, learning through inquiry began to make sense. Julie explained:

> At first, I was just going through the motions. After a while, I became excited about the possibilities. Discussion with peers was key!! That helped get ideas going about the topic. It made me realize the importance of allowing time for my students to discuss rather than me always leading and them just answering the questions. I saw how important it is to follow your own interests. At the beginning of the study, I felt that the topic, Diversity in South Carolina, was limiting. Imagine that! By the end, I realized the many thousand paths our research could have taken. We only scratched the surface of the possibilities.

Living the process, we began to grasp and believe in the power of inquiry-based education. We learned, for example, to appreciate the importance of choice within the parameters of the broader class study. Julie wrote:

> One group asked me to work with them on a topic. I said, "Yes,"
> but I finally changed groups because my heart was not in the
> first topic. That was so important for me to do. I saw right then
> that I had to follow what I valued. I knew that I needed to re-
> member not to limit my students by imposing my topics of study
> all the time. I could allow them choice within curricular require-
> ments to study a topic or concept.

In this way, the experience of engaging in our own inquiries helped us
make connections to possibilities for supporting children as inquirers.
Robbie explained:

> I think the major thing that impacts me as I head into my first
> classroom is my experience with my own inquiry into Gullah
> culture. It was so neat to participate in my own inquiry project
> even though I didn't fully understand what I was doing at the
> time. Later, as I worked on other projects and had new experi-
> ences, I was able to look back and say, "Oh! That was what we
> were doing in our project. It all makes sense now."

The following semesters, we made explicit connections to inquiry
in schools as we visited classrooms where teachers and children honored one another's questions as foundational to building curriculum.
Carly wrote, "Most of what I know about how an inquiry classroom
looks came from visiting the Center for Inquiry. Thanks to those visits,
I can envision my own classroom as a place where inquiry and investigation live." Robbie said, "It took being in a classroom, observing and
visiting schools like the Center for Inquiry and the schools in Ohio, for
the ideas to really gel so they made sense."

Misperceptions about limitations in time, space, resources, and
student populations fell away as we created opportunities to support
children as inquirers in our own internship classrooms. Robbie filled
her first-grade classroom with plants and books about plants and then
created structures to support children's investigations and presentations
of expert projects about them (Figures 3.2 and 3.3). In her MAT oral
exam, she explained the "importance of engaging children in work
based on their interests" by telling the story of one student, a struggling
reader, who "got up there and presented this project like she was the
most confident expert in the whole world." Working in a school that
drew largely from a low socioeconomic population, this was an important discovery and contradicted any misperceptions we might have had
about practices that could or could not be successfully implemented.

Similarly, Carly was impressed with the depth of questioning
exhibited by kindergartners in her internship classroom and their ability to use their own experiences and interests to support their growing

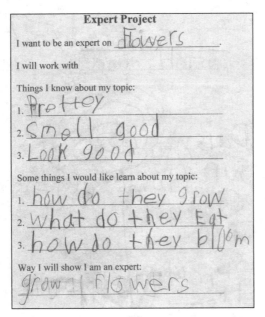

Figure 3.2. A study guide created by Robbie to support first graders' inquiry.

Figure 3.3. A first grader's expert project about plants in Robbie's internship classroom.

understandings of the world. Carly wrote, "Doing expert projects with my kindergartners, I saw exactly what happens when we have high expectations and children are supported in seeking answers to questions of importance to them." Watching children pose their own questions (Figures 3.4) and investigate answers to them, Carly saw their thinking pushed in new ways. She wrote about how they also adopted an inquirer's stance with regard to their friends' investigations: "Not only

Figure 3.4. Carly's kindergartners pose questions about animals.

did they continue to search for more understandings, but they used learning from their peers' presentations to make new connections."

Ami involved her second and third graders in a study of insects and spiders, an experience that helped her develop the conviction that a curriculum is always evolving as children's inquiries lead to new discoveries. As each of her students chose an area on which to focus, their inquiries led them on journeys to local swamplands, meadows, and forests, where they observed insects and spiders in their natural habitats. They kept journals and used multiple sources to conduct investigations. They shared their learning by creating oral and written projects, videotapes, poetry, papier-mâché models, and a collage of insect habitats that spread across one wall of the classroom.

In her internship classroom, Julie learned ways in which children's inquiries can be interwoven with curricular goals. Within the district-mandated topic of Communities, she created an environment in which her first graders wandered and wondered (Short et al., 1996, p. 161) through collections of children's literature and artifacts and then raised questions that were important to them. Julie planned for guest speakers, field studies, and read-alouds and engaged third-grade mentors to support their learning. The walls of the classroom quickly filled with student-generated work (Figure 3.5). Learning was honored in

Figure 3.5. Julie's students fill the room with evidence of their inquiries about communities.

daily class gatherings and a culminating celebration. These experiences helped Julie develop a belief in inquiry-based education as an avenue for tapping into children's natural sense of wonder and encouraging them to seek new understandings.

We left the MAT program with a desire to create classrooms in which children would uncover problems and learn strategies for solving them. We saw no value in textbook-oriented, worksheet-driven environments that would produce a guess-what's-in-the-teacher's-head mentality. Our classrooms would be places where inquiry was not just a project or a focus study but a way of life through which learning and teaching would always lead to new questions (Short, Harste, & Burke, 1996). We wanted children to know that they played a vital role in their own learning. Erin summed it up the summer before we started teaching: "I feel as if I really understand what inquiry is all about and how to incorporate it into my classroom. I think that anyone can as long as inquiry is seen as an attitude, not a time in the day or a project. By valuing students' questions, I am a teacher who supports their inquiry of the world."

Good teaching starts with expecting success and building from what children know.

Basic to every other belief we carried into the first year of teaching was our belief in starting with what children know rather than adopting "a deficit model built on repairing weaknesses" (Ayers, 1993, p. 31). Erin wrote about an incident during her internship when finding out what a child already knew became foundational to helping that child and other children continue to grow. During a shared book experience, she discovered that six-year-old Christopher, who had been struggling as a reader, could read the word *pup*. This soon became "Christopher's word." Using magnetic letters, Erin demonstrated that knowing *pup* can lead to knowing other words with the same rime (*up*), such as *cup*, *up*, and *sup*. Rather than viewing Christopher from a deficit perspective—focusing on what he could not do—Erin built on what he *did* know.

Convictions about building from what children know were grounded in our growing understanding that every child knows a lot. Before they walk into our classrooms, they have already been successful learners in their homes and communities. We were inspired by Gloria Ladson-Billings's (1994) description of a teacher who "presides over a classroom that shouts 'success' [and] insists she has never met an unsuccessful student" (p. 45). Images and ideas from the same text—*The Dreamkeepers*—stayed with us long after we closed the book. Our favorite line was about a child who had been written off by other teachers: "The school has been placing him in the kitchen junk drawer. I want him up there in the china cabinet where everyone can see him" (p. 111). We headed into our classrooms with a strong desire to put every child in the china cabinet, to ensure that our students would know they were valued in many ways.

We learn more when we are engaged in meaningful interactions with other learners; learning is social in nature.

Vygotsky's (1978) notion that we learn more through interactions with other learners was a concept we came to know and value as we lived it every day in university classes, study groups, and, eventually, our internship classrooms. Carly tells the story of Jamie, a kindergartner diagnosed with autism. He always sat with the rest of the class during morning circle time but never seemed to participate. One morning Jamie brought his journal to the community circle and indicated that he had something to share. He slowly opened his journal, placed his finger on the page, and, as if reading word for word, began reciting the names of his peers. Although Jamie had not written anything in his journal, he drew from peers' demonstrations and adopted their reading-like behaviors (Doake, 1985). Previously perceived as a child who never participated in group activities, he clearly had been an active part of the group for weeks. But Jamie did not stop there. The next day he came with his journal in hand to ask, for the very first time, for help in drawing a picture to share with his friends. In her comprehensive exam, Carly wrote, "he traveled what Vygotsky called 'the distance between the actual development level as determined by independent problem solving and the level of potential development as determined through problem solving . . . in collaboration with more capable peers' (p. 86)."

We also learned about the power of social interaction through group work in our university courses. Julie wrote about the impact of working with others during the course that introduced us to inquiry-based education:

> There are so many things that I wouldn't have gotten out of that experience if I had worked on my own. I am really glad that I had the opportunity to do group work so soon in the program. As I built my knowledge of teaching and education, I was building an understanding that there are many valuable interpretations of everything we read and did together. Working with others, I was able to build my knowledge by combining my prior experience with a powerful group experience.

Students learn best through demonstrations of skills and strategies used in the context of meaningful experiences, not through isolated skill-and-drill.

One of the strongest beliefs we held leaving the MAT program was that teaching skills in isolation handicaps rather than supports learners. We believed that immersion in meaningful experiences leads to more thoughtful learning across the curriculum and that skills and strategies are best taught in the context of those experiences. Brian Cambourne's (1988) work was particularly influential as we considered conditions that support learning. We understood that children learn best when they are expected to succeed, when they learn strategies that allow them to take responsibility for further learning, when they are supported in making approximations while receiving sensitive feedback that moves them forward, and when they receive multiple demonstrations every day while engaged purposefully. Across internship placements and school visits, we observed contrasts between classrooms where students explored ideas, skills, and strategies by doing, discussing, and interacting in purposeful contexts, and classrooms dominated by workbooks and worksheets used to teach skills in isolation.

In our internship classrooms, we had opportunities to experiment with meaning-based curricular structures such as literature circles, shared reading, interactive writing, independent reading, individual conferences, and writing workshop. Considering these experiences in contrast to others, we saw meaning-based curricular structures as more engaging and effective than teaching skills in isolation (Moustafa, 1997; Smith, 1995). As Erin said, "it felt natural and right." We began to develop confidence in being able to teach children to read without using workbooks and basal readers. We saw how more thoughtful practices could create opportunities to intentionally focus on parts of language— letter-sound relationships and structural or grammatical elements— while using those skills and strategies to read and write. During her internship in kindergarten, for example, Carly implemented daily morning messages (Figure. 3.6). As she and her students talked through the process of constructing and reading those messages, she was able to demonstrate reading and writing strategies while teaching about specific letter-sound relationships, sentence structure, and vocabulary.

In another example, Carmen tells about Juan, a Spanish-speaking child in her internship classroom. Juan had a history of struggling with the worksheets typically used in units of study, but he was able to participate actively in the class study of community helpers when Carmen's inquiry-based approach encouraged him to communicate in a variety of ways. Juan and the other children posed questions, listened to and read books, interviewed visitors, and created and presented stories, paintings, and skits to share their learning. Because he had opportunities to articulate ideas using a range of sign systems (Short, Harste, & Burke, 1996), Juan experienced success. He communicated ideas through drawing and by using both English and Spanish words as he felt comfortable. Carmen wrote, "I was proud to see Juan feel success after seeing him give up in frustration so many other times."

We all remember visiting Dan Wuori's kindergarten, where his students invited us to join them in written conversations (Short, Harste, & Burke, 1996). The moment we walked into the room, Dan's five-year-olds asked if we would write with them. Sitting with child partners, we wrote back and forth. Susi and a little girl named Kayla introduced themselves to each other through writing by asking about things they liked to do. Kayla made approximations as she wrote questions and then used Susi's responses (demonstrations) to adjust her next contribution (Figure 3.7). Through this process, we learned about another structure

Figure 3.6. Carly's kindergartners learn skills and strategies through a morning message.

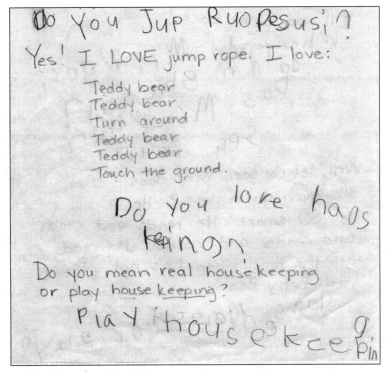

Figure 3.7. Susi's written conversation with a child in Dan Wuori's kindergarten class.

that supports children in learning skills and strategies while using them in purposeful contexts.

As a result of experiences like these, a whole-part-whole philosophy (Moustafa, 1997) became the cornerstone of our belief system. We believed that understandings about phonics and grammatical structure are important aspects of the reading process, but that they are not the whole story and that they are less effectively taught when presented in isolation from meaning-based contexts. We shared Routman's (1996) concern about an emphasis on "discrete skills and superficial learning at the expense of not teaching our students how to interpret, evaluate, analyze, and apply knowledge" (p. 6). We believed that learning to read or write, work with numbers, or understand scientific concepts is not about memorizing facts or sounding out words one letter at a time. We wanted to support children's understanding of skills and strategies through purposeful involvement in whole learning experiences. We took Mem Fox's (1993) words to heart. She wrote, "Worksheets are the dead-end streets of literacy: there's a non-message on each line, going nowhere for no reason. . . . If we want to maintain illiteracy, worksheets are perfect" (p. 69). In her journal, Julie wrote, "Out with mindless worksheets! Students need to be actively engaged in meaningful experiences that challenge them to reach their full problem-solving potential."

Careful kidwatching is key to good teaching.

In Julie's oral exams at the end of the MAT program, she said, "I really feel like assessment goes hand-in-hand with planning curriculum." This summed up our beliefs about assessment. Its key purpose should be to inform instruction. In our experience, the most helpful assessment occurred when we observed and interacted with children as they applied knowledge in real-world contexts. We learned more by listening to children and conferring with them than we did by using end-of-chapter tests or assessing skills in isolation. As we learned to use these observations and interactions to plan for instruction, we developed the belief that good teaching grows from good kidwatching—paying close attention to what children do *when they are engaged* as readers, writers, mathematicians, scientists, social scientists, artists, and musicians (Goodman, 1978). In our math methods class, for example, our professor, Irma VanScoy, asked us to look closely at one child over time. Doing so, we began to understand kidwatching as authentic, comprehensive, and reflective assessment. We got to know children as creative thinkers, problem posers, and problem solvers and used that knowledge to guide decisions about where to go next. In our literacy course, we practiced listening to and interacting with children as readers and writers to better understand what they knew. We listened to uncover their interests, concerns, and passions as well as ways they transacted with text (Goodman, Watson, & Burke, 1987; Rosenblatt, 1994; Weaver, 1994). We then focused on skills and strategies we could teach them to promote further growth. In the process, we learned about kidwatching as the act that holds curriculum together and pushes it forward (O'Keefe, 1997). As Carly wrote in her synthesis paper just before graduation, we saw students as "our best and most important curricular informants as opposed to a program written by someone who has never met our students and doesn't know anything about them."

Teachers support children as readers and writers when they provide plenty of time for children to read and write.

We left the MAT program believing strongly in the importance of providing extended periods of time every day for reading to and with children. We believed that readers grow in passion and proficiency when they have opportunities every day to read books they love and that they *can* read, to employ the skills and strategies they are learning through real reading and writing (Cambourne, 1988). We also knew that to learn to read, children need to be immersed in experiences with meaningful texts that reflect their worlds and that are characterized by engaging stories, fascinating characters, and stunning use of language. We left the MAT program hoping to build classrooms in which time for children to read and reading to children was sacred. We wanted our classrooms to be, like Joanne Hindley's (1996), places where anyone who entered would feel invited to "pull up a piece of rug and settle into a good read" (p. 84).

We also came to believe that to grow as writers, children need time to write daily for meaningful purposes. They need time to read and support for noticing strategies that writers use as they communicate story, character, information, and ideas. Writing workshop (Hindley, 1996) was a structure with which we developed familiarity and wanted to implement in our own teaching. When we visited Tim O'Keefe's second-grade and Stacie Mandrell's second/third-grade classrooms, we learned more about the authoring cycle (Short, Harste, & Burke, 1996) as a structure for supporting children as writers. We watched students using writer's notebooks (Fletcher, 1996) to record images, conversations, and impressions from the world around them that they could then access as resources when crafting extended pieces of text. As children met with peers and teachers to confer about their latest writing (Hindley, 1996), we learned about supporting individual students. We observed teachers using children's books to provide demonstrations of writers' craft through large- and small-group mini-lessons. We wanted our students to learn about writing in such a workshop environment.

Extrinsic rewards for reading books reduce the act of reading to earning points and prizes instead of learning to love reading for its own sake.

We embraced the idea that children are motivated as readers and writers when the classroom culture honors individual as well as group interests and when books are shared and discussed in meaningful ways every day. Observing children in public school classrooms and remembering our own reading experiences, we quickly realized that extrinsic reward programs trivialize the act of reading and teach students to read for points and prizes, not for enjoyment or to seek information. We saw how reading to take the literal recall tests in read-test-reward programs reduces enjoyment and limits comprehension. Questions on the tests involved children in little critical thinking. They provided no opportunities for students to make connections to their own worlds or to engage in thought-extending conversations with other readers (Carter, 1996).

The work of Alfie Kohn (1999) and our experiences with children led us to a strong belief in the fallacy of extrinsic rewards. We embraced the words of John Dewey (1916), who wrote that "no alleged study or discipline is educative unless it is worthwhile in its own immediate having" (p. 109). We believed that opportunities to read for enjoyment and in the pursuit of personal or collective inquiries were crucial to the development of motivated readers. This meant we had a responsibility to create classrooms where children would have access to books representing a range of subjects, cultural settings, and genres. Our school day would include opportunities for children to talk about books with peers and teachers (Peterson & Eeds, 1990; Short & Pierce, 1998). We would provide daily demonstrations of ourselves as passionate readers, motivating children to read in rich and lasting ways.

Opportunities for real reading and writing should permeate the classroom and the school day.

April's internship experiences in kindergarten provide examples of our belief that reading and writing should permeate the classroom and the school day. With the support and encouragement of her coaching teacher, she rearranged the classroom and constructed invitations for children to use literacy in every corner: books in the block corner; clip-boards and markers in the housekeeping area; cozy areas with rocking chairs, pillows, and baskets of books; access to Big Books and little book versions of them; and books at listening centers.

Setting up a first-grade classroom during our language arts meth-ods course was another way we learned how reading and writing might permeate the classroom. We labeled areas of the room by writing inter-actively with children. We talked about how words on walls become merely wallpaper if they are not collaboratively generated, created, and used and if they do not grow from the shared interests of the class. We learned about curricular structures that create connectedness to literacy across the day: morning message, shared reading, interactive writing, literature discussions, writing workshop, independent reading, confer-ring, kindness journals, math journals, and science observation journals.

Our understanding of each of these practices was grounded in the belief that reading and writing are not isolated processes. We car-ried this understanding into our math methods course when our pro-fessor, Irma VanScoy, asked us to complete bibliographies of children's books that could be used as springboards for talk about mathematical thinking (Whitin & Wilde, 1992). We developed engagements that en-couraged children to respond to stories mathematically. These and many other experiences left us with the belief that literacy could be used pur-posefully throughout the day. We wanted our own classrooms to reflect that belief.

Teachers have a responsibility to reflect regularly on their practices and to continue to grow through ongoing, in-depth study of theory and practice.

In her synthesis paper at the end of our MAT year, Erin wrote, "The most important conviction I have developed over the past ten months is my belief that teachers have a responsibility to continue to grow as learn-ers." We left graduate school with that belief firmly in mind—learning does not stop at the end of the preservice program. Our professors told us this, but more important, we witnessed it firsthand when teachers in our internship classrooms read current professional literature, participated actively in teacher study groups, attended and presented at local and national conferences, and viewed the supervision of interns as an opportunity to learn as well as to teach. Robbie writes about her coaching teachers as people who learned right along with her, excited about every opportunity to continue to grow:

> I had two amazing coaching teachers who were great models. They were not exactly like the teachers in the books I was reading in classes, but they were both involved in extensive professional development and were interested in learning from me as well as teaching me. They taught me that you never stop learning and growing as an educator.

At the end of our internships, our appreciation of teachers as lifelong learners deepened as we prepared for presentations of our own inquiries. Through a project developed by Susi's colleague Amy Donnelly, we collected and analyzed classroom data as we conducted investigations based on questions generated from personal curricular interests. Conducting our own investigations, we experienced inquiry as a way of life for teachers who consistently examine their own practices.

By the end of the MAT program, our belief in the importance of continued professional study and reflection was deeply ingrained. We agreed with Routman (1996) that "professional development must be viewed as a necessity not an option" (p. 39). It would be our responsibility to join national organizations; attend and present at local and national conferences; take further university courses; and read, try new ideas, reflect, share, read, try, share, and read some more.

Charged to Take on the World

During our last class session, Susi read the picture book *Miss Rumphius* (Cooney, 1982), the story of a little girl who grew up to fulfill her grandfather's wish that she "do something to make the world more beautiful." To accomplish this "most difficult thing of all," she scattered lupine seeds far and wide, creating patches of color across the countryside. Closing the book, Susi gave us each packets of lupine seeds and invited us to make the world more beautiful through our work with children. We grabbed onto the metaphor. We understood that we had a lot to learn, but we also knew that we were not blank slates; we would bring rich experiences to our new positions. We left the MAT program with definite goals for our classrooms and very specific beliefs about teaching and learning. In oral comprehensive exams, we articulated understandings with conviction and confidence. We faced the job search anxious to take on the educational world—or at least the part of it that would be a classroom of kids and a school full of enthusiastic colleagues. With them, we would work to bring our visions to life. We would become the teachers we hoped we would be.

Critical Insights from Chapter 3

We left our graduate program with convictions that defined the teachers we hoped we would be. We believed that:

- Classrooms should be warm, authentically inviting physical environments.

- We learn more when learners and teachers foster mutual respect, value and care for one another, and feel comfortable enough to take risks.

- Learners are supported when they have opportunities to inquire and reflect; respecting students' questions means that curriculum can be generated from their interests.

- Good teaching starts with expecting success and building from what children know.

- We learn more when we are engaged in meaningful interactions with other learners; learning is social in nature.

- Students learn best through demonstrations of skills and strategies used in the context of meaningful experiences.

- Careful kidwatching is key to good teaching; assessment and instruction should inform each other.

- Teachers support children as readers and writers when they provide plenty of time for children to read and write.

- Extrinsic rewards reduce the act of reading to merely earning points and prizes instead of learning to love reading for its own sake.

- Opportunities for real reading and writing should permeate the classroom and the school day.

- Teachers have a responsibility to reflect regularly on their practices and to continue to grow through ongoing, in-depth study of theory and practice.

4 We Were Going to Be Teachers *for Real*

Excited, overwhelmed, scared, and anxious. I am all of these things at once. I can't wait to meet my students, but I wonder—how much freedom will I have to implement new strategies? Will other teachers respect my views since I'm the new kid on the block? Will parents take me seriously since I'm a first-year teacher? How will the first day go? Does every first-year teacher go through this overwhelmed feeling?

With Beliefs in Hand

I am so excited about making things happen that I can hardly sit still.

With beliefs in hand, we headed out to look for jobs. We couldn't wait to put ideas into practice in our own classrooms. We looked for schools where we could use theoretical and practical knowledge to create curriculum with and for children, where teachers had autonomy and were trusted to use it, where meeting standards was considered to be a natural outgrowth of knowledgeable teaching, and where teachers and administrators saw the profession as one that could bring great intellectual satisfaction as well as joy. We sought jobs that would allow us to teach using inquiry-based approaches and implement specific curricular structures we believed to be supportive of children's learning. As Ami wrote, we wanted to find schools "where our wings would not be clipped." Carly explained, "I wanted to find a place where I would have the autonomy to teach to my students' needs and interests." We hoped to find schools where autonomy was anchored in an atmosphere of trust, respect, and caring among teachers, administrators, and parents. But learning how to recognize such places was not as easy as we anticipated.

Entering the job search, we shared a common sense of optimism and an almost giddy excitement. We had great hopes for the possibilities awaiting us. We said things like "Do I think I will be able to hold onto my dreams? I definitely do!!" and "I am so excited about making things happen that I can hardly sit still." In the following pages, we share stories about what happened next—job interviews, moving into schools, setting up our first classrooms, and first days with children. We were nervous but ready to go. At last we were going to be teachers for real!

The Job Hunt

A nerve-wracking experience

All of us found the job hunt to be, as Julie wrote, "a nerve-wracking experience to say the least." We applied for jobs and then waited and waited to be called for interviews. Repeatedly we called district offices, only to be assured that our files were in order and that we would receive calls "soon." It was frustrating. We worried that we would never get jobs. Like most of us, Robbie waited almost a month to find out if she would be offered the job she wanted: "When I didn't hear anything, I called to follow up. Then I called to follow up on my follow-up. I thought I would die while I was waiting!" Erin described the sense of urgency we all felt that summer:

> When the MAT synthesis paper was finally finished and the orals were behind me, I wanted to find a job and to find it fast. I have never been patient about anything in my life—long lines, aerobics classes that move too slowly, lectures that drag on too long— but I was probably less patient about securing a job than any other big decision I have ever made. Back when a year seemed like an eternity, I wanted to be catapulted into my future instead of taking the traditional day-by-day route. I knew I would love teaching. Did it really matter where I taught? *Impulsive* would be the best answer on a fill-in-the-blank test if you were asked to describe me at that point.

Gut feelings really do matter.

All of our first impressions turned out to be accurate, which was fortunate for some of us and unfortunate for others. We learned that gut feelings really do matter. Carly and Robbie interviewed and accepted jobs in the same school just outside of Atlanta. Their first impression was that the principal would be a caring and supportive administrator. Carly wrote:

> I went to a job fair and interviewed with three principals. The first two principals seemed bored with the whole interview process and, I have to say, very dry. Then I met Mr. Smith. He greeted me with a warm smile and we talked a lot about the wonderful lunch that the head of the cafeteria staff had cooked especially for him. He asked me very little about myself or my graduate school experiences, which was a little disappointing. I expected him to ask about teaching. So I was surprised when he called me to come in for a second interview. Later, I would discover that Mr. Smith's conversational style was actually his way of getting to know his applicants as human beings first.

Carmen found the same sensitivity when she met the principal for whom she would eventually work:

> Dr. Adkins made me feel like I was talking to a friend. I was most impressed when I realized that we shared a fundamental belief—that good teaching is based on loving children for who they are and for what they bring to you. Talking to him, I began to think that this was a place where I could feel at home; where the principal thought that it was just as vital to hug a child, know their home worlds, or attend a baseball game with them as it was to make sure that they excelled academically. It was important to me to work for a principal who understood that by doing these things, he would have a greater impact on children's opportunities for success.

Susi, thinking back to her own first job interview, remembered her gut feeling about Sam Ficarrotta. She told us about sitting in his office noticing the books on his shelf, recognizing many that she knew from her father's collection of books about the open classroom movement. From the first moments of the interview, Susi saw this as an indication that they would be kindred spirits.

Our first impressions of administrators also came from watching interactions during interviews that involved faculty members. Although it was a bit intimidating to face a crowd, interviews that included potential colleagues allowed us to observe the dynamics between teachers and administrators. After Robbie's interview with Mr. Smith, she wrote: "I was impressed by what seemed to be a very positive relationship between the principal and the other people in the interview. Their back-and-forth banter, laughter, and teasing exuded the respect they seemed to feel for one another. I left with the feeling that Mr. Smith would be a wonderful principal and that the school would be a good place to work." April had a similar experience. Her interview was with the assistant principal, Dave Tool, and several young teachers. She thought it was a good sign that new teachers were included in the process. The give-and-take of the conversation was an opportunity for her to look for and find indications of mutual respect between members of the interview team.

We wanted so badly to find what we were looking for that sometimes we saw it when it wasn't there.

It was more difficult to trust our gut feelings when we had negative reactions to our interviews. We wanted so badly to find what we were looking for that sometimes we saw it when it wasn't there. When we started the job search, Carly said that our biggest challenge would be "to search beneath the layers of rhetoric" to find a school that offered pedagogical compatibility. She was right; separating rhetoric from reality was not always easy. When we heard language that was congruent with ideas we had come to value—inquiry, immersion, meaningful context, child-centered, authentic, autonomy, best practices—we tended to think that deeper meanings would also be shared. Unfortunately, this was not always the case. Without asking for clarification, we could easily come away from interviews with inaccurate impressions about both climate and curriculum. Julie explained:

> When I asked questions, the principal gave answers that sounded in line with what I wanted to find: The grade level teams planned regularly together and he was an advocate for sharing student work and wanted this to pervade the hallways. He recognized my previous experience as a graphic designer and asked if I would be willing to use that talent in various projects around the school. He had done his homework and seemed good at seeking out a person's talents and putting them to work for the benefit of the school. He seemed very organized. These were qualities I valued. I remember thinking that he didn't seem to be very friendly, but I wrote that off as a professional stance.
>
> It wasn't until much later that I realized that I had made a huge mistake. I didn't ask the really important questions. I didn't ask if I would have professional autonomy. I didn't ask how new teachers would be supported by the administration. I didn't ask about collaboration among teachers. I didn't trust my gut feelings about personality. I didn't realize that if someone seems aloof during an interview, he might have the same unapproachable demeanor later when teachers offer suggestions, ask for something to be changed, question something, or just need emotional support.

In Erin's job interview, the principal explained that she would have to follow the district-mandated reading program but that she could do what she wanted with social studies and science in the afternoon. Having worked successfully within a mandated program during her internship, it was easy for Erin to interpret the principal's words with hope:

> When I was told that I would have to teach using a scripted, isolated skills approach, I knew that this did not support my philosophy, but I thought, "How bad could it really be?" Mandated programs were common in schools all over our area. I thought I could surely learn to address the requirements of a mandated reading program while maintaining my core beliefs as an educator. I had used the basal during student teaching but simply chosen aspects of lessons I felt were appropriate and didn't use the

rest. I thought it would be the same at my new school. I never dreamed that I would I have so little room to deviate from the script.

When the principal told Erin that she had twenty-four hours to make a decision about a second-grade position, even though her "deepest fear was that their philosophies were not aligned," she went against her gut feeling and accepted the job. Later she explained how her eagerness to get started with her teaching career kept her from trusting her instincts:

> I accepted a position quickly, not so much out of fear that I would never find a better job, but because I wanted to know my future school home. I wanted to know my room, my colleagues, my building, my students. I didn't want to wait another month, or week or even another day. *My impatience distracted me from listening to warnings that were coming from deep inside.*

I felt well prepared to answer their questions.

We all felt, as April said, "well prepared to answer questions during interviews by sharing knowledge about theory and practice," even though some of us wished we had spent more time preparing questions that *we* wanted to ask. Articulating pedagogical knowledge was often key to finding compatibility with administrators and potential colleagues. Ami felt an immediate connection with administrators Sharon Bodie and Steve Berwager. Their open discussion about educational philosophies indicated that they would be supportive of Ami's teaching style and educational beliefs. Probing beneath the surface of what might have been merely rhetoric, Ami and her interviewers questioned each other. At the end of the interview, she felt sure the position would be a good fit.

Carmen wrote that her ability to support her beliefs with theoretical understandings gave her confidence during interviews:

> I explained that I strongly believed in Vygotsky's idea that we learn more when we have opportunities to interact with other learners and that children need to be met where they are and moved forward from there. I supported my beliefs with colorful stories about engagements I had implemented during my student teaching experience.

Carmen admitted that when her future administrators explained the school's use of a scripted math program, she "felt a twinge of dishonesty" because she didn't explain that scripts telling teachers what to do and say were not a part of her belief system. She saw them as "an insult to an educator's intelligence." But she sensed that, with Dr. Adkins, she would be able to interpret the programs as she felt best:

> He let me know that he trusted and respected me as an educator even though I was new to the profession. He didn't make any demands during the interview. Our talk flowed with the easiness of a conversation with a friend or trusted colleague. I know he knew I would make mistakes, but he felt that I would do what I felt was best for my students.

During interviews I was sure to ask for a tour of the school.

During interviews, most of us asked for school tours. As we walked, we looked for signs that would provide insights into the school's culture. We peeked into classrooms, looking for evidence of teacher autonomy and innovative practices, rooms full of personality, artifacts from student inquiries, and cozy book corners. We looked to see if teachers valued variation in student work and to see if administrators valued variation from teacher to teacher: Did classroom walls and bulletin boards reflect the energy and interests of individual children, teachers, and classes? Did rooms vary in their arrangement? Did they reflect the use of a variety of instructional strategies?

Most of us felt that we were following our hearts personally and professionally when we accepted jobs.

Even though it seemed like an eternity as we waited to hear from principals and districts, we were all offered jobs before the school year started. When Carly received a job offer from Mr. Smith, she was thrilled: "I'm going to be a fourth-grade teacher! I have absolutely no idea what fourth graders are required to learn, but I feel confident that I know how to guide children in the learning process." Robbie was equally excited: "When Mr. Smith finally called, it was one of my *all time favorite* phone conversations. He offered me the job! My classroom would be a self-contained fifth grade." And Ami was elated to hear about her first-grade position: "When I accepted the job, outwardly, I was calm. Internally, I was flipping cartwheels and exclaiming, 'You bet I wanna teach here!'"

Most of us felt that we were following our hearts personally as well as professionally when we accepted jobs. Julie turned down a job that would involve a long commute so she could be closer to her daughter's day care. Carly found a job near Atlanta that allowed her to be near her boyfriend. Robbie, ready for new adventures, wanted to live in a bigger city, so accepting a position in the school where Carly would be working was a perfect fit.

Carmen's acceptance of a job in her hometown meant that she could give back to the community where she had grown up and she could be close to her family. Conversations with her cousin Bonita about the importance of making a difference led her back to Anderson, South Carolina, a small, upstate mill town. She interviewed at several schools, including her alma mater and a school drawing from a predominantly White population. When the district office called with several job offers, she struggled with the decision. The personnel officer was forthright and told her, "I hope you don't mind my saying this, but [the predominantly White school] needs some diversity." Carmen appreciated her honesty and agreed:

> My perception was that there had not been a lot of interaction between Blacks and Whites over the years in that area of town. The children and, in my opinion, the faculty needed me. And, yes, it was because I am African American. At that time, there was only one Black classroom teacher at the school. This did not make me a token teacher or any less of a teacher, but I did stop to think about being tucked away in a rural mill area with mostly White children—me, with my Afrocentric hair, clothing, and Black dialect. Because of my southern upbringing, I had my own preconceived notions about going into this school. I knew that it would be an adjustment, but I accepted the position. I would rely on my belief in loving children.

Erin, however, felt real trepidation about the situation she was getting herself into. She worried about the mandated programs in her school, but she had made a commitment and was resolved to move forward. Surely she could bring her dreams to life and still meet the requirements of the principal.

Moving into Our Schools

Our instincts were correct.

During preplanning sessions before the children arrived, we learned more about the places that would be our school homes. During that time, various incidents confirmed both our positive and negative instincts. Robbie discovered right away that Mr. Smith was the kind and caring administrator she and Carly had predicted him to be. From the first day, it was clear that he valued them and their knowledge. Robbie wrote, "He makes me feel like I am the most important teacher in the school. From the beginning, he made it clear that he was glad I was on his staff."

This feeling extended to the district level. During an induction meeting, Robbie and Carly were pleased to find a commitment to teacher autonomy. They were also thrilled to discover that district curricular requirements seemed to be closely aligned with theory and practice they had learned in graduate school. Carly explained, "An assistant superintendent spoke about language arts. He said the most important thing was for children to enjoy reading and to become lifelong readers. He expressed confidence that teachers would make this happen in ways we knew best. Robbie and I looked at each other and smiled. We thought, 'This is going to be a good year.'"

Carmen's initial impression of her principal was also confirmed during the preplanning days. One of the first affirmations that her instincts were correct occurred after she heard teachers talk about a child named Alex who had been placed in her classroom. Carmen explained:

> Susi's advice to stay away from negative teachers' lounge talk rang in my ears when I listened to teachers tell me how horrible Alex was. They couldn't understand why Dr. Adkins put him in my room—after all, he was the school terror and I was new to teaching. I'm not sure if I felt more anger or anxiety. I was angry at the constant negativity from teachers about this child and I was anxious about what to expect from him.

But then a wonderful thing happened. At a faculty meeting just before school started, Dr. Adkins mentioned putting Alex on Carmen's roster, saying that he really liked Alex and felt that she could handle him. Carmen wondered if Dr. Adkins was reflecting on their conversation during the job interview. She remembered their talk about how important it was to look for the good in every child: "Maybe there was a method to his madness. Why put this child with a teacher who already abhorred him? My feelings of anxiety faded. I sat in that meeting smiling with thoughts of how I was going to *handle* Alex. My big plan? I was going to genuinely love him and take it from there, educating both of us one day at a time."

Susi told us that her initial impression of her first principal also turned out to be accurate. He was the kindred spirit she thought he would be. The first day of teaching for Susi was also the first day of Mr. Ficarrotta's brand-new school in Clearwater, Florida. It was August 24, 1974. A newspaper article in the *Pinellas Times* described the day. Every quote revealed the principal's positive spirit: "I'm for real and this school is going places!"; "The child, the child, is the most important thing"; "We have a young, vigorous staff. We think as one." Thirty years later, Susi could still hear his voice as she read from the newspaper clipping in her scrapbook: "'Outta sight, outta sight,' Ficarrotta repeated as he checked on class after class. 'This school's going to develop into something unique.'"

I kept thinking it was all a big joke.

Affirmation of initial impressions meant that for some of us our worst fears were confirmed. In the first few days, Erin began to realize that working within a system of mandates would not be as easy to negotiate as she had thought. The first planning meeting with her grade-level team solidified her apprehension about the rigid implementation of scripted programs. Erin wrote, "We began by planning phonics instruction for the entire first week! I was told not only that I was required to teach an isolated phonics block every morning, but *how* I would teach the skills, right down to the very workbook pages my children would complete."

Erin's team leader wrote plans on the board while the other second-grade teachers copied them into their plan books. They were required to teach the same thing, each class working through the program at the pace outlined in the teacher's guide. Erin tried to collect her thoughts enough to consider how she would work around those barriers, but this situation contrasted vividly with her expectations of "a child-centered classroom brimming over with possibilities for learning":

> I kept thinking it was all a big joke. In graduate school, my peers and I planned our work by observing, reflecting, and asking, "How can we best serve these children?" Then we taught, paid close attention to the responses of each child, reflected on how things went, and considered ways to improve our teaching. This simply wasn't that.

Erin was already beginning to feel trapped in a situation she had never anticipated. It wasn't that she was uncomfortable teaching phonics, but she was frustrated by the requirement to teach it in isolation and in the same way at the same time for every child whether they needed it or not. Feeling that she could not use her knowledge about teaching and learning and about the children in her classroom to make instructional decisions, she had real fears as she anticipated the first day of school: "There is this dread that has nothing to do with being new and inexperienced. It has to do with the fact that I have no autonomy in how I teach reading and math."

Setting Up Our Classrooms

The responsibility to create dynamic learning environments suddenly became very real.

Once we had jobs, setting up our classrooms was an exhilarating but also daunting experience. The responsibility to create dynamic learning environments for children suddenly became very real. Robbie described the pressure we all felt:

> I was scared because there was no one responsible but me. If something failed, I was not just failing me, I was failing my students, their parents, and my friends in the MAT program. I wanted that classroom to be perfect. I wanted to be Bobbi Fisher, Jill Ostrow, JoAnne Hindley, Regie Routman, Susi Long, David Whitin, and teachers at the Center for Inquiry all rolled into one.

We were experiencing our first real moments of self-doubt. Everything we did *not* know began to loom large. Robbie continued:

> My school situation seemed like my MAT dream come true. No one was telling me what to do as long as I followed the curriculum and made the children, the parents, and administration happy. At the same time it was my worst nightmare. I had not been in a fifth-grade classroom since I was a ten-year-old in Mrs. Lee's class at Windsor Elementary. I had no idea what students would know or what they could do. How would I teach language arts to fifth graders? And multiplying fractions—was that when you switched them or cross multiplied or something? I hardly remembered my multiplication tables, much less fifth-grade math. I *did* know that children learn best when given opportunities to connect learning to prior experiences. I knew that it was important to know my children and generate curriculum based on their needs and interests. I knew that learning is more powerful in the context of whole and meaningful experiences. There was one last thing I knew. I knew those fifth graders were going to eat me alive!

We did a lot of rummaging in the weeks before school started.

April writes about walking into her classroom and facing an almost empty room. Her first thought was, "Where are all my materials?" The room had been an established kindergarten classroom the year before, so April expected to see it well equipped with math manipulatives, blocks, dramatic play materials, shelves for books, shelves for centers, and wordplay materials. She saw only an enormous empty shelf and a few boxes. April explained:

> I learned later that teachers often scrounge from other classrooms at the end of the year when a teacher leaves. So, by July, there was little left in my room. I was on my own to find materials and most of the furniture. As a result, I worried about getting the classroom ready in time for the first day of school. The other kindergarten teachers had been in their classrooms over the summer and their rooms were almost ready for students!

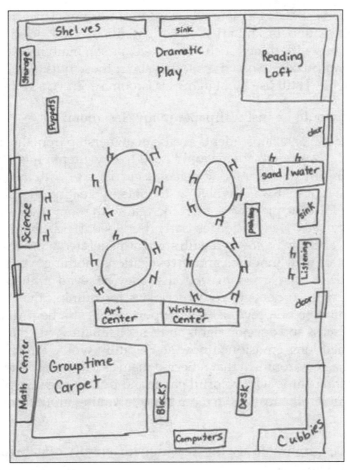

Figure 4.1. April's map of possibilities as she began to think about how to arrange her classroom.

We wanted our classrooms to be inviting places where children could relax and be motivated to learn, and we wanted to be well organized. So we did a lot of rummaging in the weeks before school started. We checked out garage sales and flea markets. We searched our own garages and attics. We gleaned ideas from fellow teachers, professional books, and catalogs. We accepted help from anyone and everyone who offered. Ami's mom came from New York with a carload of children's books and materials for her classroom. Relatives visiting Julie went to work painting bookshelves and helping her organize the room.

April began by mapping out possibilities on paper (Figure 4.1). She designed a writing area "stocked with writing tools of all kinds and a variety of paper." She planned areas for exploring science, math, dramatic play, puppets, and art. Ami bought, filled, and labeled 200 plastic shoe bins with things such as markers, paper, math manipulatives, books, and puzzles. She writes today about those bins as a "fabulous investment—I still use them in my classroom seven years later!"

Nothing would be just wallpaper in my classroom!

We wanted to give our students a sense of ownership from the first days of school. We knew that we would need to pay attention to curricular guides, but we also wanted to generate curriculum with the students. One aspect of that was involving students in creating the classroom. Carly and Robbie planned to start the year with rooms that were comparatively bare. Their vision, as Carly described it, was that "the walls would eventually be covered with student-generated work that would grow out of their inquiries and investigations; nothing would be just wallpaper in my classroom!" Because they believed in the power of working with students to construct plans for running the classroom, there would be no previously made posters of classroom rules. They would discuss and develop rights and responsibilities with the children. Robbie had long envisioned how she would involve the children in building an environment that reflected them as learners, so she covered the bulletin boards with colorful paper and put up a few inspirational quotes but left the rest of the room blank, awaiting input from the students.

We were beginning to see that teaching differently came with awkward tensions.

Enthusiasm for our dream of co-creating classrooms with students was not always shared or understood by our colleagues. In Robbie's case, a teacher down the hall didn't understand why she turned down the offer of posters and other materials. As the new kid on the block, Robbie was already beginning to feel the tensions associated with being different:

> My assigned school mentor did not love my vision about not filling the room with commercially made decorations. She brought a pile of posters into my room with definite ideas about where they should go. Not wanting to offend her, I tried calmly to explain that I did not want those manufactured things hanging in my room. She couldn't understand. I probably surprised her when I broke down in tears. I wanted to please her and make friends with a new colleague, but I also wanted to be my own teacher.

Not only did we want to avoid filling our rooms with *wallpaper*—wall displays purely for the purpose of looking pretty—but we also wanted to avoid filling our students' time with *deskpaper*—worksheets that were equally meaningless. For some of us, this meant negotiating awkward tensions when colleagues felt it was helpful to share worksheets for every skill and unit plan. Carmen explained:

> My grade-level team helped when they could, but one form of help was to give me copies of worksheets to use. Those worksheets were making things worse because I did *not* want my instruction to be worksheet-driven and it seemed to be going in that direction immediately. I worried about how I would teach according to my beliefs and still be a part of my team. My solution was to just accept the worksheets, put them in my file cabinet, and close the drawer.

We wanted to encourage children to read a wide range of literature in a comfortable and inviting place where they could lose themselves in good books.

We had a particular passion for literacy and wanted our students to be involved in meaningful experiences with print. We wanted every student to see himself or herself as a reader. We wanted to encourage children to read a wide range of literature in a comfortable and inviting place where they could lose themselves in good books. So developing a dynamic reading area was an important goal for each of us.

Ami wrote about developing her book collection by following the advice of her internship teacher. She used school funds for consumable items such as construction paper, glue, pens, and crayons and spent her own money on children's books so they would be hers forever. Ami spent much time during the summer binding and organizing her growing book collection (Figure 4.2):

> With the books I'd purchased during graduate school and the help of my mom, I already had an extensive collection, at least 1,000 titles. I bound the paperback books with clear packaging tape so they would last longer. I organized all of them into text sets based on commonalities: poetry, authors, illustrators, Caldecott winners, historical fiction, animal fiction, nonfiction, and biographies.

We did some creative searching to find homes for our collections of children's books. Ami writes about "salvaging three wooden book shelves from a dumpster and painting them bright red, blue and yellow." Carly searched all summer for the "perfect perch for my growing

Figure 4.2. Ami's organization of children's books.

classroom library," which she ultimately found in a gift shop that was going out of business. A local carpet store donated colorful carpet squares that Carly used to visually separate the "comfy reading area" from the rest of the room. Spouses, boyfriends, and other family members were often called into service as we searched for and constructed perfect places for our books. This was particularly important to Erin, who was already worried about bringing her convictions to life within a program that included few opportunities for immersion in great books:

> I desperately wanted the bookshelf beyond bookshelves for my picture books, the ones that would teach my students to love to read even within a sea of mandated worksheets. The nicest bookshelves were priced well beyond my realm of reasonable classroom spending. Dutton, my fiancé, took a good look at a coveted bookshelf in a dog-eared catalog and said he could make it. He tore the page out of the catalog and took it home with him to Valdosta, Georgia. A while later, Dutton called to tell me he had just returned from the emergency room where he almost lost a finger to a belt sander while making the nicest bookshelf I had ever seen! Fortunately Dutton's finger healed and during his next visit to Columbia, he wheeled the bookshelf into my room. It had three display shelves, was painted sky blue, and had two storage shelves on the back. It was, without a doubt, the most treasured possession in my classroom.

April was excited to find that her room had a loft—"not in good condition, but I could fix it up and use it for a reading area." She put her books along a shelf in the loft and added pillows and stuffed animals for her kindergartners to use as reading buddies. Julie made curtains and brought in houseplants, beanbag chairs, a wooden bench, a basket of stuffed animals, and a rocking chair in which she pictured herself "with children gathered around as we enjoyed books together."

Carly used student surveys to select the books with which she filled her classroom. The surveys included questions that would help her build on students' interests and backgrounds: What do you love to do when you are not in school? Who are the people you admire most? What do you like to watch on TV? Who are your favorite musicians, sports figures, famous people? Who is your favorite author? What kinds of books do you like to read?

When bookshelves had been purchased or scrounged and painted, pillows sewn, and books organized, we were proud of our literacy areas. We were pleased that they were bright, colorful, and cozy—the heart of our classrooms.

We wanted to encourage an atmosphere of mutual respect.

Many of us tried to find ways before school started to get to know our students and to set up an environment that would encourage an atmosphere of mutual respect. Robbie wrote that she wanted to base her classroom on "the respect and friendship that community can foster":

> Every day we are going to emphasize kindness and getting to know each other as real people, myself included. I want to know what my students like, dislike, and find important. I want them to know that I care about the things they are interested in. I hope that through my modeling of respect and interest in them, they will respect and find interest in each other.

Erin planned to "brainstorm classroom rules with the children" and Julie planned to begin with "one main class rule—being kind to others, like Bobbi Fisher does!" Carly drew from Dori Gilbert's kindergarten at the Center for Inquiry, where kindnesses were shared daily. She also built from the "ripples" idea learned during her volunteer experiences with City Year (Brown & Khazei, 2004):

> I plan to read Robert Kennedy's quote during the first days of school. His words were used by City Year to describe the notion that individual acts of kindness can create ripples of hope and justice: "Each time a person stands up for an ideal or acts to improve the lot of others, or strikes out against injustice, he sends forth a tiny ripple of hope. . . ." I'm going to use a small fish bowl with water and drop in a tiny staple. Then I can talk to the class about how even the smallest acts of kindness and courage (as small as even the staple) can create ripples of hope and justice. We can write down acts of kindness or courage that we notice among our classmates and place them in a jar to be read from at the end of each week.

Ami sent letters and questionnaires to students and their families to introduce herself and to ask them to share a bit about themselves. She visited families in their homes, where she listened to stories from parents and sometimes grandparents about children's gifts and unique personalities, and she shared stories about her own life. She invited families to come by the classroom before school started and asked each of them to bring a large pillow and a family portrait. The pillows and portraits helped Ami construct a classroom that reflected the lives of the children who would learn there: "One little cowboy galloped into the classroom hauling a rodeo pillow, a tiny girl tiptoed in carrying a hand-sewn patchwork creation, and many of my superhero boys had pillows and personalities matching their alter egos." The children set up family photographs around the room and added their pillows to Ami's reading area.

Julie moved her desks from straight rows into a U-shape that would allow the children to see one another and interact easily. She wanted them to feel trusted and empowered. Ami arranged her desks in what she called learning clusters—seven desks in each cluster—also to encourage interaction. Julie created a bulletin board on which students would be highlighted each week, sharing aspects of their lives that were meaningful to them and posting appreciations of one another. They would use this to learn more about one another as they began building a caring community while getting an opportunity to read and write purposefully. For the same reasons, Erin created a large Kindness Tree across one wall of her classroom (described in detail in Chapter 6) where her students would post notes of kindness.

I seriously underestimated how long it would all take.

Julie accepted her job two weeks before school began and scrambled to get the room together. We all knew exactly how she felt. At first glance, two weeks seemed like plenty of time, but those days were filled with school and district meetings that we hadn't expected, and as Julie said, "I seriously underestimated how long it would take to purchase, organize, and set up everything—labeling journals, arranging furniture, finding and painting bookshelves, and on and on." It seemed there were never enough hours in the day to attend all the meetings, organize the classroom, create lesson plans, read through all of the housekeeping memos, learn the procedures and rules of the school, and look at student files.

In the last days before school started, we spent even longer hours at school, often testing the patience of family members and friends. Carly's boyfriend, Nathan, called her at 5:00 on Friday evening when she was desperately trying to finalize plans for the children's arrival on Monday. She promised that she would be finished in "just thirty minutes." Two hours later Nathan showed up and convinced her that it was time to leave school and go with him to enjoy an evening picnic at the top of Stone Mountain. Little did Carly know that he had planned to propose at sunset. They arrived just in time.

We were excited and also a little scared.

That weekend few of us slept. We were filled with nervous energy. We had nightmares about alarm clocks not going off and being late for our first day of school. We wrote back and forth on the listserv voicing our fears: "I guess I could describe my feelings now as a combination between excitement and dread. I really don't remember being so stressed out!" "Can I really do this?" and "Say a little prayer that I can keep my sanity and create a magical environment for learning." We wondered: Would the parents like us? Would children connect with us? What would our curriculum *really* look like? What else did we need for our classrooms? And we worried about things that we had never thought would be worrisome. Erin wrote:

> I worried about things like the routine. Since I had never been through the lunch line, how would I know how to tell students to go through it? Since I'd never been on duty at recess, how would I tell them how to walk outside and which equipment they could play on? I was almost certain I would forget something. I was afraid that, in my forgetfulness, I would look unprepared and the children would misbehave. I was afraid that I wouldn't find that balance between being nice and being strict. I was nervous about phonics. I was nervous about the principal coming into my room. Basically, I was nervous about my whole first day of teaching.

Robbie finally sat down to finish planning when she arrived home at 9:00 the night before school began:

> It was then that it hit me—I was scared out of my mind. I did not have a clue. Later that night, 11:34 to be exact, I sent Susi the following email message: "Susi, all of a sudden I got really scared tonight. I have been busy but not nervous or scared until I had about twelve hours left before my first day. Do you have any last minute tips?" I didn't know yet that Susi goes to bed *really* early, so I didn't hear back from her.

The same night, Erin woke up at 1:00 in the morning convinced that it was time to start getting ready for school. She was headed to the bathroom to take a shower before realizing that it was the middle of the night. She tried to sleep again but without much luck.

Morning finally came. The first day of school had arrived. Focused on the excitement and anxieties of the day ahead, we thought about little else. In fact, it didn't even occur to Erin that it was her birthday until Dutton brought a cup of coffee to her that morning and said, "Happy Birthday!" At last it was time to greet our students.

First Days of Teaching

The kids are going to be here any minute!

A common pattern across all of our experiences was that, on the first day, we arrived at school very early. But, as early as we arrived, it seemed only seconds before the children would be there too. After running around with last-minute tasks, Erin sat at her desk thinking, "The kids are going to be here any minute, they're going to be here any minute!" Carmen wrote, "I had jitters from not knowing what to expect, but I couldn't wait for the kids to be there!"

Then they *were* there. For most of us, the first moments were hectic. Parents gave us instructions for how their children would get home while we tried to fill out attendance sheets, take up lunch money, and tell students where to put their materials. Within moments, we learned that flexibility and a good sense of humor were key to a successful first morning. Carly wrote:

> The school doors opened at 7:30 and by 8:00 I might as well have opened the window and thrust my beautiful, carefully crafted lesson plans out into the cool morning breeze. I had absolutely no concept of how much time would be spent on the housekeeping tasks of the first day of school. From organizing home transport schedules to reassuring parents who were reluctant to leave their children, I literally thought I would go insane and lose control. But, by later that morning, things had calmed down. I collected my wind-strewn plans and quickly reorganized them into something more manageable.

In April's kindergarten, the centers or interest areas she had prepared ahead of time helped to control the hectic feeling. As the children came in and put away their backpacks, she encouraged them to wander around the room to see what was there. She was thrilled to see most of the children jumping right in and getting involved.

Morning meeting: kidwatching on a larger scale

Once things settled down, we each began the day with some kind of morning meeting. We introduced ourselves, read books, and wrote interactively. Almost all of us included music. April introduced a good morning song, and Carly's fourth graders began a daily ritual—doing hand jive to "Miss Mary Mack." Carmen wrote that morning meeting with her second graders was her favorite part of the day, an opportunity to *"kidwatch* on a larger scale." She learned more about each child as they shared "the *best* stories—some sad, some funny, and some that were totally fabricated." Anxious to begin building trusting relation-ships, Carmen encouraged them to learn about her. At one point, the class engaged in what Carmen described as "one of the funniest mo-ments of the day—they argued about whether or not I was Jamaican. I'm not.☺"

Ami used morning meeting to introduce rotating classroom jobs: a botanist to care for class plants, a meteorologist to check on the day's weather, a veterinarian to care for class pets, and an accountant to take care of lunch money. Carly's class created a list of community rights and responsibilities. She was thrilled when their first suggestion was that they should have the right to ask questions.

Getting to know you

Several of us tried some variation of student interviews as vehicles for getting to know students and for them to get to know one another. In Ami's first grade, the children interviewed friends and created a book about the class. Carly's fourth graders used an interview structure to work through the processes of investigating questions, brainstorming and webbing ideas, writing rough drafts, meeting in authors' circles, revising, conferencing, and completing final drafts. Robbie described a similar engagement with her fifth graders:

> We did something that I called Getting-to-Know-You to introduce the authoring cycle. They did written conversation interviews of each other. Then they took the interviews and turned them into articles [Figure 4.3] for a classroom magazine. When it came time for authors' circles, they met in groups of three and they really took off! Without much instruction, they were engaged and en-joying it as they talked about each other's papers and then went back to revise their own writing. They really got a bang out of it and some of them were so mature about the whole process.

Carmen felt that the entire first day was about getting to know the children and letting them get to know her. She started a Kindness Journal (Figure 4.4) as a "great community builder and writing experi-ence for my students." She demonstrated writing kindnesses and "they took off from there." Carmen wrote, "It was the sweetest thing; it made my heart smile through all of my insecurities the first day. I made sure I wrote something kind about each of them."

We spent time helping children get to know their way around.

On the first day, we also spent time helping children get to know their way around. We rehearsed schedules, procedures, and routes from place

My interview was on Brian. This fifth grade boy has grown up in Stockbridge with his two brothers. He sure does love math, but if he was given three wishes, one of them would be to have no school. From one of the questions, I found out that Christmas is one of his favorite holidays. He likes it so much, another wish would be Christmas every day. The third, and final wish would be to see the Falcons play. He also wants to see the Cubs play. Speaking of sports he's thinking of being a baseball player. At home, Brian likes playing his Playstation and listening to his favorite country singer, Vince Gill. If you want to be friends with him, what are you waiting for? Go talk to him!

Figure 4.3. An excerpt from Robbie's class magazine; students introduced themselves through articles based on written conversation interviews.

to place around the school. Some of us later wished we had planned for more of this kind of thing. Others did a lot of procedural practicing, transitioning from one place to another. Ami described how she organized a scavenger hunt around the school to help her first graders learn the routes that would help them negotiate the school day:

> I put up large, colorful geometric shapes as markers outside doors around the school for VIPs and places like the school nurse, principal, assistant principal, guidance counselor, PE teacher, art

Figure 4.4. Pages from Carmen's Kindness Journal.

teacher, library, drama room, music room, custodians, etc. Then each child had a piece of paper with all of the shapes on it and what each shape represented. As we traveled around the school, they located the shapes and would say things like, "I found a red hexagon that says, 'school nurse.'" Then we would knock on the door and wave hello and the VIP would introduce himself or herself.

"Read it again! Read it again!"

Reading aloud immediately became a favorite ritual. On the first day, April read her favorite story, *The Very Hungry Caterpillar*, and was delighted when her kindergartners called out, "Read it again! Read it again!" Carly's fourth graders also begged for more when she read aloud. She wrote about how exciting it felt to "draw them into the wonderful world of books, one of my favorite things about teaching."

Robbie's fifth graders fell in love with *The Giver* as she read aloud. She loved watching them on the edge of their seats waiting to hear what would happen next:

> They are killed by the suspense! They wanted to stay after school to read on! When it gets really suspenseful and we are just about to find out crucial information, I tell them that's all I can read for now. Of course, I fully intend to keep reading, but they don't know that. It is so much fun to see them so wrapped up in a book.

Robbie also wrote with excitement about the success of independent reading time in her classroom. She started by giving students ten minutes to read with the intention of building up to longer periods, but when the timer went off the children begged for more time. She was amazed: "When I met one of my children at Open House before school started, he told me that his least favorite time of the day had always been reading. But now, after just the first few days of school, he is already so involved in reading. My kids love our reading time! I think one reason is that they get to choose what they read."

It was totally interest-directed and they were right with me!

During the first days, we were excited by the success of attempts to bring our beliefs about inquiry-based education to life. Carly wrote about the initiation of science inquiries with her fourth graders: "We talked about investigation as acting on our wonderings about our world. We observed classroom pets (birds) and discussed differences between observations and inference. We took a walk and used clipboards to jot down observations. We came back to the room and used our observations to write fiction or nonfiction stories, poems, or songs." Robbie introduced writer's notebooks and took her class outside to observe "the world around us." Back in the classroom, they shared wonderings, and when one student asked, "What grows bigger, a grasshopper or a praying mantis?," the question became, as Robbie described it, their "first classwide wonder!" Students were all raising their hands to offer views. That night she wrote to us: "Now as a class, we are going to research our questions. Without prompting they asked if they could go to the library because they needed more information to write about the topics they were interested in. I am so excited that they are taking the initiative to do their own research."

Julie was also thrilled with her students' excitement as she picked up on their interest in a frog outside the classroom window. She and her second graders launched into a spontaneous investigation that she described later that week:

During the middle of reading, a child noticed a frog outside our window. Several went to the window to discuss it. After they went back to their seats, they were still talking about it, so I decided to go with it. We discussed why we saw him on a rainy day. When they went to PE, another teacher and I caught the frog. When the students came back, I read a book about frogs and let the children's interest direct the discussion. We named the frog by creating a graph with tally marks next to name suggestions—and we were discussing graphing in math! It was totally interest-directed and they were right with me! We finally named him Bulldog, and after school on Friday, we released him into his natural habitat.

First day challenges

Many things went well, but our first days of school were not without challenges. For instance, two children were brought into April's class in tears, one kicking, screaming, and grabbing for the door. As the mothers left, April held on to the screaming child and he eventually calmed down in April's arms. April tried to interest him in the centers set up in her room, and soon he was up and joining the other children at work and play.

Dismissal also brought a few challenges. In Ami's class, "two kids took the wrong buses!" and it was well into the afternoon faculty meeting before everyone was happily on their way home. April described a similar situation: "I took some of the children to cars and the teaching assistant took others to the bus. Then one parent drove up expecting her child to jump into the car. I said, 'You told me she was going to be a bus rider!' I had put her child on the bus!" By the time everyone was safely on their way home, both April and Ami were exhausted and a bit frazzled, but they took it all in stride. As April said, "One of the other teachers had a child who threw up. At least I didn't have that!"

Erin's first day challenges were of a more serious nature and indicative of problems that were not going to go away. Because she was required to follow the teacher's guide, the day began with a scripted phonics lesson. Erin's fears were already realized as she watched children's reactions that first morning. She could already see the impact on their enthusiasm for school: "We started with phonics. The kids were so bored with it. They were yawning, putting their heads down, and playing with their books. I had to do so much reprimanding, but I couldn't really blame them for being bored or misbehaving. It was a horrible way to start second grade, but I didn't feel like I had the power to stop it."

I love it and I'm going strong, but as soon as I sit down after the kids leave, exhaustion rushes in!

For all of us, the entire first week was something of a roller coaster ride. One minute things went beautifully and the next it seemed that nothing was going well. Julie realized that fatigue played a big role in our ability to deal with ups and downs:

> On Thursday, I went home in tears. I was ready to throw in the towel. I felt like I was constantly competing with the children as I tried to get their attention. I definitely need to focus more on building community. I need to remind myself to wait until I have their full attention before I continue talking. On Friday, I had a better day. I can see that when I get tired, things get out of hand. Sleep renews me and I haven't been getting much.

We were already beginning to see that teaching was something of a juggling act. We were surprised at the number of hours we spent in meetings and overwhelmed with what seemed to be simple housekeeping tasks. We knew from our internship experiences that such tasks existed but, as Carmen said, "in our own classrooms, it was a whole different ballgame." During the first week, she wrote: "Everything is piling up quickly; I don't know where to look for anything. Other teachers constantly smile and ask, 'How's it going?' when I pass them in the hall. I smile, lie, and say, 'Everything's great' when really I don't know what my next move will be."

Julie described the flood of papers from the office and her struggle to keep up with so much all at once: "Right now, my dining room is a sea of papers. I haven't had time to stop and get organized. It's driving me crazy. Hopefully, this weekend, I can get it together."

We hated the feeling that we were flying by the seat of our pants. We couldn't wait until we had a handle on things. Carly, for example, felt "as well prepared and as organized as someone who is disorganized can be," but, like many of us, she stayed at school until almost 7:00 every night the first week. She wrote, "It's impossible to know what you need before you jump into it. I love it and I'm going strong, but as soon as I sit down after the kids leave, exhaustion rushes in!" Robbie summed up our exhaustion as she ended a first-week email with: "I'll send you more later about my week. Right now, I need to take a nap. I'm in major sleep deficit!"

Being with the kids was the best part.

Even with the challenges and exhaustion, we ended those first days with our optimistic spirit intact. Carly wrote, "In spite of my worries, I think

Figure 4.5. Being with the children was the best part (Carmen and Ami).

we did some amazing things today!" Ami ended her first day with a party to celebrate summer birthdays and a class meeting during which she asked students to share their personal highlights from the day. That evening she called parents to let them know their children were off to a great start: "The parents were so excited that I called. Many of the children had raved about how much they loved school. I felt so much better after those phone calls."

Although Erin's fears were growing about her rigid teaching environment, the children made the difference. She wrote, "I *do* love the kids already. The day went by so fast. Before I knew it, my first day of teaching and my 23rd birthday were behind me." Carmen also felt prior tensions begin to dissipate when she thought about the students: "In the midst of all the paperwork, planning, and frustration with worksheets, I had a *great* time with my kids. It was so interesting to see their personalities. Being with the kids was the best part" (Figure 4.5).

We were on the road to becoming experienced teachers. Julie exclaimed, "I made it through the first day of school!! I can't believe it! 179 days left until my first year of teaching is over and I can be a veteran!" Today as *real* veterans, we know a few things we wish we had known then (Figure 4.6), tips that might have made things easier. But we are generally pleased to look back and see the success of our first day. Our feelings about it—the excitement, nervousness, joy, and relief— were captured by Robbie as she wrote to us that evening: "I was relieved to realize that fifth graders are not as old as I thought they would be. They are still little and cute and sweet. In fact, they are terrific! And they didn't eat me alive."

If I'd Known Then What I Know Now, I Would Have:

- Been more flexible.
- Started organizing my room earlier. Everything takes ten times longer than you think it will take.
- Asked about meetings. Teacher workdays are often filled with them; you can feel very stressed about not being able to work in your room if you don't anticipate those meetings.
- Not accepted stuff (posters, worksheets, empty jars, etc.) from other teachers. It seems to come out of nowhere. You'll accumulate enough stuff of your own; don't take someone else's just because you think you might need it.
- Talked more with other teachers to get ideas for establishing procedures for morning pickup, bathroom breaks, distributing materials, going to lunch, packing up at the end of the day, getting kids to their cars and buses; and I would have practiced those routines more with the children.
- Asked experienced teachers about their systems for organizing the papers that can consume your desk: office memos, administrators' memos, meeting agendas, professional learning materials, student information, student work, technology stuff, weekly housekeeping, grades, etc., etc.!
- Shopped earlier and asked about budgets for buying supplies such as dry erase markers, paper clips, glue sticks, folders, writer's notebooks, pens, pencils, masking tape, magnets, ant killer, memo pads, laminating film.
- Dressed presentably when working in the classroom before school started; parents dropped by.
- Left more time for magical moments and been more comfortable when those moments caused me to deviate from my plans.
- Taken a few minutes to reflect in writing at the end of the first day to congratulate myself and refocus for the next day.
- Smiled more even when the going was rough; it was the kids' and parents' first impressions of me.
- Enlisted a volunteer on the first few days to take up supplies and lunch money, find out and make a list of how each student will go home, etc., so that I could have concentrated more on making the children feel welcome.
- Realized that establishing rituals, routines, and a predictable schedule means more than you think.
- Focused more on classroom community expectations and creating a trusting bond with and among the students.
- Known that it was okay to do what I wanted to do; not listened to other people who told me that I *had* to do certain things on the first day.
- Not worried so much about things that didn't get accomplished before the first day. No one else will know about that great center you wanted to create or that wonderful display. There is always time to do it later.
- Learned more about how to access resources (small grants, websites, local TV station donations) to fund the purchase of books, materials, pillows, lamps, bookshelves, and cozy furniture to make my room more inviting (see Chapter 8 for some ideas).
- Relaxed more; allowed myself to have more fun.

Figure 4.6. If I'd known then what I know now . . .

So Much Was to Happen

Looking across experiences from the job search through our first days in the classroom, we see that almost everything we did reflected convictions we held leaving the preservice program. We rummaged for furniture, pillows, lamps, and bookshelves to create inviting learning environments; engaged students in filling the classroom walls so they would feel a sense of ownership; made cozy places for reading and filled classrooms with books and other reading materials; and created opportunities for children to feel valued and to value one another. We started the day with class meetings in which songs, stories, and poetry were used to begin building shared histories and joyful communities. Many of us found ways to follow students' interests through inquiry-based experiences.

At the same time, a few red flags began to appear. Some of those flags gave us more cause for concern than others. Erin's first day stories reveal that much of her excitement was already being replaced by despair as realities of programmatic mandates became clearer. Others in our group began to sense that their views of teaching were very different from those of colleagues. They wondered about potential tensions. Some recognized the need to become more comfortable with the uncertainties of daily classroom life.

Much was to happen in the coming years. As we gained experience, our visions of great teaching broadened and deepened, sometimes with the support of those around us and sometimes because we figured out ways to grow on our own. In the process, we learned that becoming the teachers we hoped to be was about much more than merely moving into a school and setting up a classroom.

Critical Insights from Chapter 4

The Job Search

- We sought schools where we thought we could bring our teaching dreams to life. Identifying such places was not as easy as we thought it would be.
- Both positive and negative reactions during interviews proved to be accurate; gut feelings really do matter.
- In job interviews, we wanted so badly to find what we were looking for that sometimes we saw it when it wasn't there. As a result, it was easy to jump at jobs too quickly.

- Watching interactions between teachers and administrators during interviews gave us insights into the school's climate.

- Asking for a tour of the school (and paying attention to people, interactions, classroom set-ups, hallway walls, etc.) was a critical part of the interview process.

- We were glad that we had reviewed our beliefs and their theoretical foundations before heading into interviews but wish we had been more prepared to ask our own questions.

Setting Up Our Classrooms

- Accepting the responsibility to create dynamic learning environments was more daunting than we anticipated, but as we set up classrooms, most of us still felt we could bring our beliefs to life.

- Common to all of us was the desire to build classroom environments that were warm, inviting, and richly literate, and that would give our students a sense of ownership and mutual respect.

- We did a lot of rummaging around—in the school, at garage sales, in our attics—before school started, finding pillows, furniture, bins for books, bookshelves, and so on.

- We were not prepared for the number of hours spent in meetings during the week before school started; we expected to have more time in our classrooms.

- We seriously underestimated how long it would take to get ready for the first day of school.

- Even as we set up our classrooms, some of us were already beginning to feel the tensions associated with teaching differently from our colleagues.

The First Days of School

None of us slept much the night before school started; we were excited and nervous at the same time;.

- On the first day, getting used to where to go, when to go, and how to get there was something we hadn't thought could be so confusing—for us and for the kids.

- Focusing on getting to know our students, our students getting to know one another, and making school a joyful place to be was a wise choice in the first days.

- Starting out by reading aloud and using music as fundamental to the school day helped us begin with shared experiences that our students seemed to love right away.

- Connecting right away with parents by calling and sharing positive stories made a big difference for us, for them, and for the children.

- We were excited to see our students engaging as readers, writers, and inquirers in the first days.

- We were surprised at the flood of papers from the office that quickly filled our desks and dining room tables. Unprepared, we were a bit overwhelmed figuring out what to do with them.

- During the first days, there were challenges and a few disasters, but good things happened too. Kids were engaged, they learned a few things, *and* we fell in love with them.

- Although a few red flags began to appear, we ended our first days in the classroom with our optimistic spirits largely intact.

5 Living Up to a Vision: The Being Perfect Disease

Every day this week, I've asked myself why I teach. Wednesday I came home and cried so hard my eyes were swollen the whole next morning. I feel like such a failure because I know I've let my kids down, my parents down, and my principal down. I don't know why I can't seem to get the hang of this teaching business. But something keeps pushing me to keep at it. Maybe it's a subconscious knowing that one day I just might get it. Who knows?

We left the university with visions of our first classrooms in mind. We wanted to teach reading, writing, math, science, social studies—everything—in the context of authentic experiences. We wanted to fill our classrooms with enticing texts of all kinds; spark children's questions and build curriculum from those questions. We wanted to know children well, continue to build our theoretical and practical knowledge, and teach based on that knowledge. After job interviews and the first days of school, although a few warning signs emerged, most of us felt that our situations held potential for bringing those visions to life. In those very early days, we felt good about ourselves as teachers. Within weeks, however, many of us felt our dreams replaced by disappointment and our excitement replaced by seriously weakening self-confidence. We'd had no idea that living up to our visions would be so hard.

All too soon, our listserv filled with expressions of disappointment: "I had all these idealistic hopes and dreams of how my classroom would operate. It seems so far from that already. I'm not the teacher I thought I would be." Our plummeting confidence was a stark contrast to the excited anticipation we had felt at graduation just three months earlier and our nervous but hopeful outlook as we set up our classrooms and met our students. Carly's words reveal the downward spiral that many of us experienced within the first weeks and months: "There is something innate about teaching that I just don't seem to have. I don't know what that is, but I'm always behind, inevitably unprepared, eventually inconsistent, and always frustrated. There's a missing link somewhere and I have no idea if it's retrievable." At times it seemed that every other teacher was smarter, wiser, and more able. Some of us habitually second-guessed our own abilities with questions like Robbie's: "What am I doing with these children? They can't be learning anything from me. If only they were in another classroom they would learn so much more and be so much more prepared." Looking back at stories from our first years, we found incident after incident in which we met frustration as we tried to live up to our visions of an ideal. Analyzing our notebooks of data, we coded those incidents as *BPD—The Being Perfect Disease*.

Our self-doubt did not diminish much during the second year. In fact, because we thought we ought to be *getting it* by then, these feelings were often even more intense. Descriptions of the loss of excitement for the job we had anticipated with such joy were heartbreaking. Erin wrote:

> As tough as things were my first year, this year I've questioned for the first time how long I want to teach. I know it sounds like a cop-out, but I'm so burned out already. Maybe my principal last year was right, maybe they *did* give me the class that was smart and good. I know I sound pathetic but what if I just don't have what it takes?

We reflected constantly, asking question after question of ourselves as we tried to figure out what was happening. Carly repeatedly asked, "Why do I only focus on my negative feelings? Do I feel anything positive? Why is it that, when I focus on the positive, I always feel like I am lying about my true feelings? Why is there so much disappointment instead of triumph?"

We knew that our visions of great teaching would continue to evolve as we brought more of ourselves to the process, but we had an intense desire to be just like the teachers we admired in professional books, in university classrooms, and during our visits to schools. We saw their teaching as perfection, and we wanted that for ourselves. In our MAT comprehensive exams, we had articulated the idea that teaching is an evolving process, but it took us a long time to *really* understand that there is no such thing as perfection; or if there is, it lies in a commitment to questioning ourselves and our practice throughout our careers. Intellectually we understood that a static vision of the Great Classroom is merely an illusion and that the best visions are dynamic, created and re-created year to year, teacher to teacher, and child to child. In practice, however, we expected something very different of ourselves, expectations that could become debilitating. Carly wrote:

Sometimes our own destructive thoughts and voices cause the most damage to our ability to feel successful. In our first years, our own voices of insecurity could not be silenced as we lay in bed beating ourselves up once again for perceived failures of the day. While it may seem that some of us had everything we needed in terms of respect and kindness, in reality, where were we to turn for solace from ourselves?

Not an Uncommon Phenomenon

Teachers struggling to live up to a vision of perfection is not an uncommon phenomenon. Curt Dudley-Marling (1997) writes about "idealized models of the good teacher . . . created by teaching stories that efface the daily struggles of teachers, by the sanitized notions of teaching presented in teacher education programs, by reductive research that drains teaching of its unpredictabilities" (p. xii). Across the country, new teachers work to live up to such idealized visions (Beck-Frazier, 2005; Darling-Hammond, 2003). Almost fifteen years ago, Thomas Newkirk (1992) urged researchers and teacher educators to listen and give legitimacy to the voices of teachers telling hard stories, to expose the sanitization of the teaching process. In this chapter and in the two chapters that follow, we try to do just that—to share triumphs but also tensions met in the early years of teaching. In the process, we hope to illuminate issues that may help us understand why so many new teachers leave for other careers and why others remain in the profession, compromised and unhappy.

Giving Voice to the New Teachers We Used to Be

Looking back, we sometimes wonder at our expressions of despair from those first years. The fact that it takes our data to transport *us* back to that intensity reminds us how easy it is to forget or dismiss those early feelings. Although many experienced teachers face similar issues, struggles that seem surmountable or at least avoidable to an experienced teacher can be enormous in the life of a beginning teacher. So, even though we are sometimes surprised at our own words and actions from earlier years, they are important to share. They represent the range of issues met as we attempted to bring visions of great teaching to life: (1) disappointment when we saw ourselves slipping toward the status quo we hoped to change, (2) the collision of our visions with mandates and accepted practices in schools, (3) trying to pin down whirling ideas from graduate school, (4) our love-hate relationship with professional books, (5) struggling to understand and engage every child, (6) being over-

whelmed by the *stuff* that teachers have to do every day, and (7) learning how to juggle work and life. In these pages, we share stories that
helped us see these issues as critical in the lives of new teachers. By telling them, we give voice to the new teachers we used to be, as well as
the experienced teachers we are today when the "being perfect" voice
haunts us once again.

Issues We Faced as We Tried to Bring Our Visions to Life

Disappointment in Ourselves: Slipping toward the Status Quo

*Why did we see ourselves slipping toward the status quo that we so wanted
to change?*

Too many times during our first years, we felt overwhelming disappointment in ourselves when we saw our grad school dreams slipping
away. Carly wrote, "I find myself forgetting all of the great things I
learned in graduate school. Now when I hear terms that I learned, I
think, 'Oh yeah, I remember that.' Then I feel like a sell-out, because
I'm not using those ideas every day." Trying to hang on to our beliefs,
we were horrified when we saw ourselves settling for programs and
practices that could not possibly be supported by our beliefs about teaching and learning. The status quo in some of our schools and districts
was heavily influenced by fears about high-stakes testing and public
comparisons through school report cards. Even when that was not the
case, we felt alone with our visions. Erin said, "I wish I had another
teacher at my school trying the same things. I wish we could have met
today and talked about the frustrations and how we could make things
better."

We knew that our university education was only a beginning. We
had much to learn from our new colleagues. But we also believed that
we brought a solid knowledge base from our preservice experience.
Surely we had something to offer in terms of moving the profession
forward. Why was it so difficult to bring those ideas to life? It was easier
than we thought to succumb to the practices around us as our university experiences began to fade into the not-so-distant past. Robbie wrote:

> It's easy to pick up from teachers down the hall. Their ways of
> teaching may be antithetical to what you have learned in your
> teaching program, but they are there to support you, so, as a new
> teacher, if you have to make a choice between something you
> observed and read about in graduate school or something that a
> teacher can show you how to do, often you will pick up the latter.

We now realize that we were not nearly as helpless as we felt, but most of us believed, as Erin wrote, that we had little control over our teaching lives during the first years: "I would have criticized my classroom up and down a mere five months ago. The strange thing is, even though I don't like myself as a teacher, I feel so *helpless* as to how to change. Instead of ending the depressing, outdated cycle, I am passing it on."

Some of us literally began to hate our jobs and considered leaving the profession. Erin continued, "I've been trying to get through, but I really hate it. You know it's bad when you wake up dreading to go to your job like I did this morning." In desperation, Carly wrote:

> I think I'm getting to the numb point which I dread. I truly want to care but it's like, if I care too much it makes me crazy and then I begin to hate my job. I'm not sure I can settle for feeling numb, so is this where quitting comes in? I want so badly to be the exception, but the reality of it all wears me down every day.

Sheer disappointment in ourselves was expressed so often and so consistently that Susi wondered if there *was* hope. She wrote to us: "I look at the excited faces of my new MAT students and think, am I inspiring them to be something that will frustrate them endlessly? Should I take it all back and say, 'It's too hard out there. Give up while you have a chance?'" Susi tried to balance her desire to help new teachers build a vision of what was possible with the realities of the journey to make it so. She began to rethink her own practices. Already our experiences were beginning to confirm the concerns that prompted her to initiate our research. Were we also disappearing within a status quo that represented something very different from our visions of great teaching?

Being Different: When Visions and Mandates Collide

If we taught differently, would we feel alone and alienated from colleagues we wanted to know as friends and teaching/learning partners?

As new teachers, we felt particularly helpless when our beliefs seemed to be in direct opposition to real or perceived mandates or accepted practices in our schools. Carmen said, "I felt really good about what I learned in the MAT program. I was so prepared to make the ideas work. Then I realized I was in a whole new world. You go to college to learn how to teach and then you don't see it being done." The mandates we encountered were primarily connected to programs that viewed literacy learning from a skills-in-isolation approach dominated by workbooks and scripted lessons. Having developed some confidence in teaching children to read without a scripted program and with convictions about instruction and curriculum informed by in-depth knowledge about each student, we were eager to implement responsive approaches to literacy learning. When those visions collided with school and district mandates or with typical practices in our schools, we faced a dilemma. How could we teach in ways that challenged everything we knew to be supportive of children as learners? If we taught differently, would we feel alone and alienated from the colleagues we wanted to know as friends and teaching/learning partners?

We wanted to fit in, so we made compromises.

Teaching differently from colleagues was an issue that was difficult to reconcile. April wrote, "I really have to soul search to keep from doing what everyone else at my school is doing." In a few cases, colleagues seemed to resent that we did things differently; but for the most part, they were kind and friendly. Even so, it was lonely being different. April continued:

> There are many days when I see and hear about what other kindergarten teachers are doing. Sometimes I feel like I am a slack teacher even though I disagree with a lot that they are doing. I think they look at me differently because I do not believe in some of the ways they teach things. They don't disrespect me or anything and we do get along well with each other, but we do our own thing and sometimes I wonder what they think.

We wanted to move smoothly into our new school communities, so when we sensed differences, we didn't want to make our situations even more uncomfortable by speaking out against the norm. As Carmen said, "I was expected to just go with the status quo or sometimes I may have just put myself in that position so I wouldn't make waves." We wanted to fit in, so we made compromises. Describing her unhappiness with the school's reward system for reading books, for example, Julie decided that rather than take a vocal stand during her first year, she would concentrate on reading more research about extrinsic rewards while paying close attention to what motivated her students as readers. In this way, she could position herself to better articulate her argument:

> I decided that, although theoretically I know this is against my beliefs about how children should read, I had better not rock the boat this first year. I had been feeling guilty about giving in, but I'm trying to look at this as a learning experience for myself as a teacher-researcher. Then next year when I am asked to use the program, I can say that I tried it and that, based on my own expe-

rience, I will not participate. I hate to do something that goes against what I believe, but with my own data next year to back up my beliefs, I might be able to voice my opinion more and be respected for it rather than being seen as a rebel.

Another common compromise was to accept offers of worksheets from colleagues but to stash them away unused. Carmen's experience was echoed by others in the group: "I harbored hundreds of worksheets because I refused to give my children sheet after sheet, which is what I would have had to do if they were to complete work like the other classes at my grade level. I got so tired of wasting paper for those damn worksheets I wasn't going to use!"

Sometimes we compromised our beliefs when we lacked confidence in our own understanding of them. When we didn't feel that we could clearly articulate what we wanted to do and why, we were more apt to move toward the status quo. Carmen explained:

> I couldn't tell another teacher that I wasn't going to do something when I wasn't sure what I was doing myself. So, if I wasn't really sure, I wouldn't say anything. I would just go with the flow. If I voiced my opinion, it was because I thought I knew what I was talking about. Otherwise, when I was not in agreement but didn't have myself together enough to be in total disagreement, I didn't see any point in making things difficult.

In some situations, our compromise was to close the classroom door and do our own thing. While this was a solution, it was clearly not optimal. Hidden, we were able to bring a few visions to life, but without the company of colleagues who were interested in talking through ideas with us, it was difficult to sustain and build on those beliefs.

My biggest hope is that I don't forget who I am as an educator.

The most extreme example of visions colliding with mandates was Erin's environment, which allowed little deviation from the scripts: "The principal said that in first and second grade he wanted to see direct instruction, meaning isolated skill instruction and phonics drills and nothing else. He said that in the afternoon, *all 45 minutes of it*, we could do what we wanted, but in the morning, it had to be direct instruction and that was it."

Such lack of autonomy was frustrating: "As a teacher who has worked hard for her knowledge, I don't even have the autonomy in my school to decide that my children will read independently during a block of time set aside for reading." The impact of these conditions caused anger as well as despair: "I grew quite depressed. I couldn't believe I had put so much heartfelt interest into my graduate school education and I was almost forbidden to use that knowledge. I was already angry at myself for making a poor job choice."

Although Erin found some room to teach differently, the level of compromise required meant that she consistently gave up more of her vision: "I appease the principal by doing the mandated half-hour of phonics. We have to recite chants from phonics cards that I am required to keep on my wall. I have to do worksheets, but I rush through them so we'll have 20–30 minutes for silent reading and writing." Erin's compromise was to grin and bear it through the required worksheet time— "to force these worksheets to become meaningful is useless"—and use time remaining to teach in other ways. But this also meant compromising what she believed would best support her students as literacy learners. She knew she was sending them mixed messages about what really matters for readers and writers. As Erin felt her vision of good teaching slipping away, she was also losing her excitement for teaching: "I'm trying to be positive, but how can I teach with passion when I don't believe in what I'm teaching?"

Mandates, in this case, were closely tied to administrative beliefs about test scores. This led to further frustration as Erin watched the goals of education narrow to the point at which she felt she was constantly shortchanging the students: "I feel so sorry for my kids. I feel angry with myself and with the school. The way we teach is not teaching them to love reading, to love school, to love learning. It is only teaching them to do well on tests." The guilt associated with Erin's need to compromise was overwhelming. Tragically, a young educator who had been applauded for her work with children by her internship coaching teacher, professors, and peers was already losing faith in herself: "I expect a lot out of myself because I have a lot to give and I am not even close to living up to those expectations. Regardless of what we say to make each other feel better, the guilt that I feel because I'm not giving what I should will probably be there anyway. My biggest hope is that I don't forget who I am as an educator."

Myths about mandated practices are perpetuated for many reasons.

For many of us, the first year was a lesson in discerning the difference between reality and myth, separating true mandates from unsubstantiated directives that often made their way through the faculty grapevine: "*They* say you have to." Identifying and overcoming perceived mandates was surprisingly difficult. Initially, many of us bought into most of what our colleagues said without question. When we started paying closer attention, however, we realized that not every "you have to" was as threatening as it sounded. For example, after hearing a description of the district language arts program at an orientation session, Julie wrote, "I was surprised at how aligned the district agenda was with beliefs and practices from our graduate school experiences. At my school, other teachers say things like, 'If you don't implement your word wall this way, you'll be called on the carpet,' but from what I heard at the meeting, no one is saying that anything *has* to be done one way."

Sometimes mythical mandates were unspoken. They came from assumptions we made as we noticed what other teachers were doing. We quickly learned to go straight to the source of anything that sounded like a mandate. Ami explained,

> The only textbooks I used in the first weeks were from a reading program. I don't know where that pressure was coming from, but I just felt like I had to use them. I didn't like it, my kids didn't like it, and we were bored. Finally I asked my principal about it and she said, "Just put them away and don't do them." So I did. I started literature circles using trade books and my kids love it. I mean, love it, love it, love it!

Once we began to look closely, we realized that myths about mandated practices were perpetuated for many reasons. Sometimes mandates were misinterpretations of administrative suggestions. Sometimes teachers had never questioned the mandates themselves, they were comfortable with the way things were, they felt uncomfortable with change, or it never occurred to them that mandates might be myths.

Overwhelmed by Ideas: Figuring Out How to Put Those Grad School Ideas into Practice

> My struggle is that all the things I learned are going through my head like crazy. I am trying to decide how my classroom is going to shape up, but I am overwhelmed by it. I know that I have sound theoretical knowledge that was definitely firmed up by visiting the Center for Inquiry and the schools in Ohio but it is difficult to figure out how to fit it all in.

In comprehensive exams at the end of our preservice program, we articulated our beliefs about theory and practice. We substantiated those beliefs by describing the work of educators and educational researchers. At graduation, everything felt pretty much under control. Once we hit the classroom, however, we realized that a million ideas were whirling in our heads. Julie wrote, "My mind just races with all the ideas I want to implement. I find myself so anxious some nights that I wake up at 2:00 or 3:00 in the morning and have to get up for an hour or so until I can go back to bed." Having read and experienced so much in such a short period of time in graduate school, we found it difficult to recall everything we learned at a level of specificity that would help us every day in the classroom. Ami said, "Sometimes when you're reading that much professional stuff, it just starts to get jumbled. I never seem to have time to do all the things I want to do!"

The bottom line was that most of us often felt confused and overwhelmed trying to figure out how to put all of the puzzle pieces together. We tried to do it all and then realized there were so many ideas we had yet to implement. This led to frustration and, at our lowest points, to viewing ourselves as failures. Late in her first year, Julie wrote:

> I feel like such a failure. I just realized that since I have not done individual reading conferences since the beginning of the year, I really don't have a good idea of how this child is reading or the strategies he's using. I'm not familiar with any of my students individually. I realize how much of the picture I'm missing by not taking running records and then making time to conference with each student.

We longed for the support of others in our schools who would be interested in working through ideas with us. Alone, it was difficult to figure out how to pull things together even when we were excited about new ideas. We wrote back and forth to one another to express frustration, but also to build each other up. Susi frequently sent cheerleading messages: "Remember that you're terrific! You *are* fantastic teachers, it just takes time for everything to fall into place." But the cheers were hard to hear when we wanted everything to fall into place right away. In a December listserv entry during the first year of teaching, Erin voiced everyone's feelings about trying to do it all, trying to be top-notch at everything:

> When I think of how much I've changed in the short months since I graduated from the MAT program, it is amazing. It is also amazing to me the discrepancy between the teacher I wanted to be those few short months ago and the teacher I am now. I don't know if the teacher I wanted to be was even possible. I guess it's just that I wanted to be a bit of everything. When I was with you, Susi, I learned so much about how young children learn to read and write. That was your passion and you passed that on to us. I wanted to go out there and be the best language arts teacher there was. Well, when we went to Dr. VanScoy, we learned from someone whose strong area was math. We visited teachers whose pas-

sion was math. And I wanted to be the best math teacher. With Dr. Toner, it was social studies and inquiry. With Dr. Ebert it was science. With Dr. Whitin, it was building community. Do you see what I'm saying? Everyone has their strong area, an area they focus most of their time and energy on. As students we were exposed to all those areas. No wonder it was overwhelming. After starting to teach, I finally realized that there was no way I could be the best language arts, social studies, science, math, and community-building teacher there was!

The curriculum, grades, and testing dominate my reasoning for everything we do.

As ideas whirled faster and faster, it became easier to let external issues drive the way we structured our time with children. We began allowing real and perceived curricular mandates, worries about grades, and the teach-to-the-test culture in some schools to dictate our practices. It became difficult to see possibilities beyond those constraints. In the middle of the first year, Carly wrote:

> The curriculum, grades, and testing dominate my reasoning for everything we do in the classroom. With an already packed curriculum in all subjects, I feel smothered by so much to do in so little time. I never read aloud anymore. We never go outside because the transition takes too long. We don't do projects very much anymore because they take more than the three weeks that I have to teach each science or social studies unit.

Sometimes we panicked because we felt pressure to *cover* material, a concept that was at odds with our commitment to creating contexts in which children *uncover* understandings through meaningful explorations. Consequently, we found ourselves shortchanging time for children's thoughtful investigations and reflections as we felt pressure to *get through* the curriculum. Carly worried, "I feel like I still don't give my students enough time to do things because I'm worried about covering material. I get frustrated at myself for pushing ahead and not spending as much time as I would like on a topic." Her words brought together tensions that many of us felt: "My own fear and ignorance are barriers. When I feel unprepared or inexperienced about using inquiry and I am afraid I will not cover what they need to know for the test, I find myself relying on textbooks." Robbie shared a story that is a perfect example of how pressured we felt in this push to cover material:

> I got really upset yesterday by what a teacher said to me. I was in her room borrowing stuff for our project on the colonies. She said, "I don't mean to say this in a mean way, but you need to get a

move on it and get past this quickly." She was saying that I am behind in social studies, implying that I wasn't going to cover all of the social studies curriculum by the end of the year. I wanted to say a lot of things, but of course I didn't. I just said, "I know. We're hurrying" and went back to my room. My eyes were stinging. I was tired and more prone to tears than usual, but also my feelings were hurt.

With so many ideas and little or no support for making sense of them, it was easy to abandon much of our MAT learning and begin to conform to the fast-paced, teach-to-the-test climate that surrounded us. Robbie wrote, "There are so many demands, real or perceived, on teachers in the classroom, and there are so many people and teacher's manuals offering advice on how to teach, that it is difficult to remember all that you learned in a year of learning how to teach."

Sometimes we were too overwhelmed or exhausted to figure out a better way.

We felt strongly that worksheets were a waste of time. We recognized that children who accurately complete worksheets already know the skills (they don't learn skills in the act of completing the worksheet), that filling out worksheets correctly has nothing to do with being able to use the skills, and that worksheets do not in any way promote passion for reading, writing, mathematics, or anything else. We knew this, but sometimes we were too overwhelmed or exhausted to figure out a better way. Carmen wrote, "I'm not trying nearly as hard as I should be to incorporate other ideas. It's not because I don't believe in them, but figuring out how to develop them takes a lot of time. I feel like I'm barely keeping my head above water as it is right now." Carly explained that falling back on "the easy way out" typically occurred when she was most exhausted. Her words also express how easy it was to be daunted by the risks involved in trusting her own knowledge and ability:

> I often find myself in the anxiousness of wanting someone to put teaching neatly into a big how-to book. I think that happens when I'm the most tired. It's easier to follow those teacher-proof curriculum guides. We don't have to work so hard getting to know our students that way. We don't have to remember so much about methods and theory. We don't have to take risks with our own judgment.

We lacked an understanding of how to turn authentic assessment into letter grades.

Another frustration encountered as we tried to put grad school ideas into practice was reconciling our convictions about authentic assessment with the realities of number and letter grades required on report cards. Robbie wrote, "everything about number grades defies the logic behind all the theory and practice I learned while in graduate school." We believed that assessing children's learning in the context of purposeful engagements helped us better understand students' strengths and needs. We remembered the care and thought we put into writing narrative descriptions of children and using those understandings to teach responsively. We knew that authentic assessment could inform instruction in ways that numerical and letter grades could not, but we lacked an understanding of how to translate those assessment strategies into the grades we were required to put on report cards. Carly explained:

> Number grades were antithetical to the kind of teaching I wanted to provide. Therefore, every six weeks I was frantic to get even the most meaningless number grades just to be able to justify a number on report cards. Without worksheets and quizzes for meaningless stories in our reading books, it seemed impossible to give a true number grade.

Lacking an understanding of how to transfer what we knew about each child to the assessment systems required in our schools, we resorted to using end-of-chapter tests and worksheets to provide numbers and grades. While we had some experience creating rubrics that complemented more thoughtful practices, our knowledge was limited, and it was difficult to find time or support to develop them or even to better understand them, particularly when colleagues did not seem interested in working through those issues together. Carly continued, "It took most of my first year to figure out how to give grades for independent reading and writing, and I still wasn't satisfied until the very last six-week period."

We needed help in managing our days so we could find time for careful reflection and talk.

Pinning down and using ideas from graduate school was a huge frustration largely because we could not find time to think, talk, and work through ways those ideas might play out in our classrooms. We needed help managing our days so we could find time for careful reflection and talk. At the end of her first year, Carmen wrote, "This year I felt that everything was running together. I never had things the way I wanted them. This was disappointing because I had some really good ideas that I didn't get to try." Julie also struggled to manage time and ideas:

There was just too much for me to learn how to do. I was clueless about how to organize the day in which I'd get in all the subjects, all the neat community-building activities I'd learned in grad school, all the bathroom breaks, and all the questions from the kids. There never seemed to be enough time to plan a good lesson with interesting extensions and inquiries, leaving me to the quick-fix worksheets.

All of our ideas didn't have to be pinned down in the first week.

Probably the most important realization for all of us was that it was okay to try one idea at a time. At the beginning of her second year, Julie wrote:

> I'm trying slowly to incorporate the things I want to have in place. I'm starting to keep a notebook of ideas I want to implement to help me get it out of my head and onto paper. Next week, I want to concentrate on creating book tubs and getting all my classroom books into baskets by genre. I am trying to take one big to-do item and tackle it per week.

All of our ideas didn't have to be pinned down in the first week, month, or even the first or second year. In her second year, for example, Erin described an exciting and successful inquiry experience she organized for her students. Then she added, "This is the only individualized inquiry experience I've implemented this year and you know what? I am not going to apologize for that. This is simply what I've felt comfortable with." Five years later, Robbie's and Erin's words reflect how we all continued to work through ideas we learned in graduate school. Erin wrote: "It took me four years to figure out how to reflect on reading conferences in a way that didn't require hours of weekend work, and I still rethink how I will optimize my reflection time when I go back to the classroom." Robbie added:

> It wasn't until my sixth year that I finally got around to implementing literacy centers in my third-grade classroom. It was something I always wanted to do, but I never found the time to devote to making them meaningful experiences for my students. By that time, I finally had a handle on so many other aspects of teaching that I decided I could really focus on figuring out ways to give my students access to invitations that were really thoughtful.

Those Professional Books: A Love-Hate Relationship

> I can't seem to get past the betrayal I feel from all those authors who make it look like the easiest thing in the world. It seems like everything I try ends in failure. It may work for a few days or months or maybe just for a few students, but I still have no real successes.

As we entered our first classrooms, we wanted desperately to be just like the teachers in the professional books we read, the videos we watched, and the teachers we observed during school visits. This desire was what Carly labeled our "exuberant clone mentality." We constantly compared ourselves to those educators, never considering the possibility that they also met challenges every day. Julie said, "I wonder constantly if I'm the only one of us who hasn't established that wonderful classroom community that seemed so easy from reading all those books." When, for example, a child stole from her, Julie couldn't figure out why the love with which she had tried to build community didn't prevent the child from stealing: "I think back to some of the books we read in the MAT program. There seemed to be such strong communities in those classrooms that something like this would never happen. What have I done wrong? Will I *ever* be able to establish this in my classroom?" We worked hard to try to figure it out: "I'm at my wits' end here. I reflect every day. I've referred to our books time and time again. I think, 'How would Kohn or Routman do it?' Over and over I ask myself, 'What did I do wrong?' The problems have really gotten out of hand recently. It's a day-to-day struggle."

It was easy to implement engagements as if they were recipes and then to become frustrated.

This desire to be like authors of professional books, teachers we observed, and professors in courses was not a negative characteristic of our early teaching. Those distant teachers represented important points of reference and inspiration. But, in the early years, we didn't see our cloning attempts as jumping-off points. As a result, it was easy to implement specific engagements as if they were recipes and then to become frustrated when things didn't turn out exactly as we envisioned. In fall of her first year, Erin posted the following message on our listserv:

> Susi, I set it up *just* like the authors' circles were set up when we worked with third graders in our language arts course. I taught a mini-lesson about how authors use language in interesting ways. I read *Come On, Rain!* and we talked about words we loved. I read other books and we noticed great words. But when they wrote, they replaced words like "good" with words like "very good"! I'm trying my best, but it's hard not to get frustrated.

Without anyone with whom to hash out ideas, we didn't allow ourselves much room for trial and error, and we didn't have the confidence to alter ideas to make them our own. The structures and practices worked for the authors of books and teachers in videos, so we assumed they would work for us. We expected our writing workshops to be smoothly implemented structures through which children grew exponentially with every mini-lesson and writing conference. We envisioned our students moving forward as readers, writers, mathematicians, and scientists because we would know exactly the right thing to say and do. Just like the models we revered, we expected our classrooms to be caring places where a low hum of activity meant that children were interacting in congenial, productive ways. We simply didn't see classrooms in books, videos, and school visits as anything other than happily busy centers of learning. When our own attempts didn't result in the visions we anticipated, we were confused and disappointed.

They forgot this really important step—how do you get there?

We also failed to realize that not only were *we* new to these curricular structures but so were our students. They needed time, just as we did, to work though new ways of doing things before classroom life could run as smoothly as it seemed to in books and videos. A huge piece of the puzzle was missing. Robbie said, "Look at what we have to live up to. Those books epitomize everything we've learned but it's like they forgot this really important step—how do you get there?" We wanted to better understand the process of teachers' implementation of new ideas. We needed strategies to use in meeting challenges that teachers in books never seemed to face. We had tons of questions: How did they begin? How did they move forward from there? Did they ever have rough spots? How did they work through the challenges? Robbie said, "They don't tell you about the kids who only want to play video games and Gameboys. No one says, 'Oh yeah, I have this great classroom, but I do have this one child who is driving me crazy.'" Carly added, "So many authors write as if they never have one ounce of behavior problems or failed projects. All I read about is this great plan or project, the kids loved it, they learned so much from it, they all worked so hard. Do they not have those students who refuse to do anything? I feel these frustrations every day and I doubt myself every day."

Susi found it hard to believe that we thought classrooms in books and videos were always well-oiled learning environments where nothing went wrong. Sitting around her dining room table talking about a draft of this chapter, she asked, "But didn't you guys assume that there were struggles in those classrooms?" Robbie and Erin answered in unison, "No!" and Robbie said, "I truly believed that those teachers could do it without a hitch." She went on to explain:

New teachers don't realize that when you see a teacher in a video and she's having a reading conference with one child, she might have to get up and talk to a kid somewhere else in the room. Then when the new teacher has to deal with kids who are interrupting her work with other children, she thinks, "What's wrong with me? Why do I have to do that? Why didn't she have to do that?" And that's only one example of the kinds of challenges that we don't see in books and videotapes.

We all experienced some level of disillusionment when we didn't feel that we could be the teachers in professional books and videos. A few of us, in moments of deepest frustration, felt a sort of defensive anger. When we agreed to buy a new professional book published by a favorite author, one group member wrote, "No, I haven't bought the book yet. I know I wouldn't read it right now. I can't seem to get past the betrayal I feel from all those authors who made it look like the easiest thing in the world. It seems like everything I try ends in failure." Connections between the successes described in books and our own feelings of self-doubt were very real. Carly wrote, "I've been sort of scared to start reading professionally again. Isn't that crazy? It's like I'm scared to get all excited again about what someone else says is great and then I just go and fail at it again."

I sometimes overlooked the parts about struggles in books.

We realized that as graduate students, even when teachers' struggles *were* described in books, we rarely focused on those parts. Robbie wrote,

> To be honest, I think I sometimes overlooked the parts about struggles in books when I was writing all those great, inspiring quotes in my journal. When you are in the middle of your preservice program, even when books *do* tell how they got from A to Z, you don't tend to look at that when you read for the first time. You read and say, "Oh yeah, this is where I want to be."

We saw what we were ready to see. We looked for and found successes, not struggles. We focused more on product—the humming classroom—than on the process to get there.

Similarly, when professors shared their own early teaching struggles, the impact wasn't as great as it might have been, because we had not yet experienced those struggles firsthand. It took a while for Susi to understand this disconnect: why hadn't the stories she shared about her own first-year struggles been validating and reassuring? At one point, exasperated with our distress over feeling distressed, she wrote to us in a "this-is-teaching-so-buck-up" tone: "But don't you remember the disastrous stories about my early teaching years? It happens to all new teachers." Erin's response reminded us that learning for preservice teachers, just as learning for children, is about real experiences in purposeful contexts, not just about telling or reading or talking:

> I remember clearly specific things you said to us in class about the way it takes years for this to come together. Sure, we remember you telling us about your first year. I remember you telling us how you had a friend who you used to cry to and drink wine with. What you told us *is* helping me. But let's apply what we know about how people learn to this situation. We don't learn things simply by people telling us. There is no way that we, as excited and energetic preservice teachers, could really learn just by listening to you.

Of course, we highly valued and admired the books we read and the teachers we observed. That's one of the reasons we were so distressed and defensive. But we struggled to translate the pedagogical places described in books and observed in classrooms to our new teaching situations. As student teachers, most of us had opportunities to try out ideas with the steady support of our coaching teachers, our MAT peers, and our professors. We always came back together to talk about how an idea did or did not work and why. In our own classrooms, none of us had that kind of support.

In our second year of teaching, more of us felt ready to head back into professional reading.

While several of us were ready to dive back into professional books during our first year, most of us needed some distance from them as we worked to learn about life in our own classrooms. The keeping-my-head-above-water metaphor came up again as Robbie wrote:

> Reading professional books was difficult in the first year. After I graduated, I wanted to read pleasure books. I wanted to read tons and tons of the books that my kids were reading. Although I tried, I did not really want to read professional books yet. I think I was spending so much time figuring out grading, making my classroom look presentable, learning the curriculum, doing paper work, dealing with behavior problems, getting along with everything else in my life, that it was tough to read another book. I wasn't ready to do it the first year, or even at the beginning of the second year. I was just struggling to keep my head above water.

In our second year of teaching, more of us felt ready to head back into professional reading. To start, we read Regie Routman's (2000)

Conversations. Some of us read other books as well. We made time during research meetings to share ideas from readings. At one summer meeting, for example, Robbie shared how she had used *Conversations* to "completely redevelop my literature log system," and Julie shared from her reading of Georgia Heard's (1999) *Awakening the Heart*: "I love the ideas for setting up a poetry environment and poetry centers; that's something I want to get good at this year and then next year work on something else." Reading professionally in the second year was, as Robbie explained, "more meaningful because we have a year of experience to build on. We know a lot more about what works for us so we can read much more into a book. It's like going to conferences now. We can go to sessions and relate to them more." In our second year, Carly wrote, "I want to read now and I need to. When I read these days, I start to reimagine the possibilities."

Taking the time to be reflective made all the difference.

At the end of her second year, Erin used professional reading to help her think about what she wanted to do differently the next year. Taking the time to be reflective allowed her to draw from texts—in this case, Joanne Hindley's (1996) *In the Company of Children* and Katie Wood Ray's (1999) *Wondrous Words*—to connect frustrations from the year with possible solutions as she planned for the future:

> This year I wanted to have a great writing workshop, but I never really taught my children how to use their writer's notebooks. I could just kick myself for it because it was hard to teach prewriting when the children didn't even utilize their notebooks for anything except drafts. This summer, I'm going to make a long-range plan for writing workshop. I want my kids to be like Hindley's and beg me to let them start writing. I feel like I've promoted a factory in my classroom. My kids hurry up and write, hurry up and edit, and then beg for the computer to publish their work. Sometimes I have to ask myself, "How did I teach them to be this way?" I want to get better at teaching them to slow down. After reading *Wondrous Words*, I also want to get to know more children's books so I can teach more elements of writing craft through them. It's amazing the way some children really implement craft into their writing.

Struggling to Understand and Engage Every Child: Did We Really Say Those Things?

> I haven't been able to send an entry for a while because it seemed that no matter how hard I tried to be positive, my journal entries just turned out pitifully pessimistic and downright depressing. I

was having a really hard time engaging my students, and everywhere I turned everything we did just seemed to fail.

As we tried to live up to our visions of great teaching, one of our greatest challenges was figuring out how to engage every child. What do you do with a child like Marvin, for example, who "refuses to do anything I ask him to do," or the child who "walks around the classroom saying, 'I hate all your books,'" or when "one of my kids screamed that he hated me, threw his chair, and had a temper tantrum"? We all thought that building community was going to be such an easy thing. Julie wrote, "It felt easy when we were a part of communities in our university classes, when we read about classrooms that were warm and caring, and when we visited other schools. But it wasn't that easy. It was incredibly hard."

Our frustration and fatigue soon began to surface in actions and words that we never thought we would do or say. Much sooner than we care to admit, we started blaming kids and parents: "I try so damn hard not to let these students ruin it for me, but they are succeeding. I feel like they are sucking me dry. Almost all of my attention unwillingly goes to them," and "What are these parents doing? Apparently not teaching respect!" This became a vicious cycle. We didn't know how to find the time to develop deeper understandings of children, so we resorted to managing their behavior, which led, of course, to more problems, which led to our greater frustration: "I'm tired of dealing with problems when all I really want is to teach. I'm tired of taking the blame for it all. When you manage more than you teach, it's very frustrating."

Sometimes our words revealed a misplaced sense of entitlement—we went through a period of feeling that, because we worked so hard, we deserved something from our students in return. Our frustration at not knowing what to do led us to say things like "Why don't they appreciate all of the things I try to do for them?" and "It really upsets me that with all I'm doing—staying late, coming in early, trying my best—my students are not respecting me." These were the very words that we had criticized other teachers for voicing just a few months earlier.

Susi was not immune to feeling this sense of entitlement and the tendency to make quick assumptions based on a limited understanding of students' lives. Running late for her daughter's high school drama production one evening, she met with an MAT student after class. The student was upset with Susi's responses to her work. Susi wrote to us: "After all of the time that I've spent giving feedback and now I'm spending more time to talk again about this paper. I wanted to help her pass her comps, but she wasn't listening to me, instead she was upset with me." Already feeling guilty about being late for her daughter's performance, Susi fell into the same "after all I've done" entitlement stance that others of us recognized in ourselves. It wasn't until after the student graduated that Susi recognized missed opportunities for conversations she could have had to better understand issues underlying the student's obvious distress.

What's wrong with me?

Our negative reactions frightened us, which led to even deeper disappointment and further affirmation that we were not living up to our visions of great teaching. We felt frustrated and sad and wondered what we were doing wrong. When the child in Julie's class stole from her, she wrote, "I want my students to have more respect for me and for themselves than to steal. How do I do this?! An afternoon like today makes me wonder if I'm making any difference whatsoever." Erin wrote in response:

> When I read your entry this week, I just sat there and nodded my head the whole way through. I had your exact problem with a child stealing in my class. I didn't know what I was doing wrong because I tried all the community-building activities like we learned, but he still acted up all the time. I wish I had some magic answer, but I don't. Just know that you're not alone. Believe me, you're not alone.

Similarly exasperated with herself, Carly was shocked to face her feelings of frustration and irritation. This kind of attitude was antithetical to the beliefs she carried into the classroom: "What do I want—to have a class full of little robots? What's wrong with me? Listen to me! This is not what I want to believe!" We look back at emails that were achingly honest and introspective. Always courageous in the way she looked at her teaching, Carly wrote, "You know, teaching is like looking at your soul in the mirror. If you take the risk of being truly reflective, you really begin to see the true you."

Fueled by a culture of negativity

The negativity we began to see in ourselves was sometimes fueled by a culture of negativity in our schools. April described how easily productive conversations with colleagues could become destructive: "Sometimes our planning sessions turn into gripe sessions. Some teachers spend so much time complaining about children that they forget about the exciting things that happen. Sure, I have children who pull at every nerve in my body, but I try to talk more about the great things I see my children doing." Susi wrote, "It's easy to join the pity parties. It becomes habitual and counterproductive. I let myself get sucked into them and am pretty good at leading them too, but I also see that negativity just breeds more negativity." Julie added, "It's easy to fall into that pattern of behavior. Then you have to work really hard to change the way you think about children."

I didn't know how to stop my attitude.

In spite of our recognition of the problem, we had few strategies for doing much about it. One group member wrote, "I didn't know how to stop my attitude or how to rectify theirs. I let pride get in the way. I convinced myself that it was the kids. I had tried everything, so I relegated them to weeks of seatwork. 'I'll show them,' I told myself, 'I'll make the work miserable—make them see what they are missing.' Needless to say, it didn't work. They just resented me and I resented them."

Some of us found it very difficult to stop the cycle of frustration. Our frustration with kids led to frustration with ourselves, which led to further frustrations with kids. The following email is an example of how easily we jumped to these attitudes even while we were ashamed to see ourselves exhibiting them:

> Last week, every day seemed like a battle of wills—between the students and myself and between the students themselves. We were extremely sarcastic and frustrated with one another and had little patience for anything; this included me as probably the instigator. Their disrespect—I'm sure in large part because of my modeling of disrespect—increased toward me, and it seemed like the things I was doing and saying could never be forgotten or forgiven. I didn't like myself and I guess I couldn't blame them for not liking me. I was and still am terribly ashamed of the kind of teacher I had turned out to be.

When we didn't know what to do to make things better, it was easy to get defensive. Carly said, "If I'm in the moment of feeling hurt or angry about a student or parent or colleague, the last thing I need is to have someone tell me that it's really my fault and that it's all about the way I'm perceiving the situation. Although deep down I might know that is true, I'll still get defensive, maybe even more so." We tended to react this way when we were the most unsure of ourselves. The more confident we became, the more likely we were to come up with thoughtful ways to consider a problem.

What was this really about?

In both our hearts and heads, we understood that engaging every child wasn't about quick-fix solutions, but we were trying to do so many things at one time that we couldn't figure out how to find space for sitting back to contemplate deeper issues. Years later, when we stopped to consider what this was *really* about, we realized how little we knew then about getting to know children well. Our notions of building community needed to go further and deeper. We had practiced kidwatching and completed case studies of individual children during our graduate program, but we didn't know how to translate those experiences to the specific challenges we faced once we were in our own classrooms. Most of us felt like novices in terms of issues of diversity and how to connect with families different from our own. We didn't have a broader vision of how to really know and value children and their families beyond the usual homogenizing comments about loving them all. And there were no structures in our schools to support the level of experience and reflection necessary to develop such visions in the midst of everything else we were trying to do. Erin explained:

> I knew I needed to get to know students better, but I just wasn't sure how to negotiate all of that in addition to everything else. Looking back, I think now that the problem wasn't behavior, it was not knowing my kids. There is so much I don't know beyond my own cultural comfort zones.

We learned to take a different stance.

Since our first years of teaching, we have learned to take a different stance. Julie remembers that a turning point for her came after she explained frustrations about a child's behavior to a friend: "I was saying that I wanted to quit, and she basically said, 'Look, it's your job to teach these kids. You've got to find a way to do it.'" This gave Julie a new perspective:

> With the child who threw tantrums daily and had to be carried out several times kicking and screaming, I realized that I had to find something positive about him and to focus on it or I was going to face a battle with him every day. The negativity that I felt about his behavior would keep me from seeing any good in the child and would hinder any potential for teaching and learning. You truly have to search for the positive and build on that.

One of the biggest lessons we learned in moving beyond the blame game came from the wisdom of one of our internship teachers,

Donna Jarvis. Donna said something like "When things don't seem to be going too well, think about what more *you* need to know and what *you* could do differently. Look to yourself for the problem." When we were tired, worried about our teaching, and trying to do too much at once, we found it more difficult to pay attention to Donna's advice; but when we did, it made all the difference in the world. Robbie wrote:

> At one point the other day, the children stopped using good judg-
> ment about when it was time to talk and when it was not. It was
> driving me crazy. I finally realized that it was probably some-
> thing that I had been doing differently that caused their attitudes
> to change. I had to look to myself. Sure enough, changing my
> attitude and my approach made such a difference.

As we look at our teaching over the past six years, we realize how much we have internalized Donna's advice. While we sometimes have moments when deficit views creep into our lives, we are better able to recognize that perspective and shove it aside. Remembering first-year power struggles with children, Carly said, "I think I look past the be-havior now and ask, 'Why? What's behind all of this?'" Julie wrote:

> We always need to ask ourselves, "What can I do differently?"
> Reflecting on ourselves helps us take down our defensiveness
> and become accountable for the problems, instead of blaming the
> child. I could really see this with one of my children. After I
> stopped being angry with the fact that I had to deal with his be-
> havior and began trying to see good in him, I was able to estab-
> lish a positive relationship with him. I learned to seek the good
> and he learned to respect me. This taught me a good lesson—that
> it's all about how we approach our children and change our rela-
> tionships with them.

Overwhelmed by Stuff

> It's awful trying to manage all this new stuff. I feel so lost!!! Came
> home in tears today. Was in tears at school yesterday. Not getting
> enough sleep due to trying to be so prepared and then ending up
> emotional and not able to cope. How do I find balance in all this
> stuff?

Stuff. Who would have thought there would be so much of it involved in teaching? Mundane, as well as necessary and useful, tasks consumed our days. Our litany of *stuff* will be familiar to teachers everywhere. Meetings, for example, often important—but there were so many of them: faculty meetings, team meetings, meetings with literacy coaches, meetings with math coaches, parent-teacher organization meetings, meetings with instructional specialists, school and district committee meetings, hospitality committee meetings, school improvement council meetings, accreditation meetings, individualized education program planning meetings, student intervention meetings. The list of meetings goes on and on; and in our experience, there were no alternative plans for scheduling them other than after school or during planning times. In addition to meetings, there were multiple inservice sessions, some that were extremely helpful and others that were a waste of time. We were surprised to see that some sessions even contradicted each other in terms of their philosophical and theoretical bases.

But there was more stuff: mandated assessments that had little or nothing to do with planning for sound instruction, statewide checklists, grades on progress reports, unit and end-of-chapter tests, and benchmark tests. There was bus duty, recess duty, lobby duty, ordering materials, organizing materials you wanted as well as those you didn't, and paperwork to document just about everything.

Sending us furthest over the edge was stuff that was antithetical to our belief systems, such as keeping up with schoolwide behavior management systems, read-and-reward programs, and the assessment of skill after skill in isolation. Meetings, responsibilities, and paperwork were frustrating enough, but when we had to figure out what to do with programs that were in direct conflict with our beliefs, frustrations connected to *stuff* took on a whole new meaning. At the end of her first year, Carmen wrote:

> I was all set to be the best teacher ever. I figured that I knew what I was doing, right? How hard could it be? Boy, was I in for a rude awakening. All of a sudden, thousands of worksheets came my way. I thought, "Wait, I don't believe in worksheets!" So I pushed them to the side of the desk to be dealt with later. First I had to figure out a schedule with all the timed literacy stuff—10 minutes here, 25–30 minutes there. Then there was the math book that was decades old. I found myself behind a lot of the time with piles of worksheets in tow.

Too often, the pressure to get the *stuff* done—in concert with limited support for figuring out how to do it efficiently and lacking advice about how to separate the unnecessary from the essential—meant that we spent more time on stuff than on thoughtful teaching. Erin wrote, "I don't know why they call planning period a planning period. Who actually gets to plan? All you ever do is run around like a chicken with its head cut off trying to go to a zillion meetings, call parents, write notes home, clean up activities, set out activities, and get homework ready to go home."

We knew we should find time to seek deeper understandings of individual children, interact regularly with colleagues in professional study, and plan for structuring inquiry-based environments. But not only were there no structures in place to support our understanding of such endeavors, we were also simply overwhelmed by *stuff.* Erin's description of a typical school day was familiar to us all:

> I arrive at school at 6:45 and spend an hour completing preparations for the kids to come in at 7:45. Then I go strong till 12:20 when I drop my kids off for special area. During that time, I run around trying to pick up morning activities and get ready for the afternoon (this is when we don't have a meeting during planning), call parents, etc., etc. Anyway, my activity period is during everyone else's lunch hour, so it's impossible to get through to places like the district office. After a 45-minute period that feels like five minutes, it's time to pick up my kids again. At the end of the day, it's off to meetings or tutoring. I really love to go to the gym, but if I want the teacher discount (which I do), the latest class I can go to is at 5:00 and that's hard to make. When I get home, I don't have the energy to do much more than fix supper and crawl into bed. I hate to complain. I know you know the drill. Julie even has a daughter and we don't even have a dog yet!

It wasn't the hard work we minded. It wasn't the reflecting and planning that frustrated us. We loved spending time at the library finding just the right books for particular children, responding to students' journal entries, and making notes about plans for the next week's mini-lessons. But it seemed that work piled up quickly that had little to do with day-to-day teaching, planning for teaching, responding to students, and growing as knowledgeable professionals. We were more than willing to carry our share of additional teacher responsibilities, but it was frustrating when they took up so much of the day that we could not devote time to the real work of the classroom.

Juggling Work and Life

> Sometimes I wish I could have one evening with absolutely nothing to do except sit back and enjoy the beautiful fall weather.

Trying to juggle work and life is difficult for teachers throughout their careers. Today we still struggle to find balance, but in the early years it was particularly frustrating as we also worked to find our place in the profession. Within the first weeks, we were all struck by the sheer magnitude of the job and the energy necessary to accomplish it. Robbie wrote, "I always knew that teaching was a profession with homework, I just never realized quite how much!" We knew that staying grounded was important and that this meant finding time to take care of ourselves, spending time with our families, and continuing to nurture interests outside of school. We knew that life away from school feeds the soul and provides experiences that make us more vibrant teachers.

But it's safe to say that during our first two years of teaching, we could not see that we would ever have time for anything other than school. We often found ourselves giving up the things we loved. We stopped participating in hobbies like reading and exercising. We made little or no time for vacation. We neglected long-standing friendships. Julie wrote, "Teaching should not come before our families, homes, and friends and yet, for most of us, it has already crept its way into first place in our lives." Time with family and friends rapidly disappeared. This was our greatest frustration as we struggled to find balance. Julie continued:

> I love my work with such a passion, but family is my real joy. Twelve hours or more a day of work is not making for a balanced life. And I still can't get everything done. I want to be in the mental shape that I can come home and play with my nineteen-month-old and my husband. We're talking about priorities. I'm not going to miss Jessica putting on costume jewelry or dress-up clothes. I'm needed at both places, but home is my priority. I went through the master's program to do something that I want to do, but now my struggle is, how am I going to balance all of this?

It was often difficult for family members to understand why we spent so much time at work, which added tension to relationships. We couldn't adequately communicate the intensity we felt about day-to-day responsibilities at school and the energy that teaching requires. When the timing was right, however, we greatly appreciated it when family members pushed us to make time for life outside of school. Julie wrote:

> Jeff has been complaining about me not being available to do fun things. He says I'm always working and not taking enough time for myself or him. SO—tomorrow, he and I are going to the mountains for some time away together. I am not sure where he's taking me—I really don't care, as long as we're alone! He told me I can't take one thing with me that has to do with teaching. This will be a much needed break!!!!!!

Our spouses were often those who convinced us to reevaluate our lives and seek balance. Carly's fiancé was a university professor and understood more about what she was going through, but finding balance between work and home was still an ongoing process for them: "I came home at 7:00 the other night and he had already fixed dinner and had started to eat before I got there. He didn't yell, fuss, or tease me.

He just said very calmly and nicely—'I hope you won't stay that late at work every night after we get married.' That is all it took to let me know that we must come first."

When we did make time for ourselves and others, it sometimes led to more instead of less stress about work. We felt guilty and disorganized. One week, instead of staying at school late every evening, Julie left at the end of each school day to be with her family. The next week she wrote, "Now I am so behind, I feel like I need 24 hours in my classroom alone to get organized!" April described the same frustration as she tried to balance home and school: "Terry has a hard time understanding why I stay so late and still bring work home, so I have been trying to do all of my work at school and leave by 5:00 or 5:30. It's hard to fit it all in, trying to get things ready for each day and having my lesson plans for the next week. I either feel guilty at school or I feel guilty at home."

Balancing our lives was not just about finding time for family and friends; it was also about finding time to be refreshed professionally. After our first trip to NCTE's annual convention, we recognized how important it was to step back from our classrooms to spend time with other educators. Robbie wrote,

> Sometimes we don't realize how badly we need a break until we make ourselves take it. It is refreshing, isn't it? The conference gave me new energy that not even the long winter break gave me. After going to a couple of sessions and getting to talk to other teachers about things that they are doing in their classrooms, I was really renewed and excited about going back to school.

Each of us moved in and out of times when we found balance and when we felt overwhelmed to the point of complete exhaustion, but we learned that seeking balance requires a shift in attitude. It didn't mean that we cared for our students or our job less; we simply began to see things from a different perspective. Erin said, "Even though I'm working harder than ever now and I still bring work home with me all the time, I put my family first. I care about my students a great deal—that Jasmine isn't reading yet or that Jayua isn't engaged or that Marvin wasn't happy today—but my family and home and friends come first."

Things *Did* Go Well

> You have to remember that every day you have at least a little bit of success, more than you think you do, and you have great big successes too. You have to pick up on those successes. Just like with kids, you want to celebrate their successes, so we need to congratulate each other.

In a chapter filled with stories of frustration, it's also important to share good things that happened. When those moments occurred and we recognized them, as Julie said, "it was the *best* feeling in the world." Stories of success did not dominate our data, but they surfaced regularly. In the following data excerpts, we share a few representative examples— moments when we built positive relationships with children, moved away from textbooks into more thoughtful learning opportunities, and helped children as strategic readers:

> I love my kids and their idiosyncrasies. I came home Friday and by 5:30 one of the girls in my class called to tell me that her new puppy had gotten carsick. She planned to tell me when we came back from spring break but she couldn't wait. At first I thought, "Why is this child calling me at home my first evening of spring break?" But it makes me realize that I have made a relationship with this child. She wanted to share with someone and she picked me. (Julie, March 2000)

> My class is such an incredible community. Whenever anybody comes in they say things like, "your kids all love each other." My principal shared something very sweet. She talked to one of my parents who said, "Ami is great; I think she could teach any grade. We're blessed to have her." And she said that I have the happiest class in the school! (Ami, November 1999)

> I know that I am supposed to allow the children to guide my instruction, and I am getting soooo much better at that. I have finally taught a social studies unit on the industrial revolution where we hardly used the textbook! We used trade books and projects on inventions! It was really neat for me on Friday because we were doing a science activity. We made paper helicopters and flew them to make predictions. After we worked as a group, the kids worked for about ten minutes with a partner and made predictions on their own. (Robbie, January 2000)

> The days when I wished my kids had a better teacher melted away as I heard Justin say that when he came to second grade, he could read "hardly any words" but now he can "read most of them in that Superman book." Each one of these children gives me a little gift on days like this. They give me the evidence of progress and growth, and most importantly, they give me the confidence that *they* love to read. I am allowing myself the responsibility for that love. (Erin, March 2001)

The Hard-Talk Nature of Our Meetings

We look back now and wonder why we didn't focus more on successes such as these. In our group meetings, we seemed to concentrate more on hard talk about struggles even though one of us would occasionally steer the conversation toward positive stories. After one meeting, for example, Robbie wrote, "I hope that at the next meeting we will be able to share more of the joy and success instead of so much struggle because I know that everyone is doing terrific things, they are just not recognizing it." There were also times when a member of the group would point out the positive aspects of difficult situations. At the end of the first year, for instance, April reminded us:

> We have things that fail, but like Erin, she was doing writing workshop and she looked at it as such a failure, but then she saw how two little girls were doing such a good job. So, even though there were kids in the classroom that weren't doing what they were supposed to be doing, there was still some success that she could take away from it.

But even when we noted success stories, we didn't typically dwell on them. Why? Perhaps, when we didn't see our classrooms as complete representations of our ideals—as our idea of perfection—we were unable to credit the successes we *did* experience. Carly offered another explanation: "In our meetings, we always talked first about what was going well; but we picked up on what we needed to figure out. We didn't dwell on issues that didn't need resolution." We also wonder if a focus on success would have provided a safe enough place to expose vulnerabilities. As Robbie put it, "Maybe we didn't dwell on what was going well because we needed validation about what was so difficult," and Erin said, "I would have been devastated without a place to voice my fears." By sharing struggles with one another, we were able to validate them as well as do something about them. April added, "A lot of issues that were bringing us down would have gotten lost if we had only focused on success; we wouldn't have addressed the question that Susi asked going into this—why so many new teachers leave the profession or lose their visions so quickly." Without a place for the hard talk, our work would have become one more sanitized version of the teaching story.

Being Perfect Is Neither Achievable nor Desirable

I'm just trying to be a good teacher and I'm definitely a work in progress.

We were living contradictions. Intellectually, we understood that being perfect was an absurd motivation and a nonexistent quality, but there was always a nagging feeling that some version of Great Teaching was just beyond our grasp. Susi was not exactly our best role model, being a bundle of contradictions herself: "I felt awful because I knew that I wasn't giving you the answers that would solve your problems. You taught me that that's not what good teaching is about but I still have a really hard time letting go of that. I want to fix it for you. I want to have the answers." We were impatient. We wanted to immediately be the teachers we envisioned. As Carly said, "We want to be the best we can be now, now, now—not just because we know that inquiry and meaning-based assessment are much more supportive of thoughtful learning experiences, but because we enjoy planning and watching wonder come alive."

We represented disequilibrium at its best. In the second year, Carly wrote:

> I remember learning in grad school that any great learning only comes from disequilibrium. That is where we are right now, feeling a sense of being off-balance, not quite sure. Questioning is a necessary thing, an inevitable thing that none of us could really prepare for no matter how many hours we planned and read. We have such a tremendous responsibility and it *should* be overwhelming. Our fortunate and unfortunate fate is that our learning and, therefore, our disequilibrium never end.

We still believe that visions are important and that good teaching means pushing the boundaries of what is possible. But we had to let go of the illusive goal of perfection and give ourselves a break. As Carmen said, "I'm just trying to be a good teacher and I'm definitely a work in progress." When we relaxed in this way, teaching was less overwhelming and we were able to see more of the successes that were there. At the end of her second year, Erin explained:

> I used to think that being a good teacher was like having a checklist and if all your points were checked off, you were okay. When I read professionally, it felt stressful because I would read all the things I was not doing. I would get so overwhelmed because I wasn't implementing everything I thought I should be doing to be a good teacher. Now I realize that the world isn't going to end because I haven't introduced magnets in an exciting way, and I notice more things that are going well.

Giving ourselves license to implement one or two ideas at a time became one of the most important learnings of our early years. Robbie wrote:

> I've almost come to terms with the fact that I can't do it all at once and I can only do so much at a time. I think that one day I'm going to be an awesome teacher. It is just going to take me a little

while and I'm okay with that. I don't get upset with myself anymore because I am a little behind in the curriculum or if things don't work out the way I planned. There is always next year to try again and in a little different way because I've learned from my mistakes.

We are kinder to ourselves today, but we admit to relapses. The Being Perfect Disease always seems to be lurking, waiting for the right moment to attack. Sometimes the nagging feeling comes back, but we try to push it away. It helps to remember Carly's words, written at the end of her first year:

> I always thought I failed if I didn't get it right the first time. If I failed, this year was the most rewarding failure I've ever had. You go into teaching determined to do it all. Then you're depressed—you aren't doing even half of it. You feel like less than half the professional you started with. I could get stuck in this rut if I focused on all that I never did this year, but I know it doesn't have to come all at once, and it won't no matter how hard I try!

Today we also realize that our destructive thoughts were not just about us. They were also connected to larger issues in our schools, school systems, and universities. Trying to live up to some version of perfect may have something to do with personal demons, but those demons are often fed and nurtured by larger structures that we can all work to change. As explored in the following chapters, we learned that while it was important to take responsibility for our own tensions and triumphs, the struggle to live up to a vision was about more than individual teachers feeling guilty and beating themselves up.

Critical Insights from Chapter 5

- Within weeks in the first year of teaching, many of us began to feel our dreams replaced by disappointment and our excitement replaced by seriously weakening self-confidence.

- It was easier than we thought to succumb to the practices around us as our university experiences began to fade into the not-so-distant past.

- We now realize that we were not nearly as helpless as we felt, but most of us believed we had little control over our teaching lives during the first years.

- As new teachers, we felt particularly helpless when our beliefs seemed to be in direct opposition to real or perceived mandates or accepted practices in our schools.

- We wanted to move smoothly into our new school communities, so when we sensed differences, we didn't want to make our situations even more uncomfortable by speaking out against the norm. We wanted to fit in, so we made compromises.

- When we didn't feel that we could clearly articulate what we wanted to do and why, we were more apt to move toward the status quo.

- Extreme levels of compromise—when strict adherence to packaged programs was required—made it easy to lose confidence in ourselves and our visions.

- Pinning down and using ideas from graduate school was difficult largely because we could not find time or colleagues with whom we could work through those ideas.

- As ideas whirled faster and faster, it became easier to allow real and perceived curricular mandates, worries about grades, and the teach-to-the-test culture to dictate our practices.

- We wanted to be just like the teachers in professional books; when our classrooms didn't look and sound like theirs, we wondered, "What's wrong with me?"

- Our frustration and fatigue began to surface in actions and words we never thought we would do or say. It's hard to admit how easy it became to start blaming kids and parents.

- When we found ourselves taking a negative stance, one of the most important lessons we learned was to look at how our own actions might be contributing to difficult situations and to change our approach.

- We were more than willing to carry our share of additional teacher responsibilities—the *stuff* that all teachers have to do beyond teaching—but it was frustrating when they took up so much of the day that we could not devote time to the real work of the classroom.

- Learning to juggle work and life was particularly challenging as we worked to find our place in the profession.

- We had many moments of success, but when we didn't see our classrooms as complete representations of our ideals, it was difficult to see our successes.

- Intellectually, we understood that being perfect was an absurd motivation and a nonexistent characteristic, but there was always a nagging feeling that some version of Great Teaching was just beyond our grasp.

6 Administrators and Colleagues, We Need You

I really enjoy my class, colleagues, administration, and school. Everyone has really welcomed me here. We don't all think the same way, we don't do the same things, but we all support each other and are not critical of each other, of what other people are doing.

Kind, nurturing administrators and colleagues who shared our passion for continuing to learn and grow were particularly important during our early years of teaching. Even when our principals and colleagues drew from pedagogical backgrounds that were different from ours, we could be nurtured and encouraged when they supported opportunities to examine practice and make decisions based on knowledge of learning and children. Some of us began with this kind of support. Others did not. The contrasts were great. With supportive administrators and colleagues, our days were happier and less stressful and we were more likely to grow in confidence. Without them, we lost confidence to the extent that some of us seriously considered leaving the profession *and* began to do exactly what Susi questioned when she initiated the study—we began to move toward a status quo that was driven not by ideas and knowledge nor by knowing children well, but by test scores and the allure of packaged programs promising to raise test scores. When those around us fell into this pattern, it was difficult to hold our own. We trusted our own knowledge less and less. Some of us even began to lose the passion to teach. This chapter focuses on the key roles of administrators and colleagues and the impact they had on our teaching lives as some of us thrived and others barely survived.

Writing This Chapter

We talked a lot about how to structure this chapter: if we discuss administrators first, will we send the message that teachers' hands are tied without supportive leaders? We know that teachers working together can do remarkable things. At the same time, a strong pattern in our data was the role of the administrator in creating a collaborative environment in which educators thoughtfully examine their own practice, *or* in establishing something quite different. In the absence of great leaders, teachers together can make an enormous difference, but there seems to be a point at which the actions of administrators can open up or close down possibilities for those who want to learn and grow. When programs and practices are rigidly mandated, an atmosphere can evolve that lacks the warmth, caring, and intellectual spirit necessary for great teaching to flourish. We understand that many perceived mandates are, in reality, myths that need to be exposed for what they are: tradition, fear of the unknown, handed-down misinformation, and misinterpretation. But in some places, mandates are not myths, and when teachers have exhausted all efforts to initiate collaborative talk, they find that their only options are to conform, go underground, or leave.

Because our study looked at teaching experiences across seven years, we were able to see members of our group in very different administrative settings. Some, who began their careers in nurturing environments, found themselves teaching behind closed doors and sometimes even adopting practices in conflict with their belief systems when those environments changed. Others found that a change in administration opened up possibilities they had not enjoyed before. We don't underestimate the importance of colleagues, nor do we pass the buck in terms of our own responsibility, but as one group member wrote, "administration sets the tone." For these reasons, we open the chapter with a discussion of the administrator's role in the lives of new teachers. The second half of the chapter explores the important relationships between new teachers and their colleagues.

Administrators, You Set the Tone

> My principal has been so supportive. She makes me feel important and valued. As teachers we are often belittled by skill and drill programs and requirements to read the manual step by step and teach by the text. I think that mentality breaks down teachers' sense of self and certainly their spirit. Over time many educators lose their zest for teaching. My principal has never been like that. She keeps my zest for teaching alive.

Ami's confidence in her first year of teaching shouts throughout our data notebooks just as it does in the preceding quote. In journal entries and in monthly meetings, she expressed real joy in having found a supportive, nurturing administrator: "Sharon Bodie goes to bat for me, shelters me, encourages me, and supports me." If we were to describe ideal administrators now, seven years after our first days of teaching, the description would go like this: *kind, supportive learners who are as com-mitted to enriching their own professional knowledge about teaching and learn-ing as they are to making sure that teachers have the resources and autonomy to grow.* Administrators inspired us through their positive energy and creation of warm and respectful school cultures. We were encouraged by administrators who valued our knowledge as well as our fragility, insecurity, and inexperience; who built caring communities; and who created opportunities to learn alongside us. In our experiences, the pres-ence or absence of these characteristics meant the difference between new teachers who felt energized and excited about continuing to grow in productive, healthy ways and those who felt inadequate, depressed, and discouraged and considered leaving the profession.

As we write about our experiences with administrators, it's im-portant to emphasize that we realize there are many sides to every story. We understand that administrators make decisions within specific po-litical and historical contexts based on their own views of education. Under considerable pressure, they have to please a wide range of con-stituents and bosses—parents, teachers, school districts, state depart-ments of education, and legislators. This means that teachers and ad-ministrators often look at issues through different lenses. Recognizing this, we are even more grateful for administrators who make collabo-ration foundational to building educational communities in which teachers are valued for their knowledge and expertise.

The stories told in the following pages provide opportunities for administrators to see their role through the eyes of new teachers and to remember what it feels like to enter the world of teaching. We invite you to consider our experiences as you welcome new teachers, open mutually generative conversations, and celebrate the good work you do as learners and teachers together.

Trust, Respect, and Autonomy

Please don't take simple autonomy for granted. Being able to make decisions about how you will teach is something that shouldn't but can be taken away.

As Erin set up her classroom in the days before her first class of chil-dren would arrive, she created an enormous Kindness Tree from bright mural paper. It extended above and beyond a bulletin board that cov-ered the length of a classroom wall. Below the tree was a basket of leaves made out of construction paper. Erin envisioned her second graders writing appreciations to one another on the leaves and posting them on the tree. She believed it would provide one of many ways that children could use and learn literacy, and saw it as foundational to building a caring community in which she and the children would support one another as learners. Once the school year was under way, the Kindness Tree quickly became one of the most popular aspects of the classroom. Within weeks, the wall was filled with notes of appreciation. The notes spread beyond the wall and around the room, wherever there was free space—on shelves, windows, the door, Erin's desk. The children wrote from the heart in ways that led to stronger connections across the class: "Hey, Jamie, thank you for talking to me at recess when I was feeling sad" or "Ms. Miller, thanks for that hug today." A special ritual evolved at the end of each day as children took turns reading aloud the kindness notes they had written that day.

In May of that year, Erin sat down with one of her administrators for her end-of-year evaluation. She listened to recommendations to improve her teaching. One of them was to remove the kindness notes from her wall. Erin wrote to us:

> One of the suggestions was to take down the kindness notes so that I would reduce what she called, the cluttered look in my classroom. She thought that they were a great way for students to praise their peers, but they made my room look cluttered. I couldn't believe it! The kindness notes are so much more than a way for my students to praise their peers. They build community, literacy, and give the children a sense of ownership in the room. They promote reading and writing for real purposes. They make the classroom ours instead of mine. She never even asked me to explain.

Several years later, Erin received a letter from one of the children who had been in that class. The student wrote remembering Erin as her favorite teacher and said, "You know what I still remember most about second grade? I still remember those kindness notes."

Stories like this deeply affected us all. At first we were angry as we read Erin's email describing the administrator's reaction to the Kindness Tree. Then we began to wonder why such a disconnect would occur. An invitation from Erin's administrator for her to talk about the value of the Kindness Tree might have opened the lines of communication and helped them get to the heart of their differences in a mutually respectful manner. Without talk, it was easy for Erin to get the impression that her teaching decisions were not valued. At another point in her career, it is likely that Erin would have engaged her administrator in dialogue to explain how and why the Kindness Tree was supportive of literacy learners. In this situation, Erin did not feel comfortable opening such a conversation. Although some discomfort came from her inexperience, it was compounded by the limited autonomy she had experienced that year. This contrasted greatly with the comfort and ease felt by most other members of our group in opening difficult conversations with their administrators.

As described in earlier chapters, it had been made clear from the first days of school that every teacher at Erin's grade level would use a scripted reading program to complete the same lessons at the same time in the same way: the teacher standing in front of the class reading from the teacher's guide, leading the children in choral responses. The teacher's guide dictated exactly what to do and say, and teachers were expected to follow the script. Erin explained, "Worksheets are submitted to be copied and each of us receives our weekly stack." At grade-level meetings, teachers were told what they would teach each week and which worksheets to use for every lesson:

> Monday, we brainstorm words for certain sounds. Tuesday, we do word rhymes and copying words for a handwriting grade. Wednesday is the dictation of sounds and words. Thursday we hand out the response card drills and the children have to look, touch, and show the cards that make certain sounds. Friday is the day that we, as a class, all work through the same workbook pages in our phonics book.

Erin's principal came by her room almost every day, usually between 9:00 and 9:30, when she was supposed to teach the phonics section of the scripted lesson. What grew in the wake of this predictability was Erin's fear of being caught doing something she wasn't supposed to do. She said, "Sometimes it's really scary because he'll come in my room five minutes before 9:00. I know he's expecting me to end the read-aloud right at 9:00 and pass out the phonics workbooks, so I'm always nervous." One day, engrossed in reading a story to her students, Erin looked at the clock and realized it was after 9:00 and she had totally forgotten the phonics lesson. Fear came through clearly in her message to us that evening:

> We were reading a story when I realized, "Oh no! He's gonna be in here and we haven't done phonics!" So we stopped reading and got out our phonics books. I never imagined it would be this way. Please don't take simple autonomy for granted. Being able to make decisions about how you will teach is something that shouldn't, but can, be taken away.

Erin's stories—the Kindness Tree and the scripted days—reflect a real difference between her beliefs and those of the leaders in her school. Erin's professional study and her habit of paying close attention to children led her to see great value in the kindness notes, as well as in other rituals and instructional strategies, and little value in scripted programs based on worksheets and skills taught in isolation. Her administrators' backgrounds led them to believe something else. Clearly, their decisions were guided by their own beliefs about the kind of teaching that would have an impact on students in their school and by an immense amount of pressure to demonstrate high test scores. Without possibilities to explore other ways to address those pressures, however, the lack of autonomy was more than frustrating. It closed down the potential for generative talk that might have led to the development of important learning opportunities for students. Ultimately, it led Erin to begin losing faith in herself and her knowledge.

Going underground is a temporary solution but not a very satisfying place to be.

Late in the year, Erin realized that a few teachers in her school were reaching beyond the mandates, but they were hidden behind closed doors, having gone underground to teach according to their beliefs:

> It slipped out one day that one of the second-grade teachers was doing a study on fairy tales. Another teacher saw a *Ramona* book on my desk and asked if that was a good read-aloud because the *Ramona* book she was reading wasn't very good, indicating that she too saw value in reading aloud to her students. More and more, I see teachers doing more of their own thing. It's just that everything has to be so quiet and under the table.

Erin considered why she hadn't also gone underground: "Why didn't I just deal with the mandates by letting them roll off my back, put on a good show, and then close my door and do what I knew was best? Teachers have been doing this for years." But in the first months, Erin didn't even entertain the possibility that she could close her door and do her own thing. With an administrator coming in to check on her, that seemed impossible. Also, she wanted to be a team player, a colleague, and she had no idea that anyone else was reaching beyond the mandates to teach differently. Looking back, we all agreed that, even if she had tried to teach behind closed doors, it is doubtful that the relief would have been very gratifying. Refuge underground also means teaching away from collegial interactions, which is a temporary solution but not a very satisfying place to be.

Sliding into the status quo: You can only fight for so long.

Watching and listening to Erin, we realized that working within rigid mandates can mean compromising beliefs until teachers no longer recognize themselves. At one point, Erin wrote, "This can't be me up here asking my kids to look, point, and show the card that makes the mmmm sound." During Erin's graduate school experience, she had conducted her own inquiry into the intentional teaching of phonics in the context of curricular structures such as shared reading, interactive writing, and written conversations. She understood how to build phonics knowledge that children could apply immediately to real reading and writing. Exhausted and feeling alone, however, Erin found that the constant state of conflict began to take its toll. Wearing down by midyear, she wrote, "I do what they want me to. I don't even fight it like I used to. I just do what I have to do and then spend the rest of the day trying to make up for the lost time. You can only fight for so long."

An incident occurred in March of that year that jolted Erin out of the compromises that were stealing her passion for teaching. She was advised to stop giving her students time to read independently during the period allotted for reading instruction because it was not consistent with what the other second-grade teachers were doing. Feeling that she didn't even have the power to make a decision about "something as important as giving children time to read," Erin had had enough. The level of compromise she had reached was causing her to slip toward a status quo very different from what she hoped for herself as an educator: "I've given up a great deal of who I am to teach here but I'm not giving up all of me." Startled out of her own complacency, Erin made plans to look for another job: "I know a few weeks ago, I said I would stay here, but I don't see how I can now. Was I going to sacrifice my beliefs as a teacher for the comfort of stability?"

The decision to leave was an important one, but the effects of a year without autonomy were hard to shake. Even as Erin made the move to leave the school, her self-confidence wavered: "I'm angry but I'm insecure too. I'm almost 100% sure I'm doing the right thing, but I think I need to hear it. Susi, are you sure that schools exist out there that would not do this? Are you sure I'm not just being difficult and uncompromising?"

I see the most growth in my students when I use what I know.

We believe that programmatic mandates, and scripted programs in particular, are a mistake. They deprive teachers of opportunities to make informed decisions based on knowledge of teaching, learning, and the children in their classrooms. They keep us from learning and growing as professionals. However, our experiences show that, while we work to change those practices, good work can be done when teachers are supported in using their knowledge rather than simply following the teacher's guide. Looking at the experiences of another teacher in our group, we see how administrative support for teacher knowledge can make a big difference.

After staying home for a year with her twins, Julie moved to a new district to teach kindergarten. Her school administrator supported her implementation of a broad range of sound practices and respected her knowledge and ability. At the same time, there was growing district pressure to adopt the reading program that had been mandated at Erin's school. Requested by the district to review programs and provide a recommendation, Julie and other teachers at her school examined multiple reading programs. They recommended one that provided predictable texts and included many of the meaning-based literacy practices Julie had come to value. The district chose instead to purchase a revised version of the program used at Erin's school. They felt the approach used in this series resulted in higher test scores and saw the scores as useful measures of reading achievement. Julie was disturbed that teachers' views seem to have been given little credence, but she decided to give the program a try, "to see for myself what it included."

As Erin had experienced, Julie found that the program promoted a one-size-fits-all view of teaching. She was frustrated with the lengthy books used for five-year-olds rather than predictable texts that would engage emergent readers. She saw the requirement to teach phonics in isolation as limiting possibilities for children to develop as strategic, passionate, and proficient readers and thinkers. She was concerned about a program that told teachers what to say and do, leaving little opportunity to learn about and address the needs of individual children. Given the replication of testing formats in the program's day-to-day lessons, she was not surprised that children who followed it might score well on standardized tests, but she felt strongly that the tests were not good indicators of children's reading proficiency and certainly did not provide adequate information to help her plan for instruction.

Erin and Julie were far from alone in their views about scripted programs and teach-to-the-test curricula. Their unease echoes a much broader national concern. Again and again, professional literature describes serious problems associated with such views of children's literacy learning: the ineffectiveness of one-size-fits-all programs that fail to see reading as a strategic, meaning-making process and that tell teachers what to say and do (Coles, 2003; Garan, 2002, 2004; Kohn, 2000; Sacks, 1999; Smith, 2003). Even the argument that such programs raise test scores loses credibility as studies beyond those conducted by the programs' publishers show that schools using the programs are "significantly more likely to be in the bottom quartile of the [standardized tests] than schools using non-scripted programs" (Moustafa & Land, 2002, p. 10). Based on this knowledge, and feeling confident that she could provide a theoretically sound form of instruction to meet the specific needs of her students, Julie addressed the program's skills and the state language arts standards using trade books and leveled texts as well as books from the adopted series. Invited by her administrator to share her ideas, she explained, "I see the most growth in my students when I use what I know about how children learn to read, teach phonics in the context of meaningful literacy experiences, and build practice based on my knowledge of each child's needs."

The principal's genuine interest in and respect for Julie's expertise provided an experience much different from the one Erin encountered. Trusted as a knowledgeable professional, Julie was able use her knowledge to address the needs of her students. This also allowed her to grow as a teacher. Teaching beyond the script meant she could further develop her knowledge as she made instructional decisions by reflecting day to day on teaching and learning in her classroom. As a result, she was able to share practices and strategies on a broader scale through her collaborative work on the district's Kindergarten Advisory Board (explained in Chapter 7).

With autonomy . . . the heights we could reach were endless.

Carly, Robbie, April, Ami, and Carmen found themselves in schools where they felt trusted by their school administration from the first day. While they were required to meet curricular guides and address state standards, it seemed very clear that they had been hired for their expertise in using professional knowledge and knowledge of their students to do so. Given that kind of autonomy, they had support to try and to fail and then to try again. They were also supported at the district level. A superintendent's convictions expressed at the district orientation meeting let Robbie and Carly know they would be trusted as knowledgeable professionals. Robbie wrote, "I don't think that I am going to have many barriers from the standpoint of what I must do in my classroom. I think that they are going to pretty much allow me to decide how I am going to teach. That is a pretty exciting prospect!" Carly shared the same feelings: "I feel my principal will be supportive of the inquiry process; I am excited about the possibilities." Ami, reflecting on her job choice, wrote: "It's *such* a great place to work. The principal supports me in doing my own thing and respects my knowledge. I never have administrators breathing down my neck."

Eventually, autonomy came to Erin's school as well. After Erin interviewed for and was offered jobs in other schools, a change occurred that caused her to stay. A new principal came to her school, bringing a fresh outlook and a sense of trust in teachers that made all the difference. Almost immediately Erin felt a renewed sense of self-confidence and energy for trying innovative ideas. In September of her second year, she wrote:

> I have finally done it. I have let go of worksheets completely! At first, I thought I'd have to use some worksheets to appease my new administrator, but she really *listens* to me explain the reasoning behind my practices, and when she comes in my room, she's proud of what she sees! Our school is changing fast and hard!

With autonomy, teachers in Erin's school began making choices. They planned and implemented a schoolwide period of sustained silent reading every morning and opened daily schedules in ways that made curricular integration a possibility. A year later the school had changed even more as teachers made their own decisions about inviting consultants to share ideas that were not bound to scripted programs. The renewed energy for professional reading and trying new ideas was thrilling to see. Erin's messages were full of excitement about the practices she was finally able to experiment with and the new level of involvement from her students:

> I took a deep breath and dove into writing workshop, and it's finally coming together! When we met back in January, I was taking a break from writing workshop because I felt like I just couldn't make it work for me. But it didn't take long to do some more reading and want to try it again. Now we're in full swing. Sometimes I'm so proud of myself because my kids look so forward to this time, and when I look around the room, I see all my kids working their hearts away.

Perhaps the most significant change that came with autonomy was a greater sense of calm and confidence. Erin wrote, "I no longer fear that an administrator will come in and find my students reading or sitting on the floor listening to me read or writing with me. I look forward to my administrator coming in because I love to show off the learning that goes on every morning." She added, "This is how things can change when you're not restricted to a program!"

Given wings, so much was possible. With autonomy, we felt trusted. We knew that it would be okay if administrators came into our classrooms and saw children actively involved in diverse learning engagements. We knew that we could try and fail and try again and be valued for engaging in the process. The possibilities for what we could do and the heights we could reach were endless.

With autonomy comes responsibility.

We believe that professional autonomy is foundational to great teaching. We also believe that with autonomy comes responsibility. As teachers, we cannot expect support for teaching according to our beliefs if we do not demonstrate professional knowledge and a drive for continued growth. Carmen used the phrase "irresponsible autonomy" to describe teachers' freedom to "do anything they want to as long as parents are happy and test scores are high." For autonomy to be truly supportive and generative, it must be much more than complete license. It comes with strings attached. We have a responsibility to *use* the trust placed in us to continue reading professionally, try out new ideas, look closely at children, talk things through with other teachers and administrators, and make decisions accordingly. If we want to be trusted to teach well, we have to demonstrate our knowledge and the desire for further knowledge that accompanies that right.

The story of Erin's second-grade insect inquiries provides a great example of what can happen when administrators embrace this notion of responsible autonomy. With her new principal, Erin felt that she was respected as an educator with knowledge. As a result, she felt much more confident in implementing ideas she had been longing to try, and she was able to use those experiences as a basis for her own further growth:

> When I think about how different this is from the inquiry experience I tried to organize when I was in the MAT program, I am amazed. My mini-lessons have been 100 percent better, my expectations more realistic, and the depth of the study more sophisticated. Not only are the kids fascinated, but we are hitting language arts standards left and right. Most of the class is doing fantastic work and I'm so proud of them. I have one adorable little boy who *loves* science. All year, he has patiently listened to fiction story after fiction story. No matter how I tried, I couldn't get his eyes to light up about fiction books. Well, now he is in his glory! All he can talk about is this study. Every time he comes up to me for the zillionth time to show me something he learned, I can't help but smile and know that I've done something really important for this child.

Administrators play the pivotal role in establishing a responsibly autonomous school environment. This requires more on their part than merely letting us loose. It requires the creation of a school culture in which ongoing and supported study and reflection are the norm. As Erin wrote, "Teachers need to be in a place that pushes them to move forward and supports them in doing that. Otherwise, it's too easy for our passion to die."

Building a Caring Community

He had what mattered most.

As Carmen began her second year of teaching, she wrote, "Sadness permeates our school today. Our principal Dr. Adkins passed on Saturday night. He had complications from surgery. We have pretty much been zombies this week. The students were very close to him and many of them have taken it very hard. School will be closed tomorrow so that everyone can attend the services." Carmen continued:

> In the eulogy, Dr. Adkins was referred to as the *gentle giant*. He stood several inches past six feet tall. He was fun-loving and not your typical principal. He had what matters most. He genuinely cared about the kids. He made them feel special. It was always a joy to watch him interact with them. The kindergartners were the cutest when they would wrap their tiny arms around his leg. He was genuinely loved by his whole staff. Several of the teachers had worked with him for many years. They had watched his children grow and were friends with his wife. He opened his home up to the staff for Christmas parties and brought in baked goods. I remember swapping recipe ideas with him. We decided to make a tomato casserole, though we never did. There was a dark cloud over the school when the news came. Many tears were shed. That cloud will lift, but it will never totally fade. Dr. Adkins *was* Homeland Park.

Dr. Adkins cared about children *and* about teachers. He demonstrated his caring every day. He brought characteristics and commitment to his school that created the foundation for a caring community. His role was critical.

Looking across our experiences, we learned that caring comes in many packages, that there is no one right way to demonstrate caring, but that some common characteristics are important. Caring communities were created when principals got to know us as human beings, knew when to pick us up when we were down, could help us think through solutions while pointing out our successes, supported teachers *and* parents in ways that let everyone know they were valued, remembered the importance of a pat on the back, let us know they were proud to have us in their schools, enjoyed interacting with our students while showing genuine interest in our teaching, and believed that we had something of value to say and listened. Hearing one another's stories, we also learned that the presence of a caring administrator is not something to be taken for granted. And we learned that, while principals establish the tone for a caring community, we as teachers have just as much of a responsibility to make school a caring place.

He cared enough to want to spend time with them, to get to know them as human beings.

A lakeside cabin away from the hum of school building air conditioners was the setting for the first faculty meeting for Robbie and Carly. Carly wrote, "You won't believe where we spent our first school meeting! Everyone on the faculty met out at this beautiful cabin nestled in the middle of the woods and surrounded by a huge lake. The cabin had a wrap-around porch and a large meeting room where we sat in comfortable chairs for meetings and getting-to-know each other activities." Robbie continued, "Mr. Smith had pork chops and chicken on the grill with not just the cheap barbecue sauce! He had broccoli casserole, corn on the cob and homemade salad, and then pie and ice cream for dessert. He cooked all of this for *us.*"

In the scope of a new teacher's life, this gesture may seem small. But it wasn't. Robbie and Carly learned from the first days that Mr. Smith was someone who cared enough to want to spend time with them; to get to know them first as human beings, then as teachers; and even to cook for them. For Carly and Robbie, this was one way that a foundation of comfort and trust was laid. Their love for Mr. Smith and sense of safety with him grew even deeper as the year went on. They often spoke about his ability to make them feel that everything was okay even on their most difficult days. They saw his empathy for the day-to-day lives of teachers: "Our principal is so understanding that even when we need a mental health day, he doesn't question it. He really understands that you need a break sometimes."

Administrators who made time for conversation and who made us feel comfortable enough to initiate conversations created opportunities for us to communicate as one human being to another. With them, we could share vulnerabilities and concerns without fear. Carmen described how her new principal, arriving after the death of Dr. Adkins, arranged a meeting with every staff member and encouraged teachers to share their expectations and concerns: "I openly shared and he appeared interested in my thoughts. He assured me that he would have an open door policy and he kept his promise." During her years with Mr. Ruthsatz, Carmen felt that she came to know him as a person, not just as an administrator. She felt that his actions demonstrated a genuine interest in her as a teacher. For example, like everyone else, Mr. Ruthsatz got to know and love Carmen's grandmother, who frequently came to spend time with the children. When Carmen went into his office, Mr. Ruthsatz always greeted her with a smile and allowed her to articulate her concerns. She enjoyed their open conversations about everything from school issues and children to the trips to California they both made regularly. They talked frankly about struggles in education: "I appreciated that we could have open conversations about young Black boys being in crisis and we talked about our growing Hispanic population and how we were failing them." Their conversations about what could be done to support the school's Spanish-speaking children led them to taking a Spanish class together.

They helped me discover myself.

Susi reflected on her own experiences as a first-year teacher working for and with an administrative team committed to the creation of a caring community. Remembering her first-year struggles to understand and engage children, she described the sensitivity demonstrated by the school's curriculum coordinator and reading specialist: "They seemed to know exactly when I was down and needed to be picked up. They helped me think through solutions to complex problems, while reminding me of what was going well." Susi wrote:

> During my first year, there were many moments when kids were literally scrambling under and over tables. As I tried to figure out how to capture their attention, the school's curriculum coordinator and reading specialist were there for me every day. Recognizing that, as a naive 21-year-old, I was *very* wet behind the ears, Phyllis Felix and Sharon Allen came into my classroom, worked with small groups, and demonstrated strategies that worked for them. Most importantly, they spent hours talking and talking and talking *with* me—helping me figure things out, but always letting me know that they valued me as a teacher. Not once did they impose their ways of teaching on me. They had the insight to recognize the kind of teacher I wanted to be and helped me discover myself. They celebrated what was going well and even made it possible for me to become involved in literacy work at the district level, where I found another lifelong source of support in Jackie Blank, the district language arts coordinator. They saw successes in my teaching that I couldn't see. Their confidence in me meant that I always wanted to do more to justify that confidence.

Susi explained that her principal set the tone for these kinds of relationships: "He was one of the most positive people I've ever met. Mr. Ficarrotta always made me think that I was the most wonderful teacher in the world even when I felt like the classroom was crumbling around me."

Other members of our group found similar support. Carly wrote that even though her class was "considered one of the most challenging in the fourth grade," she was able to find peace with herself and her situation because of the support of her principal. Ami described how her school administrator let Ami know she was thrilled with her inquiry-based approach even when a district representative appeared less than impressed. In what could easily have been an emotionally destructive situation, the principal made all the difference because she knew what to say to encourage Ami to move forward with confidence. Ami wrote, "Thank *goodness* I have such a wonderfully supportive administrator."

She was able to balance a parent's concern with a teacher's intention.

During April's first year, the parent of a child in her kindergarten complained to the administration that her expectations for behavior were not appropriate: "She thinks that I set my expectations too high." April was worried and began to question her decisions. Her principal, Linda Hawkins, deftly calmed the parent by listening to her concerns while explaining that April was a wonderful teacher and that they were very lucky to have her in the school. When the parent relaxed, the stage was set for April to call the parent and have a productive conversation. Through the caring negotiation of her administrator, April was able to maintain her self-confidence and work with the parent to help the child make better choices in the classroom: "It was so nice that during this whole episode, I had my principal supporting what goes on in my classroom." April felt the support of a sensitive principal who was able to balance parents' concerns with teachers' intentions even when the two seemed in conflict.

Similarly, when Carly experienced her first angry parent, caring support from her principal helped her deal with the situation: "Mr. Smith was there with his ever-present support. He was wonderful. While he could see that the mother's pain was related to issues far beyond the classroom, he still managed to be firm enough to insist that she talk to me respectfully." He respected both teacher and parent. Mr. Smith's compassionate attitude continued even after the parent left. Carly explained, "I held it together pretty well during the meeting. When the parent had gone, Mr. Smith simply put his arm around me. I totally lost it then. But he just let me cry on his shoulder as if I were his own child. That's the way it is with Mr. Smith. We are all his own."

When principals made their pride and confidence in us visible, there was no limit to what we could do.

Our experiences helped us appreciate administrators who, in the midst of their many responsibilities, recognized the importance of celebrating what we did well, even the tiniest successes. When administrators were quick with a smile or a reassuring pat on the back and visited our classrooms out of interest rather than as a coercion tactic, we grew confident in our professional knowledge and were encouraged to work even harder. These administrators seemed to know that, along with all of our independent bravado, new teachers are fragile and quick to bruise. This sensitivity was not merely a nice touch; in some instances, it made the difference between whether a teacher remained in a school or sought a position elsewhere.

Carmen wrote with respect and gratitude about her second principal, who "even today, when I email the school, will always reply with a small note to let me know that he appreciated my time at his school; he assures me that a position will always be there for me if ever I decide to return." After moving to Virginia, Carmen felt the same kind of support from her new administrators. Her assistant principal's affirming observations bolstered Carmen's confidence within the unfamiliarity of a new school. Carmen wrote:

> It just keeps getting better. My assistant principal came to observe today and she left the nicest note. She wrote, "Carmen— you are amazing!" She went on to say how inviting my classroom was. When I signed the observation, I saw that she had written the most detailed notes about everything she observed. It was all good. Besides giving me a "Strong" rating in everything, she called me a superior teacher. She commented on the jazz I play in the background as the kids work in cooperative groups. She said that my kids were mannerable and she could tell that I set high expectations. It was just so much, and I must admit it made me very happy to hear it all.

Ami's principal provides another example of an administrator who understood the value of those pats on the back:

> My principal came in yesterday. We were doing interactive writing. It's a loud, active class. She was looking around the room and there was a ton of stuff up all around the walls and the room. In her review, she wrote things like, "active learning, manipulatives, books everywhere, children's work everywhere." It made

me feel so great; she was like, "It's very evident that you have very high expectation for these kids because it just shines through in everything they say and everything they do."

Even little notes written during routine reviews made a big difference. Ami's principal regularly let her know that she was proud to have Ami in her school: "Ms. Bodie left an amazing review in my box last Friday. She said to keep doing what I'm doing. It made my week!"

Positive comments from Erin's new principal had the same effect: "She even opened my room last weekend to show to her sister, who also teaches. That made me feel great!" When Erin asked her principal to review a handout she planned to give to parents, her administrator not only reviewed the letter but also thanked Erin for sharing it and told her that it was outstanding. After a challenging first year, this sensitivity to the importance of communicating pride in a teacher's work was a critical step in helping Erin regain her confidence and enthusiasm.

April experienced these kinds of responses regularly. She wrote, "Even the district person said how inviting my classroom was and that she really wished her child could come to my class. She said she's glad to see good kindergarten teachers out there. It's really a pick-me-up when you hear those kinds of things and realize that people notice." In another instance, April and her principal were discussing each other's journal entries during a professional study group session. April's writing revealed a desire to do more to support her students as writers. Her principal said, "April, you don't give yourself enough credit. You're doing really wonderful things."

In Carly and Robbie's school, Mr. Smith demonstrated his pride in them all the time. He often stopped by their rooms to let them know that he enjoyed their work and to celebrate their accomplishments. Robbie wrote, "He did something almost daily to show me that he was happy I was here. His smiles and hugs were so genuine." When a letter came from the National Council of Teachers of English commending Robbie and Carly for their presentation at the annual convention, Mr. Smith let everyone know: "After that letter came, Mr. Smith read it to all the teachers. He was bragging right and left about it. When we needed funding to go to another conference, he bragged about us at the district office and said, 'If they are doing something like this, then we have to give them a lot of money!'" This was a real boost to Robbie and Carly as new teachers. Robbie said, "When I think of Mr. Smith, I think of how he *always* made me feel so good being at his school."

This kind of support constituted a huge vote of confidence. When principals were our biggest cheerleaders and made their confidence and pride visible in multiple ways, we believed there was no limit to what we could do as teachers.

Without words of appreciation and affirmation, new teachers can begin to question their ability.

Sometimes, gestures of pride, confidence, and appreciation were taken for granted, and we didn't realize their importance until we examined situations in which they were limited. Julie's emails during her first year reminded us. She felt that there were seldom pats on the back, reassuring smiles, or "I've been there too" looks that she craved as the demands of teaching unfolded. At the time, Julie wrote, "The environment feels tense and uncomfortable. It's as if you're walking on eggshells all of the time." With few words of appreciation and affirmation, Julie began to question her ability and feel that she could never do anything right: "When I make a mistake, my principal is right there to tell me that I am wrong but never to compliment me or help me figure out how to do something better." When a parent wrote in celebration of Julie's work, Julie realized how much she missed those reassurances: "Wow, it is actually nice to get this feeling. I hadn't had that at all. It meant so much because I was starving for that. I wanted someone to say, 'You are doing okay. I'm happy you are the teacher in this class.'" The parent told Julie that a copy of the letter had been sent to the principal, and Julie wrote, "It made such an impression on me that this mom thought enough of what I had done to bring it to the attention of my principal. I don't know if my principal ever received the letter, though, because he never mentioned it to me." One day, after a difficult morning, a first-grade teacher saw Julie's discouraged look when passing her in the hall. Two children soon appeared in Julie's room with some candy and a note that said, "Cheer up!" Julie wrote to us, "You know, that's one of the most supportive things that anyone has done for me at my school."

Late in Julie's first year, she made the decision to look for a job in another school, as did other teachers from her school. By fall of her second year, she had settled into a new school where things were remarkably different. Warm relationships initiated by her principal and regular gestures of genuine appreciation changed Julie's outlook almost immediately. She described Jane Wyatt as a principal who took the time to talk and to listen. She wrote, "I wish you all could see the relationship I have with my new administrator. I'm rediscovering the true joy that comes from teaching!" Julie wrote excitedly about the welcome she experienced:

My first day was *great*! Our principal had breakfast for us and we all sat around and chatted. She had a little ice-breaker with prizes. We went through the normal stuff about textbooks, schedules, etc. She gave us bags with school T-shirts, a pencil, a stress squeeze ball and a 100 Grand chocolate bar. She said we were all worth 100 grand.

We knew that "pats on the back" didn't have to take the form of breakfasts, door prizes, and candy bars, but the point was clear. Administrators who let us know that we were welcome and appreciated made a big difference as we worked to become the best teachers we could be. Administrators who communicated that they were happy we were around and proud of our work profoundly affected our attitude, confidence, energy, and drive to continue.

While he did ask what we were doing, it was out of simple curiosity and real interest.

It meant a lot to us when administrators came into our classrooms to join our learning communities in joyous ways. These visits were tremendous boosts for us and for our students, particularly when administrators took time to chat with students, accepted invitations to participate in authors' celebrations, and showed interest rather than concern when they saw something that might seem out of the ordinary. A grand example comes from an incident that occurred during April's first year. Her administrator entered the classroom at a moment when children were up to their elbows in tubs of water doing science investigations. They were happily engaged, but they definitely required April's full attention. The principal smiled at the activity going on, left April to continue the lesson, and later told her, "I saw that you had things to deal with, but you dealt with them well, so I didn't want to interrupt the flow of things." Rather than comment on the water and the noise, April's principal assumed the best and later complimented April on her ability to handle such an active engagement. April said, "It was really good to hear those things."

Carly tells a similar story about an afternoon when her assistant principal, Mr. Hightower, dropped by her classroom to find paper, art supplies, and books strewn all over the desks, tables, and floor. The room was filled with children's loud voices and laughter. No one sat at a desk; some were sitting on tables or on the floor rifling through books to get ideas for their mural. Others stood on tables to reach the top of their mural. It took a while for Mr. Hightower to find Carly among all the busy fourth graders. When she noticed him standing there, she realized how chaotic the room looked and sounded:

> My first reaction was a combination of surprise and embarrassment. But I quickly realized that there was not one student off task. It was loud, but no one was shouting. Knowing that my children were involved in off-the-chart learning, I approached him with a big grin on my face. I *almost* apologized for the appearance of the room, but caught myself just in time and just welcomed him. While he did ask what on earth we were doing, it wasn't an accusation, it was out of simple curiosity and real interest. I loved that about him.

In the same spirit, Carmen described a morning when Mr. Ruthsatz walked into her room to observe during testing: "I found myself explaining why one child was sprawled out on the floor taking a test. The child spent so much time out of his seat, it seemed best to allow him to be comfortable instead of both of us becoming frustrated with him up and down. Mr. Ruthsatz waved at me to continue, assuring me that he would have done the same thing. I appreciated this reassurance."

Contrasts include Erin's first-year experiences with administrative visits and the requirement to teach the same thing at the same time as the other second-grade teachers. Julie also wrote about a contrasting incident that occurred in February of her first year. Her principal looked in the classroom toward the end of the day, just after the children had come in from recess:

> It was close to the end of the day and I usually have the students pack up so that we get the commotion over with and then we can focus on something else until it's time to go home. My principal watched for a minute or two while the children were packing their things. The next morning, he called me to the side and said something like, "Why were your students packing up so early?" I tried to explain that I like for the children to get ready to go home a few minutes early so we can have time to read aloud or focus in some other way before they leave. He said that he felt that, with the MAT-7 [a standardized test] coming up, I could find a better use for my time. I understand that he's feeling testing pressures, but he made a quick judgment without really listening to my explanation.

They listened, really *listened.*

Listening to us with genuine interest and the belief that we had something of value to say was a characteristic we valued highly in our administrators. In some cases, attempts to solicit our views seemed only rhetorical. In other situations, it was easy to tell that requests for our perspectives were genuine. April wrote that when her views were solicited, her principal "really listens to us; it shows in the actions taken."

In her second year, April was asked for input on hiring new faculty and felt that her views were used in the decision-making process. In contrast, Carmen wrote:

> Did I mention that I sat on the interview committee for our new principal? Well, I was knocked down by my own naiveté. We were asked for our views. I fought really hard for this guy who had worked with our type of population and who seemed to have a real compassion for what he was doing. Everyone else was on my bandwagon and I felt really proud of myself. Then someone else was hired. I was floored. The new principal actually turned out to be a great person, but the frustrating part was that we had been led to believe that our choice was important. Did we ever really have a voice?

Most of our principals listened with an openness and respect that allowed us to make suggestions and introduce changes. In Julie's sixth year, for example, the latest buzz phrase had become *differentiated instruction*. When Julie explained that she was already meeting the differentiated needs of her students through flexible grouping and one-to-one conferencing, her principal was supportive and ordered the books Julie needed to work effectively. In another example, when Julie realized that the reading program adopted for kindergarten did not include an assessment that gave her enough information to help children as strategic readers, she explained what she needed to her assistant principal and further materials were ordered.

In Carly's third year, she decided to try to change the school's implementation of a program that focused on extrinsic rewards for tests taken about books. Finding a contradiction between this model and her theoretical understandings about literacy learning, Carly formulated an alternative plan. When she shared the plan with her principal and assistant principal, "they listened, *really* listened." They gave credence to Carly's point of view, demonstrated that they respected her knowledge, and encouraged her to put the new plan into practice. Carly did not come to this conversation unprepared. As explained in detail in Chapter 7, she brought research articles that described the fallacies of extrinsic rewards and she provided alternatives. It was a bold move for a brand new teacher that could easily have been squelched, but she felt comfortable because of the caring atmosphere her administrator had created and the sense of trust and respect that had been established. Because her administrators listened respectfully, Carly's professional growth was encouraged, her leadership abilities were nurtured, and she was able to move the school in a new direction.

Learners Together

We read about new ideas together and she says, "Do it! Go ahead and give it a try."

Working with administrators who engaged in professional study with us took our teaching to a whole new level. When principals joined us as co-learners, the sky was the limit in terms of how much we could grow as teachers and, certainly, in terms of our staying power as new teachers. Ami wrote, "My principal has been so supportive. Ms. Bodie studies professional literature right along with us. As a result, she gave us the go ahead to ditch our basal readers and to focus instead on literacy groups using real books. I think having supportive and knowledgeable administrators who want to continue to learn is central to our success as new teachers and to improving education in public schools." The power of collaborative professional study with administrators was most visible in schools that were involved in long-term, intentional explorations of theory and practice. In our experiences, this came in the form of the South Carolina Reading Initiative (SCRI). Through this three-year professional development experience, literacy coaches facilitated study groups and spent time with principals and teachers in classrooms every day (Morgan et al., 2003). Although none of our schools was involved in SCRI during our first year, several of us were eventually able to participate. We could see that principals' whole-hearted commitment was key to the success of these experiences. We grew more when administrators read professional literature, tried new ideas with children, engaged in pedagogical reflection, provided release time to visit other schools, and found funding for professional books and travel to professional conferences.

Ami and April, whose principals were actively involved in SCRI with them from their second year, told stories of teaching frustrations, but in their frustration they had support to figure things out. April wrote, "I know that both the school and the district support what I am doing. I can see it. For one thing, all the principals are involved in the Reading Initiative. It really shows that they are trying to do something." Studying with our principals, we grew together in our excitement for new ideas. In the process, we got to know each other in new and wonderful ways. Ami wrote, "I've really gotten to know my principal as a person this year through the Reading Initiative class. She's a dynamite person. She's really in tune with everything that goes on in the school personally and professionally. She makes me comfortable trying anything that I want to try." In Julie's new school, she also had the opportunity to participate in SCRI, which she said was one of the most supportive aspects of her situation: "I love having the extra support of a literacy coach and learning with my principal, who is a wholehearted participant. We read about ideas together and my principal always says, 'Do it, go ahead, give it a try.'"

The Characteristic That Stood Out

As with children leaving home for the first time, freedom to learn through our new experiences was important. We appreciated administrators who gave us room to try, reflect, and make mistakes while staying close enough to provide support when day-to-day demands took their toll or we lost confidence. We felt tremendous respect for administrators who were able to support top-notch teaching in their schools without making us feel like we were under a microscope.

The characteristic that stood out as the most overwhelmingly supportive of us as new teachers, however, was administrators' commitment to learning and growing *with* us. When relationships with administrators were built on the foundation of learning partnerships with the support of organized opportunities for ongoing professional study and reflection, our confidence and potential for further growth were at their highest.

Colleagues: Mentors and the Teachers Next Door

> The biggest challenge I've faced in my first year of teaching is being alone in the struggle.

Many of us began our first year of teaching with expectations that our colleagues and mentors would be supportive both emotionally and professionally. We were accustomed to receiving such support from one another in graduate school having picked up each other's slack during hard times, sent encouraging notes to one another, worked through complex ideas together, and helped each other plan for teaching. We assumed we would have similar relationships in our schools. Once we started teaching, we found that most of our colleagues and mentors were extremely helpful in acquainting us with school routines and procedures. Some of them visited our classrooms to share words of encouragement. Most were friendly and kind. But it did not take long for a dichotomy to emerge between the level of pedagogical support we found in our schools and the support we enjoyed within our research group. Finding learning partners on the job was more difficult than we anticipated.

This section explores these issues as we describe experiences with colleagues, mentors, and in induction programs. Contrasts in the kinds of support we found were surprising. We believe now that an important reason for these differences has much to do with the school's professional climate. Even though most of our experiences were not as restrictive as Erin's, few of us found school environments that truly embraced and provided support for a teacher-as-learner mentality. The habit of examining day-to-day practice and sharing ideas was, during our first years, not a part of the culture in most of our schools. Those who did land in such settings found that many colleagues engaged readily in the easy exchange of ideas which pushed everyone forward. In the following pages, we share the highs and lows of our relationships with colleagues and mentors and the impact of those relationships in our lives as new teachers.

Mentors: Our First Colleagues

We gravitated toward mentors with whom we felt personal and philosophical connections.

Often the first colleagues with whom we had contact were the mentors assigned to us. We expected that they would play a very important role in our professional lives. Over the years, however, we have watched mentors paired with new teachers and see that the protocol for choosing them varies widely. Sometimes it's even as arbitrary as "it's your turn," "she needs the monetary supplement," or "he volunteered and no one else did." Rarely do we see consideration given to theoretical orientation or intellectual curiosity as mentors are selected. Ultimately, many of us found mentors with whom we were philosophically aligned and who shared our excitement for professional learning, but they were never our assigned mentors and sometimes they were not even colleagues in our schools.

For example, when Robbie realized that she and her assigned mentor had few educational beliefs in common, she went to another teacher for advice. She wrote: "I think I've finally found an ally in fifth grade who I can talk to while I am trying to figure things out." Julie also wrote about a teacher who, although not assigned as her official mentor, became the colleague who helped her the most: "Emily is a teacher who is always doing some small thing to help me out. She's been wonderful in that respect. She does more for me than anyone else in terms of sitting down and telling me stuff about how she organizes her teaching, but she is not my assigned mentor." One of Ami's greatest mentors continued to be her mom, who visited occasionally from New York and was always only a phone call away. Susi wrote about similar experiences as a beginning university faculty member. Characteristics of mentors to whom she gravitated help us explain reasons why "found" mentors were so supportive: "The best mentorships in my experience evolved through interactions with more experienced colleagues who held similar theoretical orientations or who genuinely honored diverse perspectives. They were always people with whom I felt comfortable exposing vulnerabilities and who knew just the right balance between validating despair when I felt defeated and working to turn difficult experiences into learning moments."

Because we found the greatest support when we gravitated toward mentors with whom we felt personal and philosophical connections, we wondered if systems might be put in place in which mentors could be found rather than assigned (see related ideas in Chapter 8). As Erin said, "How cool it would have been if we could have found mentors because of common backgrounds and interests in working together."

I think a mentor should be your learning partner.

Many of us had mentors who kindly helped us learn about procedures within our schools. Some of them dropped by regularly with notes to let us know they were thinking about us. But, while friendly gestures and organizational support were certainly helpful, we also longed for mentors who would engage with us in professional study. As one group member wrote:

> I think a mentor should be your learning partner, should work with you to improve your teaching and theirs. Mine just tells me to put down a grade I think students deserve and don't worry about it. She leaves every day by 3:15 and thinks I'm crazy for staying until 5:00. I'd go as far as to say that your mentor should suggest professional books and read them with you. I think your mentor should meet with you weekly to talk about what works, what doesn't, and new things you can try in the classroom.

We envisioned being paired with mentors whose philosophies and priorities were similar to our own. We expected that mentors would help us move our teaching forward through thoughtful conversation as we reflected together. Most of us did not find such pedagogical allies. Carmen wrote, "While it appeared to the district that each new teacher was paired with someone to guide them, in actuality, new teachers were often all alone." In one situation, the mentor was all but invisible:

My mentor was not involved in helping me find my way. It was sad. To this day, I can't believe that she still brags on being my mentor though she never stepped foot in my classroom, never helped me get organized, and never saw me teach. Now she will tell you that I'm an absolutely wonderful teacher, but she doesn't really know.

For another group member, her mentor's philosophical orientation was so different from her own that the mentor voiced opposition to almost everything she tried to do: "She kept telling me everything I was doing wrong, including wasting time on reading aloud." This relationship was a clear mismatch of teaching philosophies and styles. The mentor believed in children sitting quietly at their desks completing worksheets, while the new teacher believed in collaborative grouping and open discussion. Yet another member of our group wrote, "You are given a mentor, but often that mentor's practices are completely different from what you have just been studying, and she could care less what you learned."

Even when we were not completely theoretically aligned with our mentors, good relationships could grow when there was respect for and interest in each other's ideas. But when mentors showed little interest in questioning practice together through mutually respectful professional conversation, there was little chance for such relationships to grow. In those cases, it was easy to feel alone: "I don't have a mentor who I can talk with about ideas, so I really do feel isolated."

It is often difficult for mentors to find the time necessary to provide nurturing support.

Another obstacle to building good mentoring relationships was time. Susi found that this also paralleled her university experience. Mentoring new faculty members, she struggled to find time to establish relationships through which they could learn and grow together. She scheduled weekly breakfast meetings, but as regularly as they attempted to meet, it was often difficult to find real time to talk. This meant that some of the most important conversations were short-changed and occurred much like they do in many schools—on the run, in phone conversations, and in brief meetings when both Susi and her colleague were racing to other obligations.

As we gained teaching experience, the rest of us saw this side of the fence. When we had opportunities to mentor, we also found ourselves hurrying through the week, appearing impatient with new questions, and forgetting to offer help to new teachers. We learned that it is often difficult for mentors to find the time necessary to provide nurturing support and wondered how schools might be organized differently to make that time a priority.

Many concerns we had about mentoring programs we also had about induction classes.

In addition to mentors, our school districts typically provided some kind of induction program for us as new teachers. Many of the concerns we had about mentoring programs we also had about the required induction classes. Often the educators running the courses were not pedagogically up-to-date themselves. The classes rarely involved us in talking about issues that we felt were important to us as new teachers. We viewed the meetings as a waste of time and expressed as much in our emails to one another: "The worst are induction meetings where all we do is sit and watch those videotapes for an hour and a half as if we didn't have anything more important to do or more important issues to discuss," "Nobody asks us what we want to talk about," and "The only things I *really* dread are the dumb meetings I have to go to because I'm a first-year teacher. I get irritated because they are so pointless and boring."

Since our first year of teaching, some of our districts have moved forward in developing better induction programs. Some of them engage Teachers of the Year as leaders in mentoring programs. Some are beginning to focus on thoughtful conversation, professional reading, and pedagogical sharing. Because our experiences were very different, we are encouraged by recognition of the need to overhaul the system in ways that stand a better chance of sustaining and building from the energy of new teachers (see examples of other programs in Chapter 8).

The Teacher Next Door: What Makes a Good Colleague?

Our colleagues beyond assigned mentors—teachers next door and down the hall—had a tremendous impact on our early teaching experiences, both positively and negatively. Robbie said, "They can lend assistance and support or they can antagonize you to tears." As new teachers, we desperately needed others with whom we could share experiences, discuss professional readings, visit other schools, explore new ideas, and talk about issues basic to daily classroom life. Described in the following pages, we appreciated colleagues who dropped in to check on us, boosted us when we were down, and introduced us to the logistics of the school, but we also hoped for colleagues who would share their knowledge and who would be interested in the ideas we shared.

Simple tasks are mundane to experienced teachers, but they are daunting to someone who has never been responsible for his or her own classroom.

It was extremely helpful when colleagues took time to show us how to accomplish simple tasks such as how to take the children to the cafeteria; how to use the copy machine; where to find tables, chairs, and bookcases; how to follow field trip procedures; and how to fill out the millions of forms that appeared in our boxes. Julie explained, "Such tasks may seem mundane to experienced teachers, but they are daunting to someone who has never been responsible for his or her own classroom." We greatly appreciated colleagues' patience with our questions about those tasks and others, but surprisingly, some of us encountered impatience with our need to know. Every now and then, a message appeared on our listserv about an encounter with someone who was less than tolerant and even rude when confronted with a new teacher's questions. After a grade-level meeting, for example, Robbie wrote:

> I didn't understand about testing procedures so I was asking a lot of questions. One of the other teachers really had no tolerance for my first-year-teacher questions. She told me to quit asking them so we could "get out of there." That's something I'm going to try hard to remember—that as a first-year teacher there is so much you don't know and it is hard to ask, so I hope I take the time to lend a helping hand and answer them even when I might be really busy myself.

My colleagues always made me feel like a valued member of the team.

Ami's first-year experiences demonstrate how colleagues can play an important role in helping you feel that you belong. She wrote, "My first-grade colleagues always made me feel like a valued member of the team. Even when I moved to piloting a multiage program, they included me in the first-grade team planning meetings, field studies, and special events." Ami and her colleagues met each week to share ideas, discuss upcoming events, and plan field studies. They planned within broad themes that allowed them autonomy and creativity in supporting inquiry-based experiences, but also provided a common framework for sharing ideas and working collectively to plan special events, expert visitors, and field studies. Together, they developed a tradition called Teacher Rotation Days through which every first grader experienced some aspect of each teacher's expertise. One year, for example, a Teacher Rotation Day was centered on winter celebrations across cultural settings. There were also math rotation days, arts and crafts rotations, and storytelling days. This inclusive, generative relationship made a big difference in Ami's early teaching experiences because she felt a part of a warm and welcoming group of colleagues.

In contrast, there were times when some of us felt alienated by colleagues. It was hard to believe, for instance, when Robbie wrote to us that all of the other teachers at her grade level had planned a field trip and hadn't included her. She felt alone and hurt when she heard that her class had been left out of the experience:

> I just found out last week that seven of the nine fifth-grade classes are going on a field trip together. A colleague, one of my only allies in fifth grade, was chatting with me in the hallway and asked if I was getting excited about my first field trip. I said, "What field trip?" He explained that the fifth-grade classes were going to the Fox Theatre in Atlanta to see *Freedom Train*. He had no idea that my class wasn't included in the trip. I was so hurt that I hadn't even been invited and that my class would miss a trip that would have been amazing for them. It was my students who lost out that day. That's what hurt so much.

I really needed someone to let me know that I wasn't a horrible teacher.

One of the most supportive gestures we received from colleagues was recognition of what we were doing well. Our confidence was fragile. We were often convinced that we weren't good enough or had failed at some aspect of teaching. This was compounded when the culture of our school was not geared toward noticing what went well. One group member said, "Sharing classroom successes is something I quickly learned that teachers in my school just don't do. We all tell the behavior problem stories, but you don't just sit around and say, 'So, what happened that made you feel successful today in your classroom?'" Colleagues who made a point of recognizing the successes in their own days and helping us find the bits of wonderful in our teaching were greatly appreciated. When Carly described a teacher who did just that, she added, "I really needed someone to let me know that I wasn't a horrible teacher." Similarly, on a day when Robbie was feeling particularly frantic in her attempts to be successful at everything at once, a colleague helped by simply telling her to relax, that she would figure things out as she went along. Carly's mother-in-law, also a teacher, helped by encouraging her to celebrate even the tiniest joyful moments. She suggested that Carly "write down at least one thing every day that brought her the slightest smile."

Support like this from colleagues helped us look on the bright side even when things didn't go as smoothly as we had hoped. It helped us notice and build from our successes. By the end of her first year, Carly was able to write, "I don't fret over failures so much anymore and a big part of it is because of my administrators and colleagues. This is absolutely the best place to teach! We get support across the board. It makes mistakes much less worrisome."

Being around other positive teachers inspires me.

Colleagues who greeted us each day with a positive outlook and let us know they were glad we were in their school meant a lot to us as new teachers. In her first year, Julie wrote, "All of the teachers here are so helpful. I feel very fortunate. Several, not even on my grade level, came by to check on my day. One of them put a sweet note and a bookmark in my box." April remarked, "I am really enjoying my class, colleagues, administration, and school. Everyone around the school has really welcomed me here." Colleagues' positive spirit had a dramatic effect on our own attitudes as we negotiated our way through the maze of those first weeks. Susi remembered finding just such a person from her own first days as a teacher:

> During the planning weeks, I met a colleague who would become a best friend and mentor. Phyllis Foley had already been teaching for five years. She was, and still is, the wisest, most joyful teacher I know. There is something special about Phyllis that always draws kids to her. I'll never forget the first grader who said he liked Mrs. Foley better than me "because she wears purple tights." That was 30 years ago and it sticks with me as reflective of the positive spirit she engendered in a child. She still teaches first grade. She is vibrant and dynamic and gets such a kick out of her kids. She taught me to put things in perspective with a sense of humor and a life outside of school (although those who know me now would say that I need to relearn that lesson). From Phyllis, I learned that a good friend, a smart teacher, lots of laughter, and a great glass of wine make a very supportive combination.

Colleagues who could take a negative situation and turn it into a positive one, who laughed easily and saw the bright side of situations, and who focused on their good fortune in teaching the children who struggled the most brightened our days and led us to be more positive too. In August of her first year, Ami wrote, "I am in a state of bliss and joy! Being around other positive teachers inspires me."

We never realized how integral collaboration was to successful teaching until we no longer had those opportunities.

We appreciated colleagues who energized and encouraged us, who helped us see our own successes, and who let us know that we weren't alone. But many of us longed for someone with whom we could work through understandings of specific ideas and practices—folks who could help us figure things out. We wanted to be a part of professional communities where it was standard practice for teachers to "challenge themselves and reflect on their teaching." Erin explained, "Today, for example, we were all talking about behavior problems. I wanted to say so badly, 'Well, maybe we should look at what we are asking the children to do.' People are nice here on a personal level, but it's just that we don't share our thinking about teaching." Carly had similar experiences: "I had great friendship support, but not professional support. That's what I struggled with, trying to pin down my own ideas without having anyone to bounce ideas off of except Robbie, who was having struggles of her own."

Finding so few opportunities to collaborate with colleagues, we realized how necessary such collaboration was for us to thrive as professionals. Our listserv was filled with messages such as "I wish we could have met today and talked about frustrations and how we could make things better," "I wish I could collaborate with other teachers on ways to enhance our curriculum," "I wish I could read books and educational journals and share relevant articles with my teammates," "I know that it would be so much easier if I could talk to someone about how they approach things and so I could bounce ideas off of them too." In graduate school, there was much talk about the importance of collaboration, but we never realized how integral it was to successful teaching until we no longer had those opportunities. Erin wrote:

> It's lonely doing all this on your own. I know last year the work in the MAT program was really hard for all of us, but I do miss talking about the literature and the ways our ideas fed off of each other. I would really love to be in a school where my team read professionally on a regular basis and met often to talk about their readings. I feel like I could do anything with support and guidance from colleagues.

I'm ready to be in a place where people are eager and willing to learn and try new things.

A surprising realization during our first year was the extent of resistance to new ideas we found in our schools. One group member said, "Some teachers in my school are so resistant to change that it is scary just sitting in a faculty meeting with them." We had not anticipated the lack of innovative practices we saw in some classrooms. More than one of us made comments like: "I am both amazed and depressed by the reality of many teachers in our schools. So many people are so traditional and dry. You need to have an internal drive to inspire, teach, and spark children's lust for knowledge." Another group member wrote, "We take professional growth seriously in our research group, but we also take it for granted. Not every teacher wants to, or has the resources to take on that responsibility. In fact, *many* do not."

Colleagues' negativity toward change made it easier for us to slip toward a status quo that was nothing like our teaching visions. Another group member explained: "I have to be more independent in my thinking because a lot of people here seem to be negative or against change. I realize that I have to speak up more for what I believe because sometimes I find myself going with the majority against what I truly feel." Another said, "There are tons of people who will listen to the horror stories and gripe with you, but there really isn't anyone to pull you along the road of professional development. That is where new teachers fall into the static trap. Susi, you told us that all along. I just never knew how hard it would really be."

During job searches, we envisioned joining communities of professionals who worked together to learn and grow as they created dynamic learning contexts for children. Instead, as friendly and kind as our colleagues were, during our first year we rarely witnessed expressions of interest in such growth. We wrote: "I'm ready to be in a place where people are eager and willing to learn and try new things. That way, I will also be inspired. Here no one tries new ideas. They teach the same way they taught twenty or thirty years ago" and "I feel disheartened at the reality of some teachers today. I want to be a part of a profession of educators who are dedicated and committed to moving forward with their knowledge all the time."

If you can find even one person at your school with a similar teaching philosophy, it's better.

During our first years, we frequently made comments like "I wish there were other teachers at my school trying the same things I've learned" and "It would be nice if I had someone else to talk with among my team members about inquiry and more effective approaches to literacy." The desire to interact with like-minded colleagues was strong. Robbie explained:

> That's what I miss the most. Like the first day of trying writing workshop. It was a flop and it would have been nice to have someone to talk to, to say, "Okay, I tried something. I went out on a limb and totally screwed up and it did not work out." If I could

have at least had someone in my school to say, "Oh my gosh, let me tell you about when I tried writing workshop."

Often the teachers with whom we had the greatest philosophical congruence were fellow first-year teachers. Carmen relied on another new teacher "to wade through the waters with me." With similar belief systems, they helped each other maintain perspective: "We kept it light in spite of the treacherous tide of not knowing what to do and how to do it." When we didn't have the support of colleagues with similar backgrounds, however, it was difficult to sustain and build on our visions of great teaching. Robbie wrote:

> There are a lot of MAT graduates who have lost their dreams. They're not doing things they truly believe in. I think it's because they don't have the support from people with the same background, and it's easier to fall into a trap of doing things the easy way if you don't have people saying, "It's okay if you stumble along the way, but hold onto that dream because eventually you can make it happen."

Ami also pointed out how hard it is to "hold onto cutting-edge practice when there are not enough teachers out there doing these same things." She continued, "It's hard to keep trying new things when you don't have a kindred spirit to bounce ideas off of. Usually, if you can find even one more person at your school with a similar teaching philosophy, it's better."

It was scary to initiate professional conversations.

As much as we wanted to interact with others professionally, as beginning teachers, it was scary to initiate professional conversations with experienced colleagues. We wanted to suggest new ideas, but we also wanted to be accepted in our school settings. We wanted to get along, make friends, feel a part of a community. Erin explained, "I've always done better in a group with other ideas helping to form my own. Isn't that the whole idea behind Vygotsky? However, I don't like to be different. I don't want people not to like me. In this situation, I haven't really shared, I'm afraid of losing their approval. If I were to say something about change, I don't think I'd be liked at all."

Negativity in our schools was another reason why some of us shied away from making our views known. One group member wrote, "They complain so much that I am intimidated to voice my opinion." Hearing negative reactions about so many other things, we worried that any suggestions we might make would also be negatively received: "Do you know how sometimes you just *know* your suggestion would be seen as ridiculous? That's how I feel."

In some schools, the fear of initiating talk came from listening to colleagues who told us "We aren't allowed to" or "That won't work." It took us a long time to understand that sometimes those responses simply meant that experienced teachers had become discouraged themselves. Robbie said, "The people who spend all their time telling you, 'You can't do that here,' are not necessarily saying that you aren't allowed. Sometimes they are just tired and beaten down themselves. More often than not, their plates are too full and they don't have time for one more thing."

Sometimes we were reluctant to share ideas because we worried that we would come on too strong. Ami wrote, "Sometimes my opinions come out without my thinking about my audience, but I am so excited about doing things and making them happen that I can hardly sit still." We struggled to find a balance between expressing our excitement—we had learned so much that we couldn't wait to put into practice—and curbing our enthusiasm to the extent that we would lose our energy and drive. Julie said, "You can't come on like a bolt of lightning. This first year, I think it's a good idea to back down a little." We could see that it was far better to ease into the new worlds around us and then begin to talk about our ideas as we developed trusting relationships with colleagues.

The fear that other teachers might resent new ideas for whatever reason was disappointing, to say the least: "When you're working with other teachers who resent what you are doing and you don't have reinforcement from anyone else, it's really hard because there are all of these great things you want to do and then when you try to bring it up, you get a negative reaction." Soon many of us stopped sharing and kept our ideas behind the closed doors of our classrooms or abandoned them altogether.

We can learn by collaborating with colleagues even when we have very different views.

An important realization during our early years of teaching was that it was possible to have rich and rewarding collaborative relationships even when we had very different views. If our school cultures supported the give-and-take of respectful collegial conversation, we could share and create new ideas, knowing we didn't have to think like everyone else to do so. April explained:

> Among my grade-level colleagues, we don't all think the same way, we don't do the same things, but we all support each other and are not critical of each other, of what other people are doing.

On Tuesdays, we come together, share ideas, and plan what activities we want to do. Everyone's plans are different but may
include some of the same ideas. We are able to share ideas, risk-
free, among the whole team.

Carmen wrote about how she and her grade-level colleagues would
"plan together, but any one of us could decide that we want to do something else at any time." Similarly, Ami described working with her first-
grade colleagues:

I love teaching here because we all have different styles and different philosophies yet we are all friends and we share everything. We bounce ideas around, and each teacher is free to do
things her own way while having the same springboard as we
plan together. As a first-year teacher, this has kept me from feeling overwhelmed, and I have eight other teachers to help me generate ideas and work through problems. They allow me to be
myself and to bring my fresh ideas to the table. We don't choose
to do all the same practices, but we support each other's decisions and instructional choices as educators. They supported me
when I chose not to use basals and workbooks. Several members
of my team asked me to help them start up guided reading groups.
They know that I am passionate about children's books so they
ask me for book suggestions and recommendations. They always
make me feel important and valued. This helps nurture my spirit
for taking risks and helps me stay energized as a new teacher.

*Alone, it became too easy to abandon our beliefs and halt the momentum of
professional growth.*

Our sense of isolation was voiced probably more than any other sentiment in our data: "It's really hard being alone; I think that is my greatest challenge." We had so many questions but few partners with whom
we could explore practices, and talk thoughtfully about children. As a
consequence, it became too easy to abandon our beliefs and halt the
momentum of professional growth. As one group member wrote: "I felt
that I was basically alone, except for my one friend who was also a first-
year teacher, so I felt I had to roll with whatever they gave me with no
questions asked."

The bottom line was that to be able to bring our teaching dreams
to life and continue to grow, it was essential to find a place where we
could collaborate, reflect, and readjust our teaching in the company of
colleagues who also wanted to learn and grow. Erin said, "I've realized
that I've got to be in a place that pushes me to move further in my professional development and, basically, that will depend on the people I'm
around." We wondered what we might accomplish if we worked to-

gether not to decide who would copy the worksheets for that week or to plan generic units but to share children's work, read and talk through new ideas, and rethink practice on a regular basis.

We turned to each other.

Carmen joined our research group several months after it was initiated. To familiarize herself with our conversations, she reviewed our archived emails. Then she wrote, "After reading your emails, I felt cheated, to be honest. It was tough not having people to lean on. I need to be in touch with people that I can relate to and be inspired by. I am one of those people who need to be inspired."

When we didn't have a place for safe, collegial conversations in our schools, we turned to our research group. In our meetings, we could share in ways that we couldn't always share with other colleagues. We leaned on one another when there seemed nowhere else to go. Erin wrote:

> Sometimes I get really depressed. The thing that makes it worse is that no one really understands. People just think I'm complaining and being hard to get along with. I've decided not to discuss these issues with anyone but this research group. I really need all of you, and I think I'm going to continue to need you for a long time.

As the months went by and relationships deepened, Susi also shared that she revealed vulnerabilities to the group in ways she did with few other people. April responded, "I know what you mean; I have friends at school, but sometimes it's hard to talk to them about everything I'm feeling. With you guys I can spill everything and know I will be supported." Even family couldn't provide the same support as we talked about teaching. Julie wrote, "Thanks for letting me have someone I can say all of this to because, as loving as he is, my husband doesn't have a real understanding of what teachers go through and it's hard for him to help or give advice."

The support of like-minded professionals who met regularly not only sustained us but also provided impetus for further growth. Together, we could not possibly remain stagnant. Our comments across the years reflect the supportive nature of the group, support that was defined not merely by mutual commiseration but by conversations that challenged our thinking:

> In this group, I'm surrounded by people who push my thinking. (Julie)

This group gives me energy to think in new ways. I question so much about myself as a teacher because of the time I spend with you. (Susi)

I am always encouraged to be a better educator because of our group. (Carly)

I have learned so much about myself as a teacher. I don't think I would have evaluated myself so carefully without this experience. (April)

I have become so much more reflective through this group. I feel like I'm constantly growing and changing professionally because of our interactions. (Ami)

For some of us, the group was a lifeline that kept us going. Erin wrote, "Without all of you, I could have easily become a drained, lifeless teacher," and Julie added:

I would never have gotten through the first year if I couldn't have gone to the computer to write to all of you or to our meetings to just talk. You were the ones who helped me stay positive when I couldn't see the light at the end of the tunnel. We need each other to give a different perspective when all we see is the negative.

We kept one another from losing our visions entirely. Carmen explained, "You all were my reality check when I needed to think about ideas I might have let go of for the sake of making things easier and smoother. I feel like I'm a good teacher, but my confidence isn't always there. I need an open relationship with someone who isn't going to be critical, but who will also help me." We learned that holding on to our beliefs and growing beyond them, as Carly said, "takes people who know and care about you to not let you lose sight of who you are. It takes someone to say they believe in who you are."

Our personal support of one another's lives beyond school had a direct bearing on the level of comfort we felt when sharing professionally. We could count on one another when personal as well as professional chips where down. Support came in many forms over the years: gift certificates for massages; wedding showers; baby showers; special touches like Julie's red tablecloth at a Valentine's Day meeting; Robbie's "anonymous" gifts of printer toner (and even muffins one time!) that appeared regularly on Susi's front porch; Carly, Robbie, and Carmen literally going the extra mile as they traveled across state lines to our meetings; offers to take on extra work when someone was overwhelmed or in the middle of a family crisis; everyone taking turns helping out when Julie's twins were born; and on and on and on.

Even when we struggled to figure out how to fit *us* into our lives, our collegial and personal relationships were priorities. April wrote, "I am involved in so much with my school and my church that my days are very full, but I feel so connected with this group that I don't know what I'd do if it ended." As Julie said, "Something good always comes from us working together."

Beyond Survival

Donald Graves (2001) writes that "teachers and principals create energy for each other when they are in the process of shaping a vision together" (p. 154). This was our expectation when we headed into our first jobs. New teachers may survive without nurturing colleagues and supportive administrators, but they will certainly not be able to shape the visions that push the profession forward. Our data demonstrate that the lack of opportunities to collaborate with caring, interested, positive administrators and colleagues can make challenges faced by new teachers even more difficult. Other issues were more easily resolved when we had administrators and colleagues with whom we could take risks to talk, question, try, fail, celebrate, and grow. Leaving graduate school, we saw schools as "labs for learning about learning" (Meier, 1995, p. 140). It wasn't until we were without such contexts that we fully understood the importance of schools as "places of reflective experimentation" (p. 140) where children, teachers, and administrators are learners together.

Critical Insights from Chapter 6

About Administrators

- Kind, nurturing administrators who shared our passion for continuing to learn and grow were particularly important during our early years of teaching.
- Rigidly mandated programs took away autonomy and with it, trust in ourselves as knowledgeable professionals.
- Good work could be done in addressing mandates by using our knowledge rather than simply following the teacher's guide.
- Given autonomy, so much was possible. When we felt trusted, we found new energy for professional reading and trying new ideas, as well as a greater sense of calm and confidence. It was

important for us to know that we could try and fail and try again and be valued for engaging in the process.

- Caring communities supported us as new teachers. Such communities grew when principals got to know us, helped us discover ourselves as teachers, made time for talk, let us know they were happy we were in their schools, and listened.

- We felt supported when administrators came into our classrooms to join our learning communities in joyous ways.

- Working with administrators who engaged in professional study *with* us took our teaching to a whole new level.

About Colleagues

- Real mentoring relationships evolved as we got to know and connect with colleagues rather than through the assignment of mentors.

- Even when we were not completely theoretically aligned with our mentors, good relationships could grow when there was respect for and interest in each other's ideas.

- Colleagues' negativity toward change made it easier for us to slip toward a status quo very different from our visions of great teaching.

- Colleagues who laughed easily and saw the bright side of situations and who focused on their good fortune in teaching the children who struggled the most brightened our days and led us to be more positive too.

- Without colleagues with whom we could work through understandings of specific ideas and practices, it became too easy to abandon our beliefs and halt the momentum of professional growth. Finding few opportunities to collaborate, we realized how necessary such collaboration was for us to thrive as professionals.

7 Being Political: New Teachers, You *Do* Have a Voice

The first couple of years of teaching were so draining. To think about the world outside our classrooms seemed too daunting at the time. We could only comprehend and try to make sense of our immediate worlds, but then our understanding stretched to include the school and then the community and to the political issues that govern it all, and we realized that we had been political all along.

Being political was the furthest thing from our minds when we began our careers as teachers. At that point, most of us thought that politics meant people in suits, running for office, talking to legislators, writing letters to members of Congress, or working for a political party. Our experiences with politics and education were varied. Some of us closely followed the educational views of local and national political candidates. Some questioned the motives of politicians and saw them as overly controlling in educational arenas they knew little about. Others were aware of politics at the national level and its influence on education but didn't see much of a connection to our own classrooms. A couple of us assumed that we could leave political concerns to administrators and legislators because they were "surely getting good advice about how children learn, and we could trust them to make good decisions while we focused on teaching."

We certainly didn't recognize that anything we were doing could possibly be viewed as political activism. Although we left our preservice program ready to change the world, that drive diminished rapidly for many of us during the first months in our own classrooms. As we struggled to manage day-to-day life, our role as change agents became a distant dream. Carly voiced what many of us were feeling: "I can't even help myself, much less those around me." Disappointed when she did not see herself making a difference in ways she had envisioned, Erin wrote, "I'm trying but, in reality, I'm not changing anything at all." It wasn't until well into the process of writing this book that we recognized the political acts and strength of our voices in the big and little things we had been doing all along.

Several realizations led to the recognition of ourselves as having voice. First, looking back at data, we were able to see successes in our teaching that we hadn't recognized before. With the distance of time, we were able to see that, in spite of our struggles, we did many things well, and people around us were paying attention. When we thought we had the least control over our teaching lives, we actually *did* have a voice. We each used it in different but equally powerful ways. Then, through hours of conversation and emails, we broadened our definition of what it means to be political. Rather than seeing it as related only to governments and political parties, we began to think of *being political* as using our voices to take action of any kind to make a difference or, as Julie described it, "engaging in acts, no matter how large or small, that honor one's core beliefs and philosophies." With that definition, we realized that we had been politically active from the minute we first set foot in our classrooms.

In this chapter, we share stories of our political actions over the years. We do so to give new teachers an awareness and confidence that we didn't have. We want you to know that you *do* have a voice and that you are probably using it right now in ways you don't even recognize. We used to think that, as Carly said, "the hands of teachers, administrators, and teacher educators were pretty much bound by the mandates of policymakers." While we still find great frustration with the federal and local politics of education, we know there are many windows of opportunity for new teachers to be heard. We also know that taking such action happens in both gentle and boisterous ways and that no action is more or less courageous than another. Each has the potential to make a difference.

Taking Action by Teaching Differently: Effecting Change by Example

We can effect change without storming the gates.

From the first days of teaching, we engaged in a subtle yet powerful form of activism when we were able to quietly hang on to our beliefs and teach in ways that were supported by our knowledge. Doing this, we could effect change without storming the gates. With our classroom doors wide open, other teachers stopped by to chat. While there, they noticed and began to show interest in our work, just as we did in theirs. When there was a feeling of mutual respect in a school climate that encouraged colleagues to learn from and with one another, change happened by example and through mutually respectful conversations and

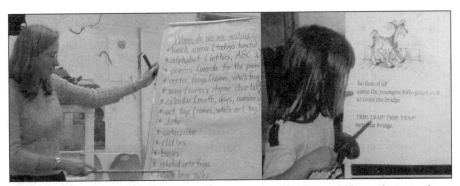

Figure 7.1. April and her kindergartners explore literacy skills and strategies in whole literacy contexts.

casual observations. Even when there were significant differences in our approaches, we could always learn something from one another.

April and Letter-of-the-Week

April has always provided the most powerful examples of gentle action that opens the way for productive collegial conversation. For instance, her decision not to implement a letter-of-the-week approach to teaching letter-sound relationships, combined with an attitude of mutual respect within the school and her nonthreatening demeanor, allowed other teachers to feel comfortable enough to express interest in her practices. Instead of worksheets and other letter-of-the-week activities, April preferred to intentionally and explicitly embed phonics instruction within a wide range of other engagements (Figure 7.1). It wasn't long before other teachers began to take notice:

> In my first year, even though I was a new teacher and wanted to be accepted by my colleagues, I decided not to do letter-of-the-week for my literacy instruction. All of the other kindergarten teachers were practicing letter-of-the-week, but I was very successful using interactive writing, written conversations, shared reading, and opportunities to write independently to support my children in learning letters and sounds. In grade-level meetings, we would share one at a time. When it was my turn, I would share what I was doing, and soon people were coming by my room asking for specifics.

Without realizing it at the time, April took action to effect change from her very first days in the classroom. Her peers noticed the impact she had on children's learning and the practices that led to that learning. It was no surprise to any of us that in her sixth year, April's peers voted her the school's Teacher of the Year.

Robbie's Timeline and Julie's Expert Projects

During the first week of her first year, Robbie introduced a timeline that eventually circled her entire classroom. She and her students began by completing timelines of their own lives and then added them to a much longer timeline that grew from wall to wall with each unit of study. Similar timelines began appearing in other classrooms around the building as colleagues noticed Robbie's idea and decided to incorporate it into their own teaching. At the time, Robbie didn't realize that her work might possibly influence the teaching of those around her. When she left the school two years later, she realized that "other teachers must have been paying attention to me because, as I was leaving, some asked me to explain practices so they could use them the next year."

In Julie's second year, her colleagues became interested in her implementation of expert projects when they saw what was going on in her first-grade classroom. Stopping by her room to chat, they noticed evidence of children engaged in inquiries as they studied plants (Figure 7.2). Soon teachers expressed curiosity and began to ask about how she structured opportunities for children to investigate answers to their own questions within mandated curricular topics.

Taking Action to Alter Mandated Programs or to Develop New Ideas

> We want a classroom where the curriculum is guided not by what everyone else is doing but by the students' needs and interests.

Sometimes, taking action to teach differently meant making alterations to or opting out of widely used programs in our schools. In most situations, we were able to use our knowledge to justify alternatives and work within and beyond existing programs and practices. For example, when Ami was asked by parents why she didn't use a popular rewards-based reading program, she was able to explain that "I don't use it because it doesn't assess higher-order questioning and thinking. Children will be more motivated to love to read by the other things we do in my classroom. They need to read for the love of language, story, authors, characters, not earning points." When Carly's school bought "a very skill-and-drill sort of language arts program," she set aside the teacher's manual and restructured the program to address skills contextually. Carly's students were able to meet the program's expectations, and almost all of her students received ratings of average or above average on the English/language arts section of the standardized test that year.

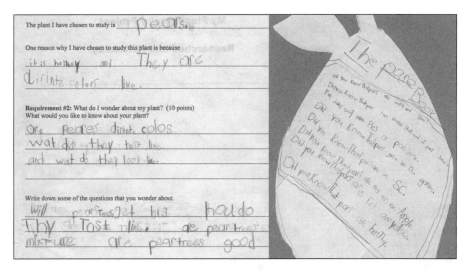

Figure 7.2. Julie's students plan and present their inquiries about plants.

Better yet, they learned those skills while engaged in meaningful reading and writing experiences across the curriculum.

In much the same way, Erin, with a change in administration, taught skills and strategies from the mandated reading program through more purposeful practices than those in the program's teacher's guide: "I took the stance that I was responsible in every way, shape, and form for teaching my students second-grade standards, but as long as I was meeting those standards, I would use a variety of resources and strategies to meet them." To reassure parents and administrators that those skills were indeed a part of her curriculum, Erin kept an ongoing list of phonics skills on her bulletin board under the heading "Look at all the phonics we are learning through shared reading!" Every time she and her students talked about a letter-sound relationship in the context of real reading or writing, they posted that skill on the board.

Ami's Multiage Program

In her third year, Ami proposed that she pilot a multiage program beginning with a first/second-grade combination in her own classroom. Her proposal was enthusiastically supported by the school's administration. As the program evolved, Ami realized that she was truly in her element: "It was heterogeneous learning at its very best. There was no ceiling on what I could do, and I was able to use the children's interests to direct our inquiries" (Figure 7.3). Within three years, the popular

Figure 7.3. Children from Ami's multiage class engage in an investigation about newts.

multiage program had grown to include 100 children and four classes—kindergarten/first grade and second/third grade—and served as a model program for other schools and districts. Many families even opted out of the Advanced Placement track (a program that compartmentalized students with high test scores into separate classrooms) so that their children could continue in the multiage classes. A local television station filmed a segment in which the state superintendent of education spoke about educational innovations as well as test scores. As an example, the cameras cut to a shot of Ami's multiage class.

Robbie and Brooke Create a Team

One Saturday in the spring of Robbie's fifth year, she and her colleague Brooke met for dinner and talked, as they often did, about their teaching lives. They began to dream about possibilities for team-teaching in the same classroom, combining their third-grade classes into one big class with two teachers. In the light of the next day, the dreams scribbled on restaurant napkins the night before still sounded exciting, so they began to articulate a plan. Nothing like this was going on in their school at that time, so it was important to build a solid argument to present to their administrators. In their proposal, they wrote:

We want a classroom where the curriculum is guided, not by what everyone else is doing, but by the students' needs and interests, . . . a place where teachers and students are partners in developing and implementing curriculum. . . . We envision a classroom that focuses on instruction that moves each student from his or her starting point, not from the beginning of third grade to the end of third grade. . . . It is difficult to implement this dream classroom when we feel separate from our colleagues. We want an environment where we can collaborate and support each other so we are comfortable implementing changes in our teaching practices.

Robbie and Brooke were given a green light to begin planning. They worked through the summer, and that fall they greeted their students as one class. Their actions continued as they articulated the positive impact of their new arrangement for "some parents who were a bit worried that their children wouldn't learn as much in our class as in a traditional one and some of the other teachers who were skeptical too." In what became Robbie's "best year professionally," their actions yielded great success as teachers and parents began to appreciate their work and encouraged them to continue. At the end of the year, Robbie wrote, "In years past, I felt that I was a decent teacher, but I was not implementing all the practices I knew were best. Working with Brooke gave me the energy and collegial support to be the teacher I had strived to become for five years."

Erin and Lindsay's Map Skills Ideas

During our second year, we received an email from Erin explaining how, through the example of her work with another teacher, also a graduate of the MAT program, a new idea had been picked up by a few other teachers. At a grade-level meeting—typically spent scheduling which skills to teach and which worksheets to use—Erin and Lindsay offered a new idea. Erin wrote to us about how their suggestion resulted in change they never expected:

Today was the best day I've had. It all happened while we were planning, as usual, as a grade level. This week and next, in social science, we are covering map skills. We've received tons of worksheets to go along with the skills. Of course, I just put them in my to-be-recycled box and went to the library and found some books on maps. Lindsay and I are having the kids read books and create their own maps. Anyway, in the meeting, a colleague asked if we could end the map skills unit early because, as she said, "I don't think we have enough worksheets to get us through till next Friday." Can you imagine?! Then she asked for suggestions about what to do since we would run out of worksheets. I told her about the activity that Lindsay and I are doing. I think they were a little taken aback. But then one teacher seemed really into it. Lindsay showed her some students' work, and our colleague was really impressed. What an awesome feeling! Another colleague took one of the books. I think she's going to do the activity too!

Taking Action by Speaking Up for Children

Sometimes we have to be the voice for kids.

Speaking up for children was, of course, one of the most important ways that we were politically active. Carmen said, "Sometimes we have to be the voice for kids who don't have anyone else to fight for them." One example comes from an incident that occurred during Carmen's second year of teaching. Nyle was placed in her second-grade class. He was also placed in a pull-out learning resource class that served children identified as having "special needs." He was, however, one of her highest-performing students. When Carmen questioned his placement in the special needs class, she was told that he was there because of behavior problems. She wrote to us: "This didn't make sense, so I questioned why he would be in a learning disability classroom when he has a behavior problem. No one had an answer." Carmen was told that if Nyle was taken out of the special needs class, it would be difficult to get him back in, logic that was difficult to understand. She worried that, rather than building an identity as a competent learner and an achiever, Nyle would soon begin to believe the negative language used to describe him and become the struggling student he was believed to be. She explained to Nyle's aunt that he had been placed in the special needs classroom because of behavior issues but that she was not seeing those issues in her classroom. They both refused to sign the papers that would recommend such a placement, wondering why there should be a battle in the first place since his test scores and class work indicated that he did not qualify as "special needs." Ultimately, Carmen's efforts were rewarded, and Nyle was taken out of the learning resource class and placed full time in her mainstream classroom.

In another example, Carmen wrote about eight-year-old Neil, who was taking medication that "put him in such a zombie-like state that it scared me." Carmen explained that she would "rather deal with his active behavior than watch the child gnaw on his nails, fall asleep in class, and not eat his lunch." She said, "His mother worries that he is fading away, but she doesn't know what to do. She has the impression that if he is not medicated, he will not be allowed to return to school." Carmen kept a diary of Neil's behavior. She kept a watchful eye on what he ate for lunch, noticing that he ate "virtually nothing." She filled out forms describing Neil's behavior so that his mother could have documentation to take to her doctor. Ultimately, Neil's dosage was reduced, which, in Carmen's view, made a world of difference. She wrote that "after that, he was allowed to *experience* school instead of going through second grade in a blur."

Taking Action by Leaving Difficult Situations

> I need to be in a situation where my philosophy of education and the goals of the school are in line.

By the end of their first year of teaching, it was clear to both Julie and Erin that they had to take action by looking for new jobs. They could no longer remain in situations that they felt kept them from living fully as professionals. Having just gone through the interview process a year before and having experienced a difficult and unhappy first year of teaching, they wanted to leave, but they were also a bit frightened to put themselves "out there" again. Revealing their decision to leave also meant revealing reasons for their unhappiness, which meant that not all of their colleagues would understand or appreciate their concerns. And what if they were unsuccessful? What if they couldn't find new jobs in better situations? Erin wrote, "I thought *getting* a job was hard. I had no idea of the repercussions that came with giving it up!"

Erin

Before making the decision to look for a job elsewhere, Erin wanted to establish once and for all that the lack of autonomy she felt and the strong difference between her pedagogical views and those of the school administration were not just school mythology. Perhaps she had misread the signs that told her she could not deviate from mandates. She made an appointment to meet with the assistant principal. In an email to our group, she explained what happened during the meeting: "I asked how much autonomy I had to decide how to teach my children. She said that we were required to use the adopted, scripted programs because they were similar to formats on the standardized tests and produced good test results. This helped me make the decision I had to make." Having practiced what she would say many times before going into the meeting, Erin explained to her administrators that she had been doing a lot of thinking over spring break and really felt it would be in her best interest and the school's if she requested a transfer: "I said that I feel the need to be in a situation where my philosophy of education and the goals of the school are in line, that I did not believe in the skill-and-drill approach to education, and that using worksheets and teaching skills in isolation as primary instructional strategies just didn't fit with who I wanted to be as an educator." Erin wrote that "it was not a matter of 'Oh, maybe I'll leave.' I knew I was going to leave that school or not teach." Then she put in for a transfer and hand-delivered copies of her résumé to almost every school in the district.

A new principal came to Erin's school just before the end of the school year, when Erin was in the midst of job interviews at other schools. As described later in this chapter, conversations with the new administrator let her know that the climate of the school would change, and she decided to stay.

Julie

Julie also knew by the end of the first year of teaching that she would leave the profession altogether if she didn't move to another school. She was miserable on a day-to-day basis. Having watched her become more and more unhappy as the year progressed, Julie's husband and our group encouraged her to take action to find a job in another school. Feeling a contradiction that many of us could understand, Julie was unhappy yet worried about leaving the familiarity of her school to start all over again. In her present situation, at least she knew the challenges she faced. But it was clearly not the right place for her: "It's really important for me to be at a school where everyone feels comfortable enough to give honest feedback regarding decisions being made and receive positive feedback and encouragement. A bad day somewhere else has got to be better than a good day here." Julie explained that her decision to move was also influenced by her desire to interact with colleagues with whom she could grow professionally:

> Except for the first week of school, we met only to discuss school events. We never really shared classroom ideas. This made me feel very alone. I would have loved to have had a group to bounce ideas off of at my school. I don't ever want to lose my enthusiasm and desire to teach students in a better way or to learn and share the latest teaching research.

Once Julie made the decision to leave, it wasn't long before she found a new position. She wrote to us with excitement, "I just want to let everyone know that I have a new job! I'm so relieved that I don't have to go back to my other school! I have so much hope that this year will be different from last year and a very positive change for me." In her new school, Julie found a caring, nurturing principal as well as opportunities for collaboration with colleagues.

Taking Action by Speaking Out

> I hope I don't sound bitter. I don't feel bitter. I feel bold!

Speaking Out to Legislators

In the wake of state and national elections and political debates, more of us began to have strong sentiments about what was going on in education. Many proposed changes didn't make sense to us. It was time to use our voices to speak out when we had the opportunity to talk to politicians. Taking advantage of one of those opportunities, Robbie attended a meeting at a local elementary school that was led by leaders from the state House of Representatives. At that time, educators, parents, and policymakers across the state were involved in a heated debate over legislation that would give parents the opportunity to receive tax credits or vouchers to pay for private school tuition. Robbie stood up at the meeting, explained her opposition to the plan, and asked about alternative plans. She used that platform to share her views about other issues that affect the lives of teachers:

> I talked about class size. I talked about teaching to the test. I explained problems in education from a teacher's standpoint and some ways I see of solving those problems. I was impassioned as I spoke. In the end, I asked the legislators to consider speaking with younger teachers as well as veteran educators when creating legislation, because we also have many ideas to offer.

In addition to voicing her views at the meeting, Robbie learned about the kind of action that would have the greatest impact in governmental arenas—writing letters, sending emails, and making phone calls to legislators at home. Inspired by Robbie, Erin began calling members of the House Committee on Ways and Means about the voucher-for-private-schools issue. She was empowered through her conversations with politicians: "I was standing up for something I believed in, and because of that, I felt strong and proud of myself. I was doing something that felt right to me, instead of sitting back and doing nothing." Carmen was also anxious to take action. Feeling strongly that a tax break to fund vouchers for private schools would take funding away from public schools, she signed letters, read articles to be better informed, and attended a meeting by the local education organization to add her voice to their rejection of the voucher program.

Speaking Up in Conversations with Administrators

Erin's new principal arrived at her school in late spring, shortly after she began searching for another job. Wanting to get to know the teachers, the administrator invited Erin for a conversation and asked why she wanted to leave. That evening, Erin described the meeting in an email to our group: "I decided to be very honest and say, 'These are the reasons why I am unhappy.' I wanted to let her know exactly what was important to me as a teacher. If she said, 'No, you can't have autonomy, you have to use the worksheets,' then I would take a job in another school." Erin continued:

> I almost didn't even recognize myself. I was so open and bold. I ran through the schedule I would like to have in my classroom. I brought in sample parent feedback forms and photocopies from the kids' reader response journals to show the value of the kind of teaching I want to do. I flat out said that I do *not* believe in using worksheets. I gave specific examples of how I could teach my children without using worksheets. I guess you could say I got on a roll. But I'm sick and tired of not standing up for what I believe. It goes back to what Routman talks about, teachers finding their voice. Well, I have found mine. I hope I don't sound bitter. I don't feel bitter. *I feel bold.*

The new administrator's reaction was what Erin had yearned for: "She thought my ideas were great and said she wanted me to share them!" This gave Erin the courage and confidence she needed. She decided to stay at the school and began to feel "really good" about going into her second year.

Making our views known to principals doesn't seem like a daunting challenge now, but after an intimidating first year, speaking out in this way took courage. By doing so, however, Erin opened a conversation that let her know whether she should go or stay. This led to greater confidence to speak out in future months and years as she took on leadership roles within the school. It allowed her to bring her full teaching self into relationships with peers and administrators. Within three years, Erin was selected by her peers as the school's Teacher of the Year. She wrote, "Isn't that wild? Knowing all that you do about my first year, I thought all of you would really appreciate that bit of news."

Speaking Out about Programs and Practices

During our first year, most of us found it difficult or uncomfortable to speak out about issues or programs in our schools. As we gained confidence and experience, we were able to speak out more and more in our schools and districts about specific programs and practices. Ending her second year, Julie wrote, "I have learned to speak out when I see things that I don't understand or agree with. My first year, I watched but said nothing about some of the things I saw going on. I don't feel like I have to sit on the sidelines anymore." To prepare for opportunities to voice our views, we often went back to journals from graduate school, notes, and, yes, those professional books. We also looked to one another for resources and support with email questions like "Could anyone help me with this issue I will be facing with textbook adoption?"; "Does anyone know any other resources that would be good for me to take to this meeting?" We realized how important it was to do our homework before we stood up to voice a view.

Julie and Erin and Scripted Programs

Julie used her knowledge about literacy learning to address issues related to program adoption and ultimately to support her work on the district's Kindergarten Advisory Board. In her fifth year, teachers at each school in Julie's district were asked to review literacy programs to consider for adoption. Julie met with other kindergarten teachers in her school "for countless hours reviewing reading programs, completing rating forms, and writing comments." As a result, they were able to make an informed decision about the reading program they felt best supported understandings about literacy learning. Hearing that the district was likely to adopt a different program, teachers at her school requested a meeting so they could share their views with district representatives. At the meeting, Julie expressed the concern that the scripted nature of this program would take away the possibility that teachers could use and continue to develop knowledge about theory and practice in making instructional decisions. She explained that good teaching occurs when teachers pay close attention to children and use their professional knowledge to plan accordingly. She was also concerned about the program's approach to reading instruction. She wrote to us recounting the opportunity to explain her perspective:

> At the meeting, the comment was made that some teachers are young and probably don't know much yet about teaching read-

ing. I explained that I have a master's degree that fully prepared me to teach reading and I have continued my professional development since receiving that degree. I explained that this reading program would do a disservice to our students because it relies too heavily on teaching phonics in isolation from application in real reading and writing. I went on to say that I fully believe that it is very important to teach phonics, but that phonics knowledge is just one part of the reading process. I explained that readers read well when they use a balance of cue systems focusing on meaning, structure, *and* phonics. I said that I teach phonics explicitly, but I do so in ways that children will immediately connect to real reading and writing. I suggested that we could help new teachers develop stronger backgrounds by providing opportunities for ongoing professional study.

Julie was not alone in her concerns. The claim that scripted programs are necessary because of lack of teacher knowledge is not exclusive to this situation. Jonathan Kozol (2005) writes about this as a misguided yet widespread assumption: "The argument is sometimes made that scripted programs . . . are essential for schools in which teachers are inexperienced and where there is high turnover rate of faculty members" (p. 274). He goes on to describe the futility of addressing school reform with prescriptive solutions that "leave little to the competence of teachers" (p. 274). In another example of strong voices frustrated by this trend, Deborah Meier (2004) writes about school systems in which "scripts downloaded daily into classrooms replace teachers' judgment" (p. 75), an approach antithetical to what we know about good teaching and learning.

At the meeting, Julie asked if the decision had already been made to select this reading series. She wrote, "The answer was, 'No,' but the hope was expressed that we would choose the program that we knew would raise test scores." Frustration with this logic again mirrors frustration felt nationally as "test scores drive curriculum [and] quick fix solutions are put into place" (Graves, 2001, p. 1). Julie wanted to do something to address the problem: "This focus on scores means that people—parents, administrators, district people, other teachers, the general public—who don't have a solid foundation in teaching reading can be easily persuaded that certain programs are necessary without truly understanding the bigger picture. How can I help to change this?"

That summer Julie joined the district's Kindergarten Advisory Committee. The group was convened to consider how the implementation of the required reading program (ultimately adopted by the district) would fit the needs of their students. The decision to get involved at the district level gave Julie the opportunity to move beyond merely voicing opposition. She realized that much of her frustration had to do with differences in opportunities that various stakeholders had to develop knowledge about children's literacy learning. Serving on the advisory board could be an opportunity to raise awareness. Within the system, Julie hoped she could work to effect change. She wrote about the committee's goals:

> We decided to make a list of sound literacy practices and then see how the adopted reading program fit that model. Then we listed the state standards and practices we felt would be supportive of literacy learning—all growing from what we know about our children and from theoretical understandings about how we learn literacy. The advisory board has a real commitment to figuring out ways to provide opportunities for teachers and leaders to build knowledge across the district. We hope that understanding literacy learning will make it possible for a more common articulation of goals so that teachers and district leaders can use a common knowledge base to make informed decisions together. We discussed a plan to hold classes that would involve district leaders, school administrators, and classroom teachers in learning together about how students learn to read and write. It's my goal, along with others through this committee, to work to make this happen.

Erin tackled similar issues during her third year of teaching. Serving as her school's language arts representative, she attended a workshop to learn about a grant that would provide funds to implement a program much like the one Julie later encountered—a scripted, sequenced package with a focus on teacher transmission of discrete bits of information. Erin saw no sound theoretical base to the proposed program. The night after the workshop, she tossed and turned, trying to decide how she would explain her disagreement with a program that would bring grant money to the school. The next morning she explained to her principal why she could not play a part in seeking this kind of funding: "I said that I don't agree with scripted programs because they contribute to the dumbing down of teachers and I find that the research this grant used to be faulty." To support her argument, she drew on theoretical knowledge and practical experience with both scripted programs and thoughtful approaches to literacy education. Erin also pointed out specific criticisms of the research supporting the grant— the narrow body of research and the limitations of the studies used to justify the program (Garan, 2002). Erin wrote to us:

I explained to my principal that I felt it was important to look at all angles of this grant and what it would mean for our children. I said that I had some literature she could read if she was interested. She was! Anyway, I feel wonderful. I don't think I'm changing anything, but at least I'm actively trying. Who knows where this will lead, but at least I feel that my principal might reconsider this grant!

Our group applauded Julie and Erin as they voiced their views. Ami wrote: "I told two teams in my school about you and they were like, 'Go Julie!' You are really inspiring!" Carly sent her congratulations: "I'm so proud of you for standing up for your beliefs!" Susi wrote, "I read your message to my literacy coaches and they literally cheered you!" We were particularly proud of Erin and Julie for backing up their views with research as well as experience. They didn't base their action on merely gut reactions. They drew on everything they knew about teaching and learning to build strong cases for their arguments.

Carly's Breakfast Book Club

Carly wasn't a stranger to the world of politics. She had been dubbed the political guru of the group in graduate school because of her strong will to speak out and offer solutions. In her third year of teaching, she took a position as Title I reading teacher. With the job came responsibility for managing the schoolwide implementation of a computerized system that emphasized extrinsic rewards for reading books. This almost caused Carly to turn down the job. She was fundamentally opposed to everything about the rewards program and had no idea how she could endorse it. That summer she spent many hours researching, reading, and thinking about how she might communicate her concerns and program alternatives to her administration. A few weeks before school started, she met with her principal and assistant principal, data in hand. Carly described the meeting in an email message written to us the next day. Carly's message communicates her well-thought-out actions and carefully chosen words, as well as her respect for the administrators' points of view:

> I began the meeting by describing the professional reading I've done this summer and what I've learned from two years of teaching reading. I was careful to point out that, just as they, as administrators, are supportive of teachers' professional beliefs and practices, I want to be supportive of their commitment to the program. Then I explained how I take serious issue with the intent of this program. I got straight to the point. I said, "I know that

testing is a reality and I know that accountability is the big scare now. Yes, some research does point out that this program will provide a quick fix and it just might lead to raising those reading scores a few notches. But, as an educator, I can't settle for quick fixes just to save my behind. I'm extremely concerned about what this does to a child in the long run. Study after study shows that when offered an extrinsic reward, *especially* for something that is intrinsically motivating, we inevitably devalue the act. I can't knowingly make that sacrifice." We talked about the kinds of things they liked to read, and I said, "Just like you, when children find something they are interested in, they will be motivated to read anything they can get their hands on." That, I argued, is the difference between intrinsic and extrinsic motivation, which makes all the difference in developing lifelong readers. Finally, I shared ideas that I thought might provide alternatives. First, I would create two book clubs that all students in the school could join. Another idea was to create a weekly *Book Talk Live* in-house television program that would give students an opportunity to share favorite books, magazines, etc., with peers. To make a long story short, they told me to do whatever I needed to do to make my ideas happen. They even said that we can do away with the trophy that is given for the class that earns the most reading points—even though they just ordered a new trophy! They want me to present all of this to the teachers, individually and in small groups instead of in a whole staff meeting. *No more points*!!!

Carly began holding book club meetings after school and in the early morning: "On the morning of the sign-up, you should have seen the shock on our faces to see a line of eager students wrapped around the school entrance and into the cafeteria—students from all instructional levels. Many teachers were shocked to see their most struggling students begging for membership in the book club. It was truly one of the most rewarding days I've had as a teacher."

Taking Action by Making Ourselves Aware of Local Issues

Before becoming a teacher, Carmen says, she always shied away from political conversations. She saw politics as primarily a national endeavor revolving around Republican, Democratic, and Independent debates. She voted as a civic duty more than anything else. Then a local zoning issue convinced her of the importance of being better informed. In her small town district, an elementary school with a predominantly Black student population was closing at a time when two new elementary schools were opening. Carmen explained, "When the lines were drawn for the new schools, it became known that a somewhat affluent elementary school would have to take a large portion of the poor kids and children from the African American community. The school was in an uproar about their free- and reduced-lunch populations doubling and the potential for test scores to go down." In spite of a city council meeting called to address the issues, zones were creatively altered, resulting in many of the African American children traveling beyond the school closest to their homes to another school. Carmen wrote, "How do they expect kids to feel with this kind of foolishness going on? I am not going to sit on this. I have a co-worker who is in this with me. We're going to the next meeting so we can be fully informed."

Taking Action by Attending National Conferences and by Sharing Our Research Findings

> It made it hit home as far as the importance of it all.

Sharing our research is always exciting, but we are most exhilarated when we venture beyond our own communities to do so. Presenting at our first national conference—NCTE in Denver in 1999—and at others through the years—NCTE in Atlanta and Indianapolis (Figure 7.4) and three times at the annual convention of the American Educational Research Association (AERA)—we began to fully appreciate the magnitude of our work. Preparing to present and then engaging in conversations with attendees, we discovered that our research findings became clearer and our message grew stronger. Watching heads nod in empathy and agreement, and fielding questions during our presentations, we realized that issues we faced were those faced by new teachers across the country. After flying back home from a New Orleans conference, Carmen wrote, "The plane was loaded with people who had been to the conference. I talked about our research. They were so receptive. It made me feel really good about what we're doing. The importance of it all really hit home."

It was not just the act of presenting our work that helped us find our voice. Attending conference sessions played an important role in giving us courage to go back to our schools and teach differently. After an NCTE conference, for example, Robbie wrote, "The session about literature circles gave me energy to get back to my classroom and implement some neat things. As I sat in the session, I could feel the energy flowing to my brain again. I began to get new ideas immediately, thinking of particular children in my classroom and what I might do differently." Carmen captured the potential impact of attending national conferences on teachers' ability to take action locally: "What if everybody

Figure 7.4. Carly, Julie, Robbie, Carmen, and Susi at the 2004 NCTE Annual Convention.

had it this good? Would professional development opportunities like this make teachers more equipped to deal with the struggles of teaching? Would more teachers stay in the field?"

Taking Action through Workshops, University Classes, and Leadership Roles

> Taking leadership roles in our schools also allowed us to bring our voice to specific issues.

Conducting inservice workshops for other teachers, speaking to university classes, and taking leadership roles in our schools and districts also allowed us to bring our voices to specific issues. At the university, we spoke to education majors about the findings from our research. In our schools and districts, we led workshops to share practices from our classrooms. We supervised student teachers and practicum students and welcomed visitors to our classrooms. We took leadership roles as grade-level team leaders and as members of school and district curricular committees. We presented at state conferences and served as district expert teachers and as school representatives in parent-teacher organizations. We organized parent education programs and volunteer training. We wrote grants. We took further graduate courses. Carmen, April, and Erin worked toward and were awarded National Board certification. Julie and Ami are working toward their certification as we complete this book.

Taking Action by Building Knowledge

Knowledge *is* voice.

Continuing to build on knowledge from graduate school gives us confidence and courage to take action. Knowledge is our best resource. Our data are filled with instances when we used theoretical and practical understandings to support practices and to suggest changes in classrooms and schools. Carly and Robbie drew on theoretical knowledge when colleagues asked why their students had not yet accumulated any points from the school's reading rewards program. They were able to explain that extrinsic rewards are fleeting and only motivate children to earn points and prizes, not to become passionate, proficient readers (Kohn, 1999). They were able to provide alternatives: motivation through daily read-alouds (Fox, 2001; Krashen, 1993), literature discussions and book clubs (Peterson & Eeds, 1990; Short & Pierce, 1998), and authors' studies (Ray, 1999). In the same way, Julie was able to draw from her theoretical understandings to talk knowledgeably about the importance of contextualized reading instruction that helps children grow as passionate, strategic readers and writers (Moustafa, 1997; Smith, 1997; Weaver, 2002). The examples go on and on: Ami, writing the proposal for her multiage class; Robbie and Brooke, proposing their team-teaching idea; April, explaining why she did not use a letter-of-the-week approach to teaching phonics; and Erin, sharing articles with administrators about the importance of contextualized skill instruction.

While theoretical knowledge was important, we found that it was just as important to have solid understandings of national and local policies that affected our schools, our students, and their families. In her first year, Carly wrote, "I am making a point of becoming more knowledgeable about federal and local education policies so I can better help people inside and outside of education understand the issues." Erin said, "In my first phase of activism, I feel that it is my responsibility to become as educated as possible in current policies and the political climate. I'm reading and having conversations now. Who knows where that will lead?"

Being informed about policy and building knowledge about theory, practice, and children was a powerful combination. It gave us voices with clout. Whether using knowledge to teach well on a day-to-day basis, share a curricular structure with a colleague, justify a classroom practice to an administrator or parent, write to a legislator, or present to a school board, it became clear to us that knowledge *is* voice.

Taking Action Begins with Talk and Noticing the Silences

> When there is no space for reflective talk that urges us to pay attention to what we do not say as well as to what we do say, silences go unnoticed.

We have written elsewhere in this book that our opportunities for reflective talk over long periods of time were critical to understanding our experiences. We also see talk as foundational to taking action. Writing together and talking at length about feedback from outside readers, we recognize something else. It's not just about the talk; it's about noticing the silent spaces in the talk, the unexplored aspects of conversations. For us, one of the most visible examples of the need to examine the silent spaces comes from our talk related to issues of race. For example, during Carmen's second year of teaching, she wrote to us about one of her second graders, who told the class that he had to go through *niggertown* to get to his new apartment. Another student told the biracial children in Carmen's class that people would die and become ghosts if they married or lived with a Black person. Carmen wrote:

> I talked to the class to try to bring some understanding to all of this, but after my heartfelt speech about respect, friendship, treating each other with kindness and using kind words, one of the children went back to his desk and called a classmate a *nigger*. I've never had this problem before, so I have my work cut out for me in more ways than one. I know you are astounded that my kids would say those things in front of me, but I wouldn't have it any other way. I can't deal with the problem if I don't know it exists.

Carmen talked with parents of the children who had made the remarks. Their conversations required that both Carmen and the parents come to a common understanding about honoring each other. As she talked with one parent in particular, Carmen made it clear that, "I will not have that kind of talk in my classroom," but they also openly shared perspectives on interracial marriage. After a year in which Carmen offered spoken and unspoken invitations to help students better understand multiple ways of being in the world—a year in which parents and children grew to trust her open ways of dealing with difference—she wrote to us: "Remember the little girl who made the comment about marrying a Black person? Well, she was allowed to come to my house, a Black woman's house, for an end-of-the-year barbecue."

Several other incidents involving race emerged in our data stories: a child in Robbie's class explained that she changed schools because her parents felt that she had too many Black friends at her previous school, a little boy in Julie's kindergarten used the word *nigger*, Carmen told about the zoning inequities in her district, Erin and Julie asked Carmen for insights about African American boys in their classes, and Ami wrote about frustrations with the continued existence of White-flight private schools across the state. Examining those issues again in the process of writing this book, we began to understand the importance of noticing the silences in our conversations, or as Newkirk (1992) writes, "silences in our narratives as teachers" (p. 21). Looking at our data stories about race, we wondered why we hadn't used them to explore further: When the children in Carmen's and Julie's classes used racist language, why didn't we talk more about the issue? The children never used those words again within their teachers' earshot, but that doesn't tell us much about deeper issues that remain or the use of language in ways that may be more subtly racist. When Erin and Julie talked with Carmen about African American boys, why didn't we talk about issues of identity and Black males? When Carmen faced the zoning issue, why didn't we talk more about societal structures and community biases that perpetuate situations like creative rezoning? Why didn't we attempt to do something about it?

During our book-writing conversations, we considered reasons why such silences existed in our talk. Maybe we had been so focused on survival that we didn't make time to delve into potentially volatile issues. Maybe, as close to one another as we felt in the beginning, we weren't comfortable enough to open those conversations or to push them forward once they were opened. Carmen said, "One of us would put it out there, but we never really talked about it." Susi wondered about her own role:

> I think a big part of it is that I didn't make those conversations foundational to what I do as a teacher educator when you were MAT students. We read Ladson-Billings, and Gloria Boutte [1998, 2001] came in to talk to us about bias, but I didn't know how to go beyond that. I remember Carly being very upset and I didn't know how to help us explore those feelings in productive ways.

We wondered if, being a group of predominantly White teachers, we didn't see or feel the issues as deeply as we might have. Carmen said:

> If you don't feel that it plays a large role in your life as a teacher, it won't be talked about. It's always going to play a large role in mine. That's not to say it's not important to anyone else, but of course it's going to ring more with me. When that little boy talked about niggertown, he thought nothing of it. It just happened to

be in a Black teacher's classroom. My thought is that it happens a lot, but many White teachers are not really as conscious of it. It might not be something that is as visibly offensive as using the word *nigger* and so it may not get the attention that it would get from me. Race relations are always going to be near and dear for me because I'm a Black woman. I've experienced it, and it hurts me to see my Black boys the way they are. There are so many misperceptions teachers have. I told Susi about this little boy whose teacher said, "All he needs is a little TLC." Well, how does she know he's not getting any TLC?

As we send this manuscript off to press, this is where we are—beginning to notice the silences in our talk and wondering what that means for us as educators who want to take action. Carmen said, "I don't know if it's too late for our book, but I think we should include that this isn't something we addressed and now we're thinking about it. This is what's to come. This is how further growth will happen in open conversations," and Ami said, "We know that we want to have these conversations now."

An important learning for us was that it takes time, intentionality, and a strong relationship to recognize that such talk is necessary and to make a place for it. As Carly said, "conversations about silences or harder issues can only happen when teachers take time to involve themselves in discussion of their work." Erin added, "You don't just sit down and begin that kind of talk. It took years for us to build to it." We also know that making a place for talk over time is only a beginning. We can't guarantee that questioning the silences will lead to action or even to further talk, but it is the beginning of action when we walk away from the conversation with new questions. If there is no space for reflective talk that urges us to pay attention to what we do *not* say as well as to what we *do* say, silences go unnoticed, and there is not even the possibility that action will be taken.

Taking Action by Writing: A Book Reveals Itself

> Our study is important not because it's news. This stuff has been happening for a long time. It's important because it's *still* news.

During Carly's oral exams at the end of the MAT program, one of our professors commented on her passion for "taking an active role instead of just complaining" and said, "The work you're going to be doing with Dr. Long, that's an opportunity to become politically active too. You're going to be studying together for a year." Who would have thought that our one-year study would turn into a seven-year experience? It has become our most complex, reflexive, comprehensive form of political action to date. It has become this book.

As ideas for this book began to take shape, we sent our thoughts to several publishers. One suggested that our seven years of research might best be written in a "tips for teachers and administrators" format. By that point, we were far beyond the tips stage in our own view of the work. Carly wrote: "It really irritates me that the world is so hung up on quick fixes. Is that the game we have to play to get the word out? Tips for administrators will not even scratch the surface of understanding and solving the problem of nurturing and retaining new teachers." For us, our work means much more. Early in our experience, Erin wrote, "The more I struggle through my first years and listen to my peers struggle through theirs, the more passionate I feel about our work. We really do have something worthwhile to say, and it needs to be said to other teachers, parents, administrators, and even the public in general." Robbie put it well: "Our study is not important because it's news. This stuff has been happening for a long time. It's important because it's *still* news."

One evening at Robbie's house during our fifth year, we sat down to write and talk about what it meant to be political through our writing. Robbie wrote, "We want to do something, really *do* something to help so that teachers, especially new teachers, can grow and learn in environments designed by people who are educated about education." We all agreed with Robbie while sharing a concern voiced by April. She wondered if our first-year voices would be taken seriously: "Will people listen to new teachers? Will they accept our stories? That's what I worry about." Ami remarked that all we could do was put our stories "out there." She went on to say that it was sometimes too easy to "shut our doors and do our own thing [but that] by doing that, we aren't changing the system." We felt strongly that our writing should not be, as Carmen said, "just full of emotion without an angle for change. We can't just put out there what's wrong; we have to offer solutions."

Nieto (2003) describes the act of writing about one's own experiences in the company of colleagues as "a public way of understanding and improving" (p. 81) those experiences. This was indeed the case with us. Erin's description of taking action through our work encapsulates its impact in our lives as well as the broader political impact we dream it might have for others:

> This book has been empowering to me. I no longer have an excuse not to do anything when I am angered or upset. When we became angry at what we went through as new teachers, we put

our feelings into words. Ultimately, we put our words into a book that will hopefully change things for new teachers, if in no other way than letting them know they are not alone. That is the greatest accomplishment I have yet achieved professionally.

Being Political: Addressing Larger Institutional Issues

Change needs to start with us.

While we believe that institutional failures cannot be used as excuses, it is important to consider our own political actions in the context of "the systematic use of economic and political power in institutions (such as schools) that leads to detrimental policies and practices" (Nieto, 2004, p. 37). We see the influence of institutional structures most profoundly in our data as we look at the impact of high-stakes testing in our teaching lives. At some level, it touches every issue discussed in this book. In her second year, Carmen wrote:

> What is essentially happening is that we're teaching to the tests. I hate it. My team hates it. Just today we were saying that teaching is starting not to be fun anymore. Another teacher says she has lost her confidence. I feel like I'm just touching on material and then I have to move on even if students don't get it, because I have to get to what's on the test. It breaks my heart to see my kids tested on something that these people have decided they should know by now. So I spend five days cramming.

In Erin's fifth year, she wrote: "I'm discouraged by the whole testing frenzy because we lose sight of what really matters. At one point, our whole school was governed by tests. A curricular model that doesn't dramatically raise test scores isn't even considered. I believe in accountability and assessment. I really do. But it's the high stakes with which I don't agree. Test scores, test scores, test scores. That's all you hear."

Although before entering our first classrooms we knew that testing pressures existed, we didn't realize the extent of the emphasis put on them. As one group member put it, "Test scores completely shape the world of public education." Today, members of our group feel an even greater sense of urgency to change the system than they did seven years ago. They watch as test scores are posted teacher by teacher in school hallways, presented on overhead transparencies in faculty meetings, and printed in newspapers. Even when scores aren't posted, as one group member remarked, "everyone knows which teachers are known for their high test scores and which are not." Carly expressed her frustration about how this intense focus on test scores can thwart teachers' courage to take risks in their practice:

We're encouraged to look to these teachers whose students have high test scores as models of good teaching. It's like a false celebrity status. Even some of my friends that are known as having the highest scores feel that they've had to sell out to teach-to-the-test programs. They will admit that year after year they give up more of what we all know is best practice, because they don't want to risk taking a year or more to work through the natural trial-and-error process of reflective, innovative practice. I wonder if other teachers even know that they are selling out their kids. Or have they so totally succumbed to the institutional structures that they actually buy into the status? This is what scares and frustrates me the most.

We are most distressed when we see ourselves succumbing to the status quo because of pressure from the testing rhetoric that surrounds us. We watch students disengage when teacher-proof curricula have little meaning in their lives and when instruction is doled out in testable portions. We see testing systematically eliminate learning opportunities for many children. In her fifth year, Erin captured the marginalizing impact of high-stakes tests as she reflected on her work with Chris, a first grader who came very close to being permanently labeled by a test-driven system. Having helped Chris read strategically and purposefully, she saw how easily he might have slipped into a future dominated by skill and drill:

> I want to hug Chris, but I am afraid to interrupt his reading. I am so afraid that the moment will be lost if I interrupt him. Finally, he reads, "I am a whale. I live in the sea." I do hug him. We celebrate. I wonder if he knows? Does he know that he just read the hardest book he has ever read? Does he know that now he won't have to have an academic plan or a score "below basic"? I wonder if he knows that now his teachers won't shake their heads in desperation when they look at his test scores. He won't have go to an after-school tutor only to chant, "Block A, Block A, A, A, A." Does he know that he just unlocked a very important door that will impact the rest of his life?

We now believe that being political means taking responsibility for teaching well within existing structures while working to change structures that are unjust—the structures that cause us to want to rescue children like Erin's Chris or Carmen's Nyle from being sucked into institutional traps that would label them for a lifetime. Our experiences push us to ask: Are schools and school systems set up as places that nurture teachers as intellectuals (Nieto, 2003), or are they driven by federal, state, and local pressures to produce numbers on tests? Do schools and districts support smart, knowledgeable teachers whose jobs revolve around opportunities to study, pay attention to children and families, use knowledge to inform instruction, and collaborate with other smart colleagues? Or are teachers drowning in a sea of mandates to teach to the test and race through testable curricula? Donald Graves (2001) describes this "senseless work in the midst of high pressure [as] a prescription for significant energy loss . . . and a discouraged profession" (p. 3). This is precisely the way many of us felt as new teachers. Some of us feel the same pressures today. But we also believe that institutions will change only through the actions of individuals engaging other individuals in honest dialogue—actions large and small that new and experienced teachers can and do take to make a difference. Ami said it well: "I always thought we were up against the system, but really, we are the system. Changes need to start with us."

What Does This Mean for New Teachers?

> I can speak my mind about what I believe, and every time I do, it doesn't have to be a big event. I can have a voice and say what I believe without the catastrophic results I imagined.

Paulo Freire (1973) describes education as always political. As experienced teachers, we finally recognize the political voices we had all along. In subtle and not-so-subtle ways, we actively contributed to the quality of our lives as new teachers and to effecting change in our schools. Recognizing that we have voice, we use it even more. We speak out. We also realize that change takes time, the process is not always easy, and there are times along the way when we may lose sight of our vision. When that happens, we need the help of like-minded colleagues to regain it. Finally, we know that using our voice does not mean we will always achieve our goals, but speaking up for what we believe is, in itself, an empowering act. It contrasts sharply with feeling silenced. As one group member said, "the outcome might not go your way, but if you are troubled, you feel better if you let your voice be heard."

Looking back at the younger versions of the teachers we are today, we wish we had recognized the power of the positive actions we took five, six, seven years ago. As Erin observed, that recognition in itself gives us more courage:

> I spent my whole first year being miserable because I didn't realize that I had the power to change things on my own. I guess I didn't know I had a voice or that I had the power to do anything. I didn't see myself as enough of a professional to act like one. I would never have dreamed of standing up for what I believed in

a team meeting or with my principal. I just had to realize a few things: I am an adult, I know what I'm doing, I'm good at what I do, and I'm getting better every day. With those realizations, I can speak my mind about what I believe, and every time I do, it doesn't have to be a big event. I can have a voice and say what I believe without the catastrophic results I imagined.

Recognizing retrospectively that we *did* effect change for ourselves and others helps us understand that new teachers have a responsibility to use their voices to improve their own situations. You may not land in a school that fulfills your vision of an ideal, so while you work to change the structures that stifle innovation, you have a responsibility to figure out how to create dynamic learning environments within those contexts or to look for a new job. *You are not powerless.* New teachers can open doors to dialogue and can contribute to creating positive experiences for themselves and others. We don't recommend storming the gates, but we do know that, through quiet example that becomes respectfully louder and louder, new teachers can effect change from their very first days in the classroom.

Critical Insights from Chapter 7

- When we thought we had the least control over our lives, we actually *did* have a voice.

- We came to define *being political* as engaging in acts no matter how large or small that honor one's core beliefs and philosophies.

- Taking action happens in both gentle and boisterous ways, and no action is more or less courageous than another; each has the potential to make a difference.

- Change is most likely to be effected when actions are backed up by well-thought-out, carefully articulated, soundly based arguments.

- Taking action begins with talk and recognizing the silences in the talk.

- Recognizing our voice and using it does not necessarily mean we will achieve our goals, but speaking up is an empowering act in itself.

- We may not land in a school that fulfills our vision of an ideal, but while we work to change the structures that stifle innovation, we have a responsibility to figure out how to create dynamic learning environments within those contexts or to look for a new job.

- We don't recommend storming the gates, but we do know that, through quiet example that becomes respectfully louder and louder, new teachers can effect change from their first days in the classroom.

8 How Can You Help?

Each of us has the power to perpetuate the cycle of despair that causes some teachers to leave teaching and others to lose the drive to move the profession forward. But together we can work to put real changes in place that will make a difference.

Every year we lose far too many new teachers to other professions or to a disappointing status quo. But we can do something about this situation. Based on our experiences, we offer advice—our two cents—for administrators, colleagues, directors of induction and mentoring programs, university faculty, internship coordinators, job seekers, and new teachers themselves. We share what we've come to believe every educator can do to support the energy, fragility, knowledge, and drive that new teachers bring to the teaching profession.

To Administrators

Our advice for every other educator can be more fully actualized with your support.

In this section, we write directly to principals, assistant principals, and district leaders, but we hope you will also read our suggestions for every other educator. You are our educational leaders. Our advice for others can be more fully actualized if you are supportive of their roles as well as your own. We understand that administrators are often under great pressure because of district and state mandates, high-stakes testing, and school report cards. We know that you are the "educators in the middle" (Graves, 2001, p. 153) who deal with advice, input, requests, and directives from every corner of the educational world. Our experiences suggest, however, that action taken with regard to issues outlined below can make a significant difference in the life of your school and certainly in the lives of new teachers. Embracing new teachers' knowledge, enthusiasm, and initiative can help you enrich the vibrant school community you've already established. We can also work in partnership with you and our more experienced colleagues to turn around communities in need of revitalization. By involving us in these ways, you nurture us *and* stand a much better chance of keeping us in the profession. In this section, we draw on our experiences to suggest specific ways that administrators can help to keep new teachers'—all teachers'—energy, passion, and knowledge alive.

Know that scripted programs insult our intelligence; they constrain the heights we can reach with our students.

Teaching is intellectual work (Nieto, 2003). Scripted programs are the antithesis of teaching as intellectual work. Sonia Nieto, recognized in 2005 as the National Council of Teachers of English Outstanding Educator in Language Arts, writes about frustrations with scripted programs from her own early teaching days, programs so rigid that they "included not only the daily objectives and lessons that teachers were to cover, but even the very words they were expected to say" (p. 11). Like Julie and Erin in our study, Nieto found that such prescriptions "soon tested my patience and thwarted my creativity" (p. 11). Jonathan Kozol (2005a) aptly labels scripted programs as "intellectual straitjacket[s]" (p. 274).

Linda Darling-Hammond (1997) writes that "a teacher-proof curriculum is also student-proof [because] it ignores the fact that students come to the classroom with different preconceptions, levels of understanding, and styles of learning" (p. 51). She explains that "there is no prepackaged set of steps or lessons that will secure understanding for every learner in the same way" (p. 13) and that "highly prescriptive curriculum inevitably . . . reduce[s] learning to memorizing lower-order skill bites that fail to stimulate and challenge students' aptitudes for thinking and doing" (p. 79). In our study, we also found this to be true. Scripted programs took away the possibility of using and building teacher knowledge and severely limited what we could accomplish with children.

We ask administrators to guard against falling prey to the allure of canned curricula with enticing publicity, compelling jargon, and test score promises that lead to a "stifling uniformity of practice, . . . stripped-down curriculum and instruction devoid of passion and meaning" (Kozol, 2005b, p. 131). If you are worried that students will not learn specific skills within meaning-based practices, allow us to demonstrate how to nurture children's sophistication as inquirers while helping them develop language and computational expertise. If we struggle with this, work with us and other faculty members to develop that knowledge rather than asking us to simply follow someone else's program.

When scripted programs are rigidly mandated, we eventually begin to second-guess ourselves and our ability to teach. When we are told what to do and say, it is difficult to sustain our roles as knowledgeable professionals. We have no avenues for growth. We are robbed of opportunities to use and build knowledge and confidence that would otherwise allow us to contribute in dynamic ways to your schools and to the field of education. Teachers and students become automatons not thinkers, learners, innovators. Eventually, we become battle weary. We lose the energy and the drive to do what it takes to move the profession forward. When we find ourselves in a profession that is nothing like the intellectual community we envisioned it would be, too often we leave.

Stand up with your teachers for what you know is right.

Institutionally, we live in a frustrating time. Directives that result from the governmental love affair with high-stakes tests narrow the realm of what is possible for learners in schools. Deborah Meier (2004) reminds us that "standardized tests measure only a very small portion of what is vital for adult success in contemporary life" (p. 77), and yet we continue to enforce teach-to-the-test programs, excessive testing, and the demeaning practice of publicizing results. In the process, we send confusing messages to new teachers, who often enter the profession with the belief that teaching is about creating contexts for children to develop as human beings who can think critically, pose questions, and seek solutions for the purpose of making the world a better place.

The institutional embracing of high-stakes tests leads to problems that are often at the root of struggle for new teachers. The testing panic leads schools and districts to mandate packaged programs for the purpose of raising test scores in the misguided belief that high scores are correlated with the development of insightful, knowledgeable human beings. New teachers find their beliefs compromised within systems that consistently narrow curricula to address testing needs rather than the needs of each child. They begin to lose faith in their ability to use knowledge of children and of learning to make instructional decisions. Teachers find themselves racing through material at the expense of deeper understandings as they worry that children will not score as well as their peers next door. As Carly writes, too often teachers compromise good teaching when pressured to succeed in the grand competition:

> You worry that you aren't presenting the material in a way that will make it stick in students' heads until test time. You worry that half of them will not care enough to do as well as you know they can do on the test. But worst of all, you agonize that you are selling out your students for the glory of being a teacher praised for high test scores. There is this push for education to become more about winners and losers instead of real learning.

With no evidence that the imposition of high-stakes tests produces "better citizens, neighbors, employers, or college students" (Wood, 2004, p. 44), we ask administrators to stand up with teachers for what you know is right. Work with us to examine the testing craze in which we are currently mired. Engage us in figuring out ways to address testing issues without compromising great teaching. While you stand up with us to ensure that delight and fascination in teaching and learning are not suffocated, help us work to change systems that promote tests that "reflect a shallow kind of learning and at worst indicate only a better ability to take tests" (Wood, 2004, p. 35).

Make time for regular professional study and conversation a priority.

To bring our beliefs to life and continue to grow, we need time for collegial conversation that will help us consider ideas from professional literature and our preservice experiences in the context of our new settings. We need support in evaluating programs and practices so that we can teach within and beyond existing systems without selling out. Simply put, we need time for talk, opportunities to build "critical and long-standing relationships" (Nieto, 2003, p. 78) with our colleagues as we work to define and redefine ourselves as educators.

Members of our group regularly posed questions on our listserv and reflected in ways that could have provided perfect openings for productive collaboration in our schools. In the second year, for example, Julie wrote, "I'd like to watch that video again of Joanne Hindley conducting her writing workshop. I'm not quite sure what to do to make my writing workshop better." Erin wondered, "How can I hold children accountable for my mini-lesson, and what do you do about the kid who wants to conference every day, even when you've given him enough suggestions to last a lifetime?" And Carly asked, "How can I make children better listeners and critics of each other's writing so that I am not the only one in the classroom who is pushing their writing forward?"

During our first years, these kinds of questions were never voiced or heard in our schools. There were no vehicles for regular conversation between like-minded or at least curious colleagues who were intrigued by similar dilemmas. Even though our research group provided support, it was not the same as day-to-day collaboration with dynamic, knowledgeable teachers next door. Remembering the collaborative experience of our graduate program, we wanted more. Erin explained, "During the MAT program, after all of the books we read, I felt like anything was possible. Those readings and discussions geared me up. It is clear to me that the biggest things I'm lacking this year are professional support and interaction."

Not only do we need time for professional conversation, but we also need time and support for experiences that will promote productive talk. Make it possible for us and our experienced colleagues to visit exemplary schools, view professional videotapes, and read professional literature. Provide financial resources to pay for books and trips to national conferences. Build in plenty of time for reflection about implications for our classrooms. Think beyond typical structures to consider creative uses of time in your schools. It does us little good if opportunities for professional conversation are on top of an already overflowing agenda. With a commitment to ongoing professional study, we can work together to figure out ways to embed those opportunities regularly within our school days.

In our experiences, many problems were surmountable when we had this kind of support. When we were on our own, it was easy to feel defeated, incompetent, and confused.

Initiate conversations with us; ask us how things are going and show interest in how and why we do what we do.

You will help us gain the confidence to initiate conversations with you and to share what we are doing in our classrooms if you pave the way. Although we believe that new teachers have the responsibility to open conversations about ideas and issues, we also know that it can be intimidating to initiate such talk. We need administrators to take the lead. Ask us how things are going. Show interest in what we are doing. Ask us to share ideas. If it becomes clear that our ideas are different from yours, share your perspective and encourage us to share ours in interested, open, collegial ways.

Create an atmosphere in which it is safe to take risks.

In many of our situations, it was not customary for teachers to risk exposing vulnerabilities about their own teaching. The prevailing feeling seemed to be that teachers should already *be there*. As a result, some of us experienced an enormous barrier to sustaining and building on our visions of great teaching: We did not feel safe enough to risk examining our own practices—to trust that we could try and fail and try again.

Administrators, your leadership is key to creating an atmosphere that encourages risk-taking. In such an environment, teachers are delighted at the sound of the principal's footsteps coming down the hall. It means that one more interested teacher-learner is about to join us and our students. In such an atmosphere, testing issues are put in perspective, and teachers work to address those issues without feeling pressured or humiliated by the public announcement and reification of scores. In a risk-taking environment, there is room for talk as teachers share data from children's work, read professionally, try new ideas, and then read and try again. A risk-taking environment is one that reveres teachers as experimenters, thinkers, and learners, allowing us to build knowledge so that we can make better instructional decisions for ourselves.

Join us as co-learners.

We were grateful when administrators created structures that allowed us to take risks, study, and grow. It was even more helpful when administrators joined us in the process. When you participate fully as learners, you provide important demonstrations about what it means to be an educator who can't stop learning. Typically, advanced degrees in educational administration include only a few courses in the study of pedagogy or curriculum. Participating in professional study with us allows you to fill that gap. Read and discuss professional literature with us. Jump in and get involved regularly in our classrooms. Take risks with us to try out new ideas with our students. Show a genuine interest in ideas they are pursuing or books they are reading. Engage us the same way. Become a part of and contribute to the exciting buzz of children and teachers learning with one another. We will welcome you as a co-learner. We will look forward to your presence in our classrooms and professional study groups as we teach, reflect, revise, wonder, and learn together.

Celebrate our excitement about innovation; help us see our successes.

Trust that you hired a good teacher and let us soar. Embrace the energy and ideas that new teachers bring. Encourage innovation. Test scores won't suffer because teachers are committed to trying new ways of doing things. Create a culture in which the mutual sharing of innovative ideas is the norm. Help experienced teachers find a supportive balance between sharing their own expertise and valuing new ideas that new teachers might have to offer. Help us respect the experience of our colleagues. Give our new ideas the chance of time. In this way, you help us build on the excitement with which we accepted jobs in your schools. Know that our energy and enthusiasm can be easily destroyed. Be aware of situations that rob us of the optimism, confidence, and energy we need to move forward.

When you drop by our classrooms, focus on and celebrate the positive things going on. Sometimes we do not recognize our own successes. Feeling good about ourselves makes us want to be even better teachers. As Carly wrote:

> It makes such a difference when your administrator celebrates your successes and helps build your confidence by rarely pointing out your weaknesses. That, all by itself, makes you want to be better so you can justify their confidence. Mr. Hightower's comments make me feel like I want to be the phenomenal teacher he says I am. I know there are a lot of weaknesses that he could focus on, but because he doesn't do that, it makes me want to be better and better.

Build an environment defined by positive talk.

Lisa Delpit (2002) asks, "What happens when . . . we convince [children] that they come from brilliance, when we encourage them to understand their amazing potential?" (p. 46). Accept that challenge. Help us look for the brilliance in every child. As new teachers, it was easy to jump to a deficit perspective, looking only at what some children could not do. Overwhelmed and frustrated when we did not know how to engage every child, we found ourselves thinking and saying things about children and parents that we never thought we would say. Sometimes this was fed by a culture of negativity in our schools. We need your help to remain focused on what children *can* do so that we will build curriculum from their successes. Listen to teacher-talk around your school. Notice if the negativity habit seems to have taken hold. Look for signs of negativity—conversations that are punctuated with comments like "That family never reads to their children," "My kids are so low," or "You can't get those parents in the school." Build an environment defined by positive talk.

Encourage positive views of children by making it possible for teachers to reconsider use of time and resources so they can move beyond the school walls to get to know families and communities in new ways. Involve teachers in "cultural immersion activities such as visiting students' homes, exploring their communities, interviewing residents and community leaders, and researching the history of the students' community" (Irvine, 2003, p. 76). Encourage teachers to do this by looking through a new lens, the lens of teacher as learner who sees family and community members as experts in the lives of their children (Volk & Long, 2005). Make time for reflection and conversation that helps us consider implications for day-to-day life in classrooms. Reflect with us about institutional structures that reinforce inequitable practices and that relegate the same children to failure year after year. Do so with the goal of ridding your school of a deficit perspective and a culture of negativity. In the process, you will help us, as new teachers, become more positive-thinking, effective teachers of all children.

Make a caring community foundational to everything else.

We have more energy and desire to go the extra mile and to grow as professionals when we live and work in a caring environment. Principals dedicated to building caring communities made us, our students, and their families feel welcome, knowledgeable, and valued every day. They listened. They were genuinely interested in what was going on in our classrooms. They spent time with us and with children in joyous ways. They put genuine caring first—before test scores, before lunch counts, before accreditation reports. For them, everything else paled in comparison. In a caring community, administrators set the tone for mutual respect.

Building a caring community also means letting us see you as a real person with interests, fears, and fascinations. Sometimes, because of the hectic pace of your job, we see only the side of you that is worried about test scores. Share your own stories of tension and triumph so we can learn from your wisdom and experience. We love Kozol's (2005b) description of a principal who "was a warm and glowing woman who refused to let her natural expressiveness be tightened up by jargon" (p. 168). Recognize that the language you use and your actions throughout the day set the tone for how comfortable we will feel coming to you when we really need to talk.

Get to know us—our values, passions, questions. Let us know that we are not alone. Care about our frustrations. Be available. Create special times when we can chat with you about any question, concern, or idea. Remember Carmen's long talks with her principal, Mr. Ruthsatz? They enrolled in a Spanish class together as a result of discussions about how they could be more helpful to children and families. Their discussions grew out of a mutual commitment to building a caring community.

Give colleagues and mentors time to mentor.

Look creatively at the use of time and people. Figure out how to make time for us to engage in regular, thoughtful conversations with mentors as we learn in one another's classrooms. Consider Carly's thoughts as she looked at mentors through the eyes of an experienced teacher:

> Going back into the classroom, it is more apparent to me that perhaps the biggest challenge we face in terms of mentors, col-

leagues, and administrators has got to be their lack of time to give us what we need as new teachers. Maybe I realize this because many of my administrators, mentors, and colleagues are now also my friends. This helps me see that the willingness is there, but the time is not. Yes, there are always going to be a few unwilling, even nasty, folks. But on the whole, I think they face the same time constraints that we face. Mentors, in particular, are given this extra duty with no real resources, *especially* time. And they are already loaded down with the other responsibilities that go along with being a veteran teacher: committee chairs, technology specialists, leadership team members, grade-level chairs, curriculum chairs, and the list goes on.

Provide opportunities for mentors and new teachers to get away from school to get to know each other as human beings. Mentors and new teachers could meet for long breakfasts while administrators take their classes, or they might be given time once a month for a long lunch together. Fund substitutes to cover classes one morning or afternoon a week so that mentors and new teachers can spend time together. The Partners in Education program in Boulder, Colorado, is one of many that sees time as a critical factor in successful mentorships in which "mentors are fully released from their own classrooms to concentrate on the needs of their inductees, . . . assist[ing] novice teachers in setting up their classroom routines, forming relations with parents, and other initial preparations. Mentors subsequently work with teachers in their classrooms each week all year" (Kelley, 2004, p. 442).

Making time for mentoring requires careful planning and juggling of resources, but it can give energy to, rather than sap energy from, both mentor and new teacher. (Please see the section in this chapter written directly to mentors for further suggestions.)

Simplify our lives.

Turn meetings into explorations of ideas; we can read announcements in a memo. Remember that meetings don't always have to have an agenda; ask us what we want to talk about. Plan fewer meetings, but, when meetings, paperwork, and reports can't be avoided, let us know in advance so we can anticipate and plan for them, particularly during the planning days before school starts. Experienced teachers know what to expect. As new teachers, we assumed that those days would be spent working in our rooms. We were surprised to find out otherwise. Resist adding more to our to-do lists. Hand over responsibilities a few at a time with lots of support.

Enjoy kids and us.

Remember why you went into education in the first place. Help us hang on to the same joy and conviction. Know that, just like you, we entered the profession to make a difference, but also like you, we came to teaching with a crazy mixture of confidence and insecurity—charged up to change the world but unsure about what was in store for us. Support our excitement as well as our nervousness. Show us every day that schools are wonderful places to be. Enjoy children and us. Laugh a lot.

To Colleagues

> Felicia has always been so patient with me. She is, by far, everyone's favorite choice for support. Hers is the room where a crowd of teachers are always gabbing about this or that. I feel guilty sometimes always using her as my go-to girl because I know she is that for everyone else. Felicia is, however, always ready with a smile and she's just—always there. Her passion for teaching is unmatched and it often keeps her at school late into the evening despite the number of years under her belt. She'll tell you humbly that it's because she's so disorganized and far behind, but if you ask her for ideas about any subject, she knows exactly where to find the perfect thing. She's been this way from the first day I stepped into the school six years ago.

Felicia is a remarkable colleague. Carly doesn't take her for granted. So many of her attributes are those that were basic to supporting us as new teachers—helping us learn the ropes, making us feel welcome and at home, and simply being there. Colleagues, we need you very, very much. If we do not have you to support us in times of frustration, confusion, and triumph, we are lost. You are one of the most important keys to our success. During our first years, we were endlessly grateful to teachers next door and colleagues down the hall who supported us, cheered us on, and sometimes even dried our tears. We were devastated by those who shut us out, ridiculed our work, and talked behind our backs.

Reassure us that we're doing okay, that we're not alone.

Ladson-Billings (2001) writes that "new teachers are among the most vulnerable professionals in schools; they need to be nurtured and supported in the profession" (p. 23). We were no exception. Heading into our first jobs, we didn't realize just how vulnerable we would feel nor how much nurturing we would need. We longed for reassurance that we were okay, that we were still good teachers even when lessons flopped and our classrooms did not hum with the sounds of engaged and delighted children every minute of every day. We needed reassurance that we were not alone and that our struggles were also experienced by veteran teachers. We needed interactions with other teachers who would help us develop strategies to use in moving beyond those struggles. In earlier chapters, Susi wrote about Phyllis, her friend and colleague who gave unconditional emotional as well as pedagogical support during Susi's first years of teaching. Phyllis had a way of making Susi feel that she was a great teacher, even at her lowest moments. Every new teacher needs his or her own Phyllis—someone who teaches next door or down the hall who can provide validation of our feelings, a sympathetic ear, and mutually supportive and respectful dialogue. As Robbie wrote, "Sometimes when we are at our lowest, we don't want to know how someone else does something successfully, we just want to know that someone who understands is listening, just listening."

Offer assistance that builds from what we are doing well.

Support from colleagues in its highest form was not telling us what to do, but talking through possible solutions to problems while helping us feel good about ourselves as teachers and learners. Some of us were so overwhelmed that we struggled to see anything we did as significant. We needed someone to help us value baby steps as big successes. Experienced teachers, as you notice new teachers' struggles, offer assistance that builds from what we are doing well. If our teaching styles and philosophies differ from yours, respect our views while helping us learn to respect other ways of teaching. Be sensitive to comments that might unintentionally degrade or make fun of the ideas we are trying. We know that you don't intend to degrade, but sometimes our insecurities lead us to hear you in that way. Even when we struggle, find something wonderful about our classrooms and our teaching. Compliment us. We'll learn more if we feel that others see potential in us and that we can build on success.

Protect our time.

We were also grateful when colleagues protected our time. When volunteers were requested for various school tasks, committee responsibilities, and other jobs that would add too much to our lives, some colleagues looked out for us by jumping in to volunteer themselves. In at least one situation, the reverse occurred:

> In our grade-level meeting, the team leader said that one of us
> had to volunteer to tutor children after school. Of course, no one

said anything. We're all bogged down as it is, but she said, "Well, someone has to do it. I can't take on anything else right now so it has to be one of you." It felt like she locked her eyes right on the two first-year teachers. What were we supposed to do? Now we're doing tutoring every day after school.

These kinds of examples are, unfortunately, not uncommon. You can help by working with teachers and administrators to create a sane division of obligations for everyone.

Know that we can collaborate even when our views are different.

Donald Graves (2001) writes that "listening to a colleague does not necessarily mean agreeing" (p. 65). Many of us learned to appreciate this firsthand. Ami writes about working during her first year with an extremely supportive yet philosophically different first-grade team: "The first-grade team has been a fabulous support. We are very different, but we care about and support each other professionally. We collaborate, share success stories and frustrations, and are always there for one another as friends."

Collaboration with colleagues can be an incredibly supportive experience even when we teach differently. Share teaching ideas in the spirit of collaboration, not indoctrination. Express interest in our ideas and maybe even try a few of them in your own classrooms while we try some of yours. We can learn from one another as we support one another's right to different beliefs. Together we can share, question, and find joy in one another as people who love working with children.

Steer us away from negativity.

Project a positive view of teaching and help us find the positive in every child. While not diminishing the struggles, help us focus on what is wonderful about being a teacher, about individual children, about the school, and about the profession. Steer us away from negativity. Work to change the teachers' lounge culture that often thrives on an "I have it so bad" mentality. When you see us heading down the negativity path, validate our distress, but then help us find and focus on what we can appreciate and admire about the children who worry us the most. Help us use that positive outlook to move forward in addressing challenges.

If you are teaching behind closed doors, let us know you're there.

Remember Erin's first year of teaching? Because of rigid mandates in her school, much of the innovative teaching that was going on was happening behind closed doors. The year was almost over before she found out that some experienced teachers were reaching beyond the scripted program to implement more interesting practices. If you are teaching "underground" or below the radar screen, let us know you're there. We will feel alone if the practices we hope to employ do not appear to be typical in our school. You can make a tremendous difference in our teaching lives if you let us know there is more to the school than meets the eye.

Look out for us; be a friend.

It was extremely comforting when colleagues looked out for us. "Looking out" came in many forms. Some colleagues regularly stopped by our rooms simply to ask how things were going. Some offered to include our classes in field studies and special days. Some helped us understand the logistics of the school day, office procedures, and paperwork. Chat with us about how you balance home and school. Your advice helps.

We know that you are busy with your own work and life, but we would love to get to know you over a meal, a drink, or a cup of coffee. We may be a little uncomfortable asking. Invite us. Be kind. Be a friend.

A Few Words for Mentors and Directors of Induction Programs

Allow mentorships to evolve as teachers get to know each other.

For us, true mentorships evolved from relationships between professionals who respected each other. Occasionally, assigned mentors provided the support we needed, but more often, real mentors grew through associations that began with mutual interests. We wonder if it's more realistic to think of assigning someone as a new teacher's *guide* for the first few weeks, someone who knows the ropes and can help new teachers with logistics such as learning how to get around the school, negotiating paperwork, and understanding procedures. Then, through well-planned opportunities for new and experienced teachers to explore pedagogical questions and to talk informally, new teachers and their colleagues could gravitate toward more natural mentoring relationships that would result in a more productive fit.

Mentors should be teachers dedicated to staying on the cutting edge.

As described in Chapter 6, our mentors were very kind, but few expressed interest in professional study. We know this does not need to be the case. A description of the Partners in Education program mentioned earlier outlines some of the elements that we felt were missing in our experiences: "Mentors are chosen for their demonstrated teaching excellence, dispositions toward collaboration and inquiry, commitment to professional growth and change" (Kelley, 2004, p. 442).

Carmen wrote that mentors should be teachers who are dedicated to "staying on the cutting edge," who are familiar with current professional literature or who are at least interested in exploring it. We hope that mentors are chosen or volunteer for the right reasons—because they sincerely want to support, teach, and learn with new teachers; because they want to share their wisdom but continue to grow as well.

Induction programs should build from the assumption that teaching is an intellectual pursuit.

In our state, work is currently being done to develop more effective state and district induction programs. During our first years, however, our evaluation of programs designed to induct us into the profession were not positive. When asked what suggestions we would make to improve these programs, our answer was to eliminate them or change them drastically. A tongue-in-cheek recommendation was to "take the money and send new teachers to a spa." Although that solution is a bit cynical, it is not as far-fetched as it might seem. Providing an arena and support for new teachers to relax and laugh together, to build joy in relationships, and to talk about issues that matter to them is key. We wanted someone to listen to us and to design support from what we wanted and needed to talk about. At best, our induction programs provided Band-Aid solutions to complex problems. A tips-for-teachers approach can be helpful in the short term, but it is only a stopgap measure and perpetuates the notion that teaching is a superficial profession.

The quality of induction experiences seems to vary widely across the country. An example of a highly regarded program is Great Beginnings in Fairfax County, Virginia. The program builds from the assumption that teaching is an intellectual pursuit and that learning to teach requires ongoing, thoughtful interaction between peers (Auton, Berry, Mullen, & Cochran, 2002). New teachers are supported in cohorts, coached by experienced teachers from other schools, and mentored by teachers in their own schools. Coaches are chosen through a selective interview process. The program includes monetary compensation as well as time to mentor. Mentors receive five days of release time to spend with new teachers in classrooms and an annual stipend of $2,500–$3,000.

Mentorship and induction experiences like these treat new teachers as professionals who are interested in both theory and practice. Such programs also see the learning-teaching relationship as reciprocal. New teachers and mentors learn from and with each other. We see this as essential to building the confidence, optimism, and strength it takes to succeed not only as a new teacher but also as a school.

To Universities (Undergraduate and Graduate Teacher Education Programs)

Make the process and the challenges visible.

By the end of her second year, Julie had a piece of advice for university instructors: "Don't paint a rosy picture. Don't portray teaching to be just like what you read in professional books. It sets teachers up to feel like failures when they don't think they have met that mark." When we left our preservice program, we knew there would be challenges, but we thought we could successfully create contexts that engaged every child and moved children consistently forward, contexts that would allow us to look across the classroom and see fascinated inquirers at work all the time. We were easily seduced into expecting too much too soon, and we were certainly not equipped to deal with opposition to our ideas and dreams. Our data helped Susi see that, while it was important to send new teachers out with a vision of what is possible, that vision can become debilitating when it is not tempered by an understanding that the reflective nature of teaching can be difficult and frustrating at times. As Robbie wrote, it's easy for new teachers to come away with the feeling that everything comes effortlessly to great teachers:

> We looked up to experienced teachers who have all that know-how, and what seems like ease of teaching, and we want to be those teachers right away. We didn't think about all the struggles they went through to get where they are. We didn't think about all the times they tried something, threw it in the trash, went back to it, threw it in the trash, then *finally* figured it out. I think that sometimes we overemphasized the good things, without talking about some of the struggles, but I also think that we needed something to strive for.

While we would not want Susi or others in her position to change their stance about what is possible, we wonder how universities might equip us to deal with realities that challenge our knowledge. A greater emphasis on the process and potential barriers would help. Robbie suggested:

> One thing the university could do is to be explicit by saying things like, "I want you to see this video and afterward talk about how

teachers in videos and books might have gotten to that point."
Or, "What might the other children be doing as the teacher meets
with this child?" Then talk about how you might articulate the
importance of a strategy or structure when mandates might dictate otherwise.

Take us to visit classrooms where we can see innovative practices
at work. It helps us envision the possible. As Carly wrote, "I am encouraged by the fact that the schools we visited were so successful with inquiry. It gives me a goal. I know I can succeed and grow as an educator
once I get it all figured out." At the same time, use visits as opportunities for us to gain insights into ways that experienced teachers deal with
challenges. Encourage us to ask questions that will help us think about
process, about the realities of trial and error. From great teachers, we
wanted to know: How did you begin? What challenges did you face and
do you continue to face as you work to bring your teaching dreams to
life? How do you overcome these challenges?

We also need to understand how to negotiate within, while working to change, systems that may reflect little of our professional beliefs.
Create opportunities for us to ask great teachers questions such as: How
do you deal with district and/or school mandates that are antithetical
to your belief system? How do you address testing pressures? How do
you give letter and numerical grades using authentic forms of assessment? How do you teach within standards-based systems?

We can also learn about challenge and process by reading care-
fully selected texts. A few that make the challenges visible include Tim
O'Keefe's "Letter from a Teacher" (Mills, O'Keefe, & Jennings, 2004),
Nieto's (2003) *What Keeps Teachers Going?*, Dudley-Marling's (1997) *Liv-
ing with Uncertainty: The Messy Reality of Classroom Practice*; Ray's (2001)
*The Writing Workshop: Working through the Hard Parts (and They're All Hard
Parts)*, and Hankins's (2003) *Teaching through the Storm: A Journal of Hope.*

Help us learn how we might work within existing programs without compromising our beliefs.

Create specific engagements that support us in using our knowledge
of theory and practice to evaluate and work within and beyond required
or typically used programs in schools. Help us articulate how such programs and practices do or do not measure up to what we have come to
understand about teaching and learning. If they don't measure up, help
us develop strategies for bringing our knowledge, style, and voice to
existing programs while working to change or eliminate those that de-
tract from opportunities for thoughtful learning. In other words, pro-

vide structured opportunities through which we might consider ways to create the classrooms we envision in the midst of contradictory programs and mandates while taking action to effect change. At the same time, let us know that some mandates may be myths. Guide us in learning to distinguish between the two—to get to the bottom of the "they say" comments we will hear.

Explore strategies that allow us to support children as competent test takers while not compromising our beliefs about teaching and learning.

High-stakes testing issues came up again and again in this study and continue to be a serious issue in our lives as experienced teachers. As new teachers, we felt fairly confident in our ability to articulate reasons why tests of skills in isolation do not effectively measure student knowledge, and we could explain why those kinds of assessments provide little information that supports us in helping individual children. We understood that a focus on such tests detracts from curricula that help students grow in the ability to "make connections, find new patterns, and imagine new possibilities" (former New York Commissioner of Education Thomas Sobol, quoted in Kozol, 2005b, p. 131). But we did not know how to help children transfer knowledge learned in more thoughtful contexts to the testing genre. As a result, it was easy to fall into the trap of thinking that teaching to the test was the only way to help children succeed on them. While we work to change the high-stakes testing culture, we have a responsibility to ensure that every child can succeed on tests that often open doors to further opportunity. We can do this without compromising our beliefs and without allowing testing issues to dominate our teaching. Help us understand how to show children that they know a lot, and that their knowledge can be used in many ways, one of which is to answer questions on tests. Support us in developing ways to explore, with our students, the testing genre and its emotional, political, and societal ramifications, just as we might study poetry, biography, informational texts, and so on.

Encourage us to take it easy and to let go of the guilt.

University programs could also caution us to take it easy—to be comfortable selecting a couple of curricular structures to understand well during the first year of teaching before venturing further. At graduation, we knew we should take things slowly, but it was easy to lose sight of that advice once we were in our own classrooms. In her first months,

Carly wrote, "I'm impatient, and even though I learned last year that it takes practice, practice, practice and then you still never quite get there, I want to skip all this preliminary junk and get right to the meat of teaching and learning. I want it all so badly, right away, right now!!"

If becoming comfortable with one curricular structure at a time means using worksheets or some other temporary measure while we work to understand some other aspect of the school day, help us to let go of the associated guilt. When some of us used worksheets as a stopgap measure, Susi pointed out that our disappointment in ourselves demonstrated that we had not succumbed completely to the worksheet culture around us. She wrote, "You know, the worksheet thing is not that big of a deal, because you are so aware of what you're doing and why. You realize that kids aren't learning from worksheets and that's huge." We knew Susi wasn't advocating the use of worksheets forever, but it relieved some of the pressure to know that she didn't think we had sold out if we used a worksheet or two in the beginning.

At the same time, help us see that alternatives to worksheets are about developing a way of life in classrooms rather than creating elaborate "activities" every day. Susi didn't realize until very late in this study that we left the university with the impression that the most effective practices require hours and hours of preparation. As a result, it was easy to fall into the trap of resorting to worksheets when we were tired or in the process of figuring out a new approach. Help us see that there are more productive ways to take a deep breath—giving students more time to read and talk about texts related to a focus of study, for example, giving them more time to read books they love, or simply settling in for a few more read-alouds that day.

Help us begin to think about how to pin down the whirling ideas with which we leave our preservice programs.

We realize that we cannot design our future classrooms during the preservice program because we do not yet know our students, their families, and the school in which we'll be teaching, but it would be helpful to have support for beginning to organize ideas before we leave the university. We don't mean planning hypothetical units or lessons—those are not helpful. They are artificial and arbitrary and have nothing to do with the children we will come to know. But we could begin to think about how our classroom might look and how we might incorporate key structures and strategies into the first weeks of school. We might decide on a few structures with which to begin the year and then create a priority list, including resources that will help us when we are ready to venture further. Carmen wrote, "I wish the university had asked me to plan a possible first day or how I would set up my classroom as a part of my portfolio. Instead, I just let a thousand ideas swirl around in my head." Provide opportunities for interns to collect data in a variety of classrooms and from a range of professional literature about ways that different teachers organize time, space, people, and ideas. Then create structures through which we might use those data, in conjunction with our own growing knowledge, to begin to envision possibilities for ourselves.

Support us in learning how to find funding.

As we rummaged for bookcases, plastic bins, pillows, and rocking chairs for our first classrooms, funding was a problem. For most of us, the money came out of our pockets or we went without. During our first years, many of us learned about seeking grants to fund materials such as sets of books for literature discussion groups, throwaway cameras for home and community projects, and so on. As we entered our first classrooms, however, we didn't have a clue about the resources available to fund our dreams. Learning to write grant proposals and becoming familiar with a variety of funding sources (often through state departments of education, local television stations, and online) could be a helpful addition to the preservice experience.

Help us better understand and value worlds beyond our own.

During graduate school, we read about the importance of recognizing and honoring difference. We wrote at length in journal responses to *The Dreamkeepers*, a text that introduced us to the notion of "culturally relevant methods" (Ladson-Billings, 1994, p. 25). We were drawn to ideas like the importance of "taking care not to ignore color [as the beginning of] the journey toward acknowledging and valuing difference" (p. 31). We articulated these ideas in our comprehensive exams. But we left the university with superficial understandings of what it means to seek and value multiple perspectives and varied ways of knowing. We didn't know what it all meant day to day for our classrooms.

   We now wonder how deeper explorations of lives beyond our own and consideration of implications for the classroom might have helped us in the struggle to engage every child. When other studies of new teachers suggest that connecting with parents is one of the most frequently cited challenges (Alliance for Excellence in Education, 2004, p. 12), this seems even more important. Making that connection, however, means something very different from "getting parents in" or "teaching them to help their children." It means moving beyond the school walls to learn from and with family and community members. Professional literature is just beginning to suggest ways in which schools might work with communities so they can learn from each other (Botelho, Turner, & Wright, 2006; Boutte & Hill, 2006; Compton-Lilly, 2004; Jacobson, 2003). For many preservice (and inservice) teachers, this may represent a new and somewhat uncomfortable way of thinking— to acknowledge the importance of going beyond our own worlds to better understand and validate communities different from our own. But teacher education programs can work to change that norm. It means encouraging "student teachers to look outside of themselves" (Schultz, 2003, p. 11) as they ask, What can I discover by putting myself in the position of learner in homes and communities? What might that mean in terms of my ability to engage every child and connect with every parent?

Help student teachers work with teachers in schools to think beyond the typical home visit. Create opportunities for them to learn about how children and families use language and literacies, what they value, what concerns them, what brings them joy, and the funds of knowledge and networks of support they use to get along in the world (González, Moll, & Amanti, 2005). Help interns look for the other teachers in children's lives and consider what schools might learn from the ways these other teachers support learning in homes and communities (Gregory, Long, & Volk, 2004). Create structures through which preservice teachers begin to value difference rather than default to narrower views of what constitutes right and wrong (Sleeter, 2001; Villegas & Lucas, 2002). Help them use their learning to counter inaccurate assumptions about children and families too often perpetuated in teachers' lounge conversations based on limited knowledge or narrow perspectives about difference.

Jonathan Sacks (2002) writes that "difference does not diminish, it enlarges the sphere of human possibilities" (p. 209). Universities can do a better job of creating opportunities to examine that wisdom in light of its potential for constructing environments that will help us understand, value, and engage all children.

Explore with us complex definitions of building community.

Dudley-Marling (1997) writes about his realization that, as a university professor going back into the classroom, his initial attempts to build community "were based on simplistic, arrogant, and, perhaps, dangerous assumptions about the meaning of community" (p. 3). Similarly, we see how easy it may be to come away from preservice programs with a rather romanticized view of what it means to build classroom community. Excited and touched by the impact of community-building strategies we enjoy, we may not pay close enough attention to how our professors deal with more difficult issues as teachers. It will be helpful if you make visible the ways you work through conflict, concern, and frustration as issues emerge in our courses with you. As we venture into talk about valuing worlds beyond our own, for example, it is likely that we will encounter conflicting perspectives. Help us use moments like these as opportunities to define communities as inclusive of disagreement and difference as well as of happy stories and shared experience. Point out ways we work through the chaos of misunderstanding. Alert us to the silenced voices within the group and invite them in. Bring in classroom teachers to share how they do the same with their students. In this way, you will better prepare us to address similar realities within the beautifully complex groups of students we will learn to love. A few resources, among many, that may be helpful for university educators as they consider these issues include bell hooks's (2003) *Teaching Community*; Fine and Weis's (2003) *Silenced Voices and Extraordinary Conversations*; Irvine's (2003) *Educating Teachers for Diversity*; and Cochran-Smith's (2004) *Walking the Road*.

Help us build knowledge and learn how to use it while not reifying it.

As we grew to recognize our political voices, we realized how lucky we were to have theoretical as well practical knowledge to use in justifying our views to others. Like the interns in Harste and colleagues' (2004) study, we found that we could be more "effective change agents [when we] used theory as a vision of what might be" (p. 27). We felt fortunate to have theoretical understandings from which to draw when we were faced with conflicting programs and practices. Our theoretical understandings also helped us generate curriculum and extend possibilities beyond those we read about in professional texts.

At the same time, we realized the importance of not standardizing any body of knowledge as a set of "incontestable truths" (Nieto, 2003, p. 90). As we learn about theory and practice, it's easy to lock in ideas as finite rights and wrongs rather than as interpretations and perspectives that will change as we come to know more. Erin explained, "My first year, I saw the world as this way or that. It had to be either a scripted program or meaning-based teaching. The world to me was perceived as a straight line, and I felt I was headed in the wrong direction." We hope universities will help students look at any idea critically. Susi wrote:

> A few years ago, I began to wonder if my teaching was just one more prescription. How different was it from the packaged programs that teachers meet in schools? At one point, it began to feel as though I was sharing the same litany of ideas year after year. It's my job to grow as new understandings enter the field, but do I make the tentative nature of my own learning visible to my students—or the fact that mine is but one perspective? Because of my work with you guys, I want to do a better job of encouraging university students to consider any text, idea, or concept with a critical eye as opposed to buying into even my party line without question and to know that while I believe there are some ideas that will probably always be fundamentally important for each of us, every idea is fluid and subject to change.

Help us with the job search beyond cheering us on and writing references.

When we came together for meetings the summer after graduation, everyone shared their latest job interview stories. There was a sense of excitement but also of urgency: "What if I don't get a job?" Susi worried that such urgency might cause us to make decisions we would regret, but she didn't say much to that effect. She wonders now why she didn't play more of a role beyond staging mock interviews, writing recommendations, and cheering us on. It would have been helpful to have practiced listening to interview rhetoric—language that administrators often use to describe programs and expectations—and developed questions that would help us get beneath the rhetoric. The Job Seekers section of this chapter could be used by university faculty to help us ask better questions, interpret answers, and ask probing follow-up questions.

Don't drop us at the schoolhouse door.

The support we felt from our research group convinced us that contact with the university should not stop at graduation. The continued presence of familiar faces and our shared pedagogical history provided continuity, a place where we could touch base as we negotiated new worlds. For several of us, the presence of our group kept us from giving up entirely. It gave us a community when, as Ami said, "too many teachers have to walk alone a lot of the time." Erin wrote, "Crucial to being able to implement my beliefs was the strong professional connection I maintained with our research group. This kept me in the loop and allowed me to stay afloat amid frustrations." We believe strongly that universities need to figure out ways to systematically maintain strong connections to graduates. As Robbie pointed out, "If the university expects students to take away any of the latest and greatest knowledge of teaching and keep it, they can't just drop us as we enter the classroom." Even something as simple as co-creating—with preservice teachers—a list of readings could provide a helpful beginning. Ami explained, "That way, new teachers would have a list that they can pick up when they are ready to try something new. That would be a great way to continue to grow. It's hard to know where to begin." Carmen recommended stronger liaison relationships between the university, new teachers, and public schools to provide support for everyone involved:

> What if you had a person from the preservice program as a mentor, like your internship supervisor? What if that person followed you into your first year? That way, they would be familiar with your student teaching experiences and philosophies and they would be able to guide you through your first year.

Robbie suggested a listserv connection: "After graduation, you could start a listserv. This would be a means of keeping new teachers in touch with a university liaison and peers, people you are already familiar with. Graduates already feel comfortable letting each other see their vulnerabilities, whereas they may not be as apt to share with new people. Plus you have the added bonus of shared beliefs."

Learn about our experiences as we leave the university and during our first years of teaching. Use those data to not only revise preservice programs but also continue your involvement with us. Carmen explained:

> It is imperative to show that you care about us in the same way that we are expected to show our students that we care. I remember filling out a questionnaire at the end of the program, but that is not enough. That is paper. Graduates need support when they leave the university, because we have to walk alone a lot of times. We're out there with no sense of direction. Maybe we should have to meet at least once a month for the first school year to complete the program. We could get regular teacher's pay and then adjust it to the master's degree level at the end of that year.

There are, of course, challenges to such plans. How would university structures have to change to make a place for collaborative relationships with schools so they are not superficial or merely rhetorical?

When there are few university faculty and many graduates, what systems could be created to maintain contact sensibly? But by not abandoning us, everyone benefits. It's worth figuring out.

Get involved at the school and district administrative levels.

We believe that an enormous difference could be made if universities developed closer relationships with school and district leaders—if they worked together regularly to examine issues of theory and practice. Often university faculty members are involved in the exploration of pedagogy with teachers but rarely with school and district administration. Such collaboration could result in important insights and actions for all parties—and in better support for new and experienced teachers.

To Internship Coordinators (university profs, please read this too)

Remember that internship placements matter *a lot*.

Our internship placements had a tremendous effect on our ability to internalize ideas we read about in professional texts *and* to make those practices our own during our first years of teaching. But in some instances, systems for selecting student teaching placements seemed, as McCann and colleagues (2005) write, "rather haphazard" (p. 131). We struggled when we were placed with teachers who were not interested in their own continued growth. One group member wrote, "My internship experience was not a good one. I missed out on so much. I felt cheated. They have got to put interns into classrooms that have quality teachers." Another wrote, "Student teachers should be placed in classrooms where teachers are aware and supportive of new teaching strategies that the intern may bring into the classroom. I would love to see coaching teachers learning along with the student teachers." We learned little in classrooms where teachers "enforced worksheet after worksheet and ridiculed the practices we hoped to implement." We were the most successful when we were placed with teachers who were learners themselves, who "loved and respected children [and] encouraged them to take risks and to learn from one another" (Mills et al., 2004, p. 160). Internship placements also had an impact on our ability, as new teachers, to hang on to our beliefs, remain committed to ongoing professional learning, and persevere in spite of challenges. One group member wrote, "Internship placement has got to be one of the most important facets of the program, and it is not being taken seriously enough."

Put us with teachers who welcome us and encourage us to try new ideas.

One of the keys to successful internships had to do with our coaching teachers' welcoming stance and encouragement to try new ideas even if those ideas were different from typical practice in their classrooms. Erin writes about how her coaching teacher's warm welcome made a real difference in her level of confidence. Betty LeClair's kindness and thoughtful attention helped Erin feel immediately at home. Betty's welcoming stance included her openness to letting Erin try new ideas. Erin wrote about how this made an important difference in her growth as a teacher:

> Seven years after my semester in her classroom, I ran into my coaching teacher in the grocery store. She seemed happy to see me and, in a brief conversation, we caught up on life in general. I sent her a birth announcement after Livie arrived. She sent me a beautiful card with a personal note. It reminded me of how she opened her arms to me the year I was student teaching. The first thing she did was devote a small table near her desk for me to use. This seemingly small gesture showed her respect for the work I was doing. She gave me freedom to complete my assignments and thus grow as a preservice teacher.

When we were given opportunities to experiment with room arrangements, strategies for building community, use of time and space, and specific curricular structures, theory became real. Carly wrote: "I began to see that these theories and strategies really worked and weren't something I was just having to read for class." In such settings, we were able to make connections that we couldn't have made otherwise. Erin said, "Had I been in a classroom where I wasn't allowed the freedom to experiment like this, I would have never gotten a real feel for how what we were learning and reading affected actual teaching."

We learn important lessons from teachers who are excited about their own learning.

Another hugely supportive quality in internship placements was the excitement that teachers had for growing along with us. For those of us placed with teachers who read current professional literature, used their observations of and interactions with children to inform instruction, and consistently questioned their own practice, the advantage was great. Witnessing teachers' commitment to ongoing growth was an important learning experience in itself. Robbie wrote:

> Both of my coaching teachers taught me a lot about the importance of continuing my own professional growth. Both of them

actively pursued new ideas and tried what they learned. It was good for me to observe their transition in thinking as they transformed their classroom practice. It allowed them to be open to me trying new things, and it made me feel better to see that experienced teachers become frustrated by not knowing exactly how some new ideas will turn out. Their openness to my ideas and willingness to allow me to fail gave me the experience I needed.

Put us in internship classrooms where we can learn from and with educators who teach based on knowledge of theory, practice, and knowing children well; are excited about working with interns; will take time to talk, study, and figure things out with us; and know how to address mandates without selling their soul. Place us with teachers who will invite us into the processes of their own learning and talk with us about how they deal with challenges on a day-to-day basis.

Teachers who live the ideas we are studying make a huge impact.

Placements with teachers who lived the ideas we were studying allowed us to deepen understandings while gaining the confidence to sustain and then build on that knowledge once we were in our own classrooms. Ami explained, "During my internship, I learned how to incorporate all the fabulous ideas from graduate school. Each idea was then tweaked and used in my own classroom my very first year." We left such internships able to say, "I've seen what this is like in practice; I know it can work; I've worked with teachers who value and persevere with these ideas, so I can do it too." When this wasn't the case, the experience could be pleasant, but we missed the kinds of collegial conversations we might have had. Another group member explained:

> As an intern, I was paired with two teachers who made my experience fairly pleasurable, though I worried about what they thought of me as a teacher. Since they taught differently from what I wanted to try, I wondered if they were really able to see my knowledge and passion. They supported me by allowing me to try new and different things with their children, but they were not able to offer much advice. Neither of my cooperating teachers had the same knowledge base I had.

Placements in classrooms in which practices were philosophically incongruent with those we studied in the university classroom *and* in which coaching teachers demonstrated little enthusiasm for new ideas meant that it was difficult to develop the understanding and confidence necessary to sustain learning as we moved into our own classrooms. Those internship experiences were disappointing and disheartening. One group member wrote:

I still do not understand why I was placed in a classroom with someone who was definitely not in touch with anything that was new in education. So there I was, expected to come out of there ready to teach. But I wasn't learning. I was actually losing ground as I was in the program. She never asked about what I was learning. She lifted her brow more times than enough, and I didn't feel the support that would give me the confidence I needed to try what I was learning. Yeah, I tried some things, but support is everything and so is modeling. I do feel the program failed me in that respect. It could have been avoided. They didn't take the measures necessary to see what that teacher's beliefs were. Her beliefs should have sent up a red flag. I kept all of this to myself and just waded through the experience. However, the frustration came from me not learning anything from her. My yearning to learn was not being fed.

We receive important demonstrations from teachers who know how to find the positive in every child.

Put us with teachers who are kind to children, who love teaching and learning, and who look at children and families with a positive spirit rather than from a deficit perspective. Often before we realize it, a deficit view can creep into our approach to teaching. Teachers in our internship classrooms can set a positive or negative tone that will stay with us throughout our careers. Please put interns with teachers who refuse to buy into the "I have all the low kids" and "That family" trap. It will make an important difference in the kind of educators we become.

To Job Seekers

Job seekers, you recently left the comfort of a preservice program ready to make a new life in a new learning environment, your very own classroom. It is an exciting and yet nerve-wracking time, but you can approach the job search and interviews in ways that will have a positive impact on your first years in the classroom.

Relax; do your homework.

First, know that, if you are worth your salt, it is very likely that you *will* get a job. So relax. Second, do your homework. Find out about districts and the schools from a variety of sources, including parents and other teachers. Ask: What is the reputation of the district and school in terms of strict mandates? Are mandates perceived or real? What do parents like or dislike about the school? Third, take your time. Pay attention. Look for a school where your views will be respected. That does not necessarily mean a school that enacts all you have learned; it does mean a place where good teaching is closely tied to ongoing professional learning. Most important, look for a school where it is easy to detect, as Kozol (2005b) writes, a real "happiness in *being* with children" (p. 286).

Look beneath the surface.

To find such a school, you have to look beneath the surface. Remember that the potential for difficult situations was easy for many of us to miss or to ignore in job interviews. Excited, full of hope, and anxious to find jobs, we didn't probe beneath administrators' use of professional language that, on the surface, sounded encouraging. Our optimism sometimes kept us from listening critically or from believing what we heard. Don't make the same mistakes. Ask principals and teachers about their belief systems. During interviews, listen—really listen—with discerning ears, eyes, heart, and intellect. Don't allow your panic about finding a job to override your intuition. Feel comfortable telephoning teachers and engaging them in conversations about their autonomy, the school's philosophy and goals, collaboration, pressure to conform, opportunities to study and grow as professionals, and the attitudes of staff toward one another, administrators, and the children. Interview principals and think about what they say. Look and listen with a critical eye.

Look for a teaching position in a school where teachers "give energy to each other" (Graves, 2001, p. 3). Don't settle for less than what you are looking for. As Ami wrote, "Follow your gut and don't go into a school where you will feel repressed. There are some phenomenal schools out there. Take your time and find your best match."

A Few More Thoughts for Job Seekers

Before the interview

- Practice articulating—out loud—your vision for a dynamic classroom and specific beliefs about teaching and learning that support that vision. Back up your beliefs by demonstrating your knowledge of respected research and connecting it explicitly to the practices you hope to put into place.
- Think about what makes you special for kids and classrooms. What do you bring to education that can make a difference in a child's life and in the life of a school?
- Find out about school- and district-mandated programs; be prepared to describe how you will use your knowledge to work within and beyond them without compromising your convictions.

- Check out state and district standards and standardized tests; be prepared to explain how thoughtful practices address those standards and support successful test taking.
- Prepare questions to ask of *both* teachers and administrators, questions such as:
  - ◆ I see that the district has _____ program. How is this program used in your school?
  - ◆ How much autonomy will I have to create curriculum based on children's needs and interests and on my professional knowledge?
  - ◆ How is teacher knowledge nurtured at this school? What opportunities are provided for ongoing professional study and interaction?
  - ◆ What kind of funding is provided for attending professional conferences? For subscribing to professional journals? For visiting exemplary schools?
  - ◆ What do you value and appreciate about your students, their families, and the community?

During the interview

- Smile. Relax. They're going to love you!
- Present your beliefs honestly; acknowledge that your aim is to continue to learn and grow.
- If teachers are involved in the interview, pay attention to how they interact with one another and with the principal. This can tell you a lot about how teachers are respected and treated.
- Get beneath the rhetoric. Ask for clarification and deeper explanations. For example, ask what is meant when administrators use language such as "child-centered curriculum," "our population needs structure," "we follow the reading program," and "skill teaching."
- Ask the principal to take you on a tour of the school; on the tour, consider:
  - ◆ Are doors open?
  - ◆ Is there a warm feeling of welcome as you walk down the halls?
  - ◆ Is there joy and laughter? Does this school feel like a happy place to be for children, teachers, and families?
  - ◆ Do teachers seem natural and relaxed as the principal walks into their rooms?
  - ◆ Does the principal relate well to the children? Does he or she show genuine interest in children as people and as learners? Do children comfortably approach the principal?

♦ Do teachers and administrators talk about children and families with a positive spirit rather than from a deficit perspective?

♦ How are classrooms organized? Pay attention to the walls in classrooms and hallways. Do you see evidence that you will have soul mates here?

♦ Is children's work diverse and authentic?

♦ Are classrooms clones of one another or is it clear that teachers construct environments based on responsiveness to children and current theoretical and pedagogical knowledge?

After the offer

■ Think long and hard before taking the job. Will this school be a good fit for you? Will you be able to grow as a teacher and a learner? Will you be respected for what you know while provided opportunities and support to try new ideas and continue learning? Go with your gut feelings. Trust your instincts. Accept a position in a school that you feel will be a good match for you.

To New Teachers

Have a life.

Some of us do a better job than others at finding balance in our lives, but we recognize how important it is to set boundaries so we don't neglect the rich parts of our lives beyond teaching. In the long run, that makes us better teachers. Robbie said, "The weeks when I work my guts out and end up doing all that extra stuff, I'm not as good with the kids. I'm not as patient. I have to remember that sometimes I have to step back and not do as much." We need to put our teaching lives in perspective by taking time to be with family and friends, getting away for a weekend, or, as Erin wrote, "sitting back with a beer to blow off steam and start a new day with a fresh outlook." At the end of the second year, Ami wrote about her personal growth in terms of making time for life: "I take better care of myself now. I read for pleasure, travel, and spend time with family and friends. I have learned to take time for me so I can better nurture my kids."

In the early days, before some of us were married and had our own children, it was easy to be judgmental about teachers who left school as the bell rang at the end of the day. As we began to settle into making a life with our own families, we thought differently. Erin wrote, "To be very honest, I can tell you that I personally did look at teachers who left at 3:30 with nothing in their arms and see it as a lack of commitment to the profession. Then I had kids. When my own family needed me at home, I learned to leave stuff at school." Carmen explained, "After I got married, I had to realize that I couldn't come home every day and work. I asked Ken to bear with me for a couple of weeks and promised to make a change. I made it too. I try to go in extra early when he is at work so then I can come home at a decent hour to spend time with him." Julie described how she learned to bring balance to her life:

> I try not to bring things home in order to keep my family time separate. I allow myself only one (or two if necessary) days a week to stay late until 4:30. I leave school no later than 4:00 on the other days. I try to find new ideas or ways to teach, such as adding technology to a lesson. I enjoy the support of teacher friends with whom I can talk, laugh, complain, share successes, and reflect. I try to do things that I really enjoy during my time away from the classroom so that I come back re-charged and enthusiastic.

Pace yourself, keep a sense of humor, know that teaching *is* hard.

It's okay to take things slowly. Working on the implementation of one area of the curriculum or one classroom structure at a time is an important way to gain confidence and expertise. But it took us a while to trust this process. Julie wrote, "I was so overwhelmed and unhappy at first because I kept thinking I wasn't living up to the teacher I was capable of being. Now I've decided to try my best to come as close as possible to perfecting one area of my classroom. When I have a handle on that, I'll move on to another area." Carmen also wrote about the importance of setting priorities, pacing yourself, and keeping a positive outlook and a sense of humor:

> I do what I can in the best way I know how (*most* of the time) and try not to complain. Complaining takes away from what you could be doing if you weren't spending so much negative energy complaining. My students are my first priority. I make sure they're taken care of and let everything else fall into place. Sometimes I falter, but I keep moving ahead knowing a better day will come. And, I laugh a lot.

It helps to acknowledge that what you are trying to do *is* hard work. Of course, it would be easier to take out the teacher's guide and follow the instructions, but that would tragically limit the realm of possibilities for teaching and learning for our students and for us. We appreciate validation from experienced teachers like Tim O'Keefe (Mills et al., 2004), who reminds us that trying to figure out teaching every day is exhausting but well worth the effort:

> Teaching responsively is taxing. . . . But think of what your life would be like if you weren't planning with and for your students. Imagine if you had absolutely no say in what went on in your room. So the stress . . . may be balanced by knowing how miserable it could be if you had to teach using someone else's agenda entirely. (p. 173)

Look for your successes; don't give up.

We are motivated to keep trying when we recognize the things that are going well. Look for the joys, no matter how small. Identify at least two successes every day and congratulate yourself. Keep a diary of magical moments on your own, with students, and/or with colleagues. Noticing successes will give you strength, hope, and optimism. Within two weeks, you won't believe all of the positive experiences you have had. And give yourself a break. As Carmen wrote, "It will get a little crazy sometimes. Then just erase the slate and start over. When something isn't working for the kids or for you, don't be afraid to chuck it." The key is to give yourself time and permission to learn and grow. At the end of her second year, Robbie explained:

> I know that some days I'm going to be great and other days I won't be such a great teacher. Some lessons are going to be wonderful, some awful. Some days you think will never end and you wonder why you became a teacher, and others fly by so quickly you wish you had become a teacher long ago. Don't give up. Change takes time. Persistence is the key. Keep your heart strong and your ideas handy.

Find like-minded colleagues with whom you can share your professional lives.

New teachers—all teachers—need regular opportunities for professional collaboration between colleagues *within* their school settings. Julie said:

> You need access to someone who can relate to you and to your beliefs. If not a group, a buddy system would be great. It wouldn't even have to be formal, but someone to keep up with and bounce ideas off of without feelings of intimidation, at least for the first year when you need that security blanket to feel like you know what you're doing.

Professional literature tells us this again and again: "Try to find at least one other colleague willing to read and try" (Hubbard & Power, 1999, p. 8); "organize support groups united by a common vision, curiosity, or interest[,] . . . an important network of colleagues who share a common vision" (Salas, Tenorio, Walters, & Weiss, 2004, p. 41); "It is so important to have colleagues you can run ideas by, brag about your students' accomplishments to, to brainstorm and commiserate with. You need someone you can admit your mistakes to, someone to prop you up and to laugh with" (Mills et al., 2004, p. 165).

Listen to those voices and to ours. Even though we enjoy the company of our research group, it is not the same as having colleagues in our schools with whom we feel comfortable enough to take the risks necessary to learn and grow. Learning partners next door or down the hall make a tremendous difference in your growth, in the strength you find to make it through the rough spots, and in the depth of joy you find day to day. As Ami wrote, "having support is essential to sticking out the bumps and challenges." Look for colleagues who will be kindred spirits, but know that you might have to look hard. They may be behind closed doors. Find them.

Know that you can teach well next door to someone who teaches differently.

Don't try to be someone else. Be yourself and be true to your beliefs, but know that it is possible to construct a classroom that reflects your beliefs while honoring neighboring teachers' different views. Respect their beliefs and their right to teach as they feel comfortable. Engage them in respectful conversation as you learn and grow together. At the end of her second year, Robbie wrote, "Don't ever think that a teacher has nothing to offer you. I thought one of my coworkers was an awful teacher, but then I found out that she has a special way with difficult students and she had a lot to teach me." Ami commented, "Most teachers love children and love teaching. There is unsurpassed dedication in education. There may be a few bad apples, but most teachers really care. We can teach differently and respect that about each other."

Use distant teachers as inspiration.

Distant teachers—teachers in books, videos, and classrooms we visited—had a tremendous influence on the visions of great teaching we developed as preservice teachers, but it took us quite a while to be able to use their work as inspiration rather than as recipes. Ami said, "You can get advice and ideas from a book, but ultimately, it's got to be about who you are and how you are going to orchestrate life in your own classroom." Erin found this to be true as she learned to draw from the expertise of others while growing into herself as a teacher:

> I used to read our books and think, "Okay, I have to do this, this, and this in my classroom." It was overwhelming. Now I can read a book and take from it what I take from it. For example, from Katie Wood Ray, I learned about reading like a writer, but, at first, I was too by-the-book, trying to do it exactly like she did or like Susi demonstrated in class. Now I've internalized the idea and made it my own. I used to go crazy trying to structure a class exactly like Katie's but, from her structure, I've learned to read and write better myself *and* how to teach my students to read and write better.

Now that we are more comfortable in our own skin as teachers, we can honor the work of other educators without feeling that we have to *be* them. Erin continued:

> I don't think I'll ever have a classroom like Jill Ostrow's. But, honestly, I don't think I'd ever be comfortable with one exactly like hers. There are things we learned in the MAT program that I choose not to do. I probably would have never admitted that a while ago, but more than anything I feel confident about my teaching now. I don't feel like I have to be like everyone in the books. I used to feel so guilty about it, but I don't anymore. I used to think you'd be disappointed in us, Susi. But you're not, are you?

Stay away from negativity.

In the planning weeks prior to Carmen's first day of school, she wrote about colleagues' negativity as they talked about Alex, a child who would be in her class. April wrote about how teachers' tendency toward negativity can draw you in if you aren't careful. Negative talk about children and families is all too common. For some teachers, it is habitual. It is very easy to fall into the negativity habit when we do not intentionally pull ourselves away from it.

Sometimes negative conversations began to feel like contests: Who has the worst class? Who has the most *low* kids? Who has the most difficult parents? Don't fall into that trap. When you hear yourself saying things like "Those kids," "Those parents," or "That family," let that be a huge red flag. Stop yourself from getting sucked into the deficit habit. Be aware of it when it is happening. Negative teacher-talk can sap every ounce of positive energy and destroy excitement about teaching faster than almost any other condition in a school. Refuse to buy into it. Recognize that fatigue and frustration at not knowing how to reach individual children fuel these kinds of reactions. Push yourself beyond defensive responses. Put yourself in the company of colleagues who will do the same. Look for real solutions that build from positive views of children and their families. When other teachers say things like

"It's the parents' fault" or "It's the district's fault" or "It's the kids' fault," turn those comments around and look for what *is* going well.

Look for what children know and can do and build from there.

Know that you are not a bad teacher just because a few kids aren't engaged today, but look beyond their surface behaviors by going the extra mile to build relationships that allow you to see children in a new light. Create opportunities within and beyond your classroom to learn about and celebrate difference. For example, when Carmen moved from South Carolina to California and then to Virginia, she made a point of learning about and honoring differences she found in each setting:

> I'm very conscious of race and cultural difference as I plan for my classroom. I choose books that will promote conversations about how cool it is to be different. With music, although I had mostly White kids in my school in South Carolina, they loved R&B and rap. At my school in Virginia, kids love country. I try to be aware of what works for them. I don't own any country music, but I encourage them to bring it to play during prep time. The *best* was doing the cha cha slide with them today. It's a line dance, but it's R&B. They were hilarious, but they *loved* it. I'm sure I gained a little more love with that one. I believe we have a responsibility to know more about each child's community and culture. Yeah, you love them, but you have to let them know you value that connection.

Irvine (2003) writes that students often struggle in school "not because their teachers do not know their content, but because their teachers cannot make connections between subject-area content and their students' existing mental schemes, prior knowledge, cultural perspectives" (p. 47). Carmen began by learning about students through their music and through conversations prompted by books she chose to read aloud. Music and carefully selected read-alouds are a beginning. Build from there by spending time in homes and communities. Look for what children and families know and can do, what they care about, what worries them, what delights them, what they love about their children and each other. Learn from the strategies used by the other teachers in children's lives—parents, siblings, grandparents, neighbors, Sunday school teachers. In doing so, remember that you see the world through the lens of your own experiences, definitions, and knowledge. Acknowledge that you may not have accurate perceptions of others: "Look beyond stereotypes with genuine *respeto* (respect) to see what's really there" (Zentella, 2005, p. 178). Use your broadened perspectives to inform day-to-day practice in your classroom.

While working to change it, learn to work within the test-driven culture without compromising your beliefs.

We have deep concerns about the powerful position of high-stakes tests in our society and believe that teachers should work together to change systems governed by them. But because tests are currently used to determine who will have access to opportunity, we also believe that teachers have a responsibility to support all students as critically insightful problem seekers and solvers who are also competent test takers. You don't need to set aside your visions of great teaching to help children succeed on tests. We can help children grow as proficient and passionate learners *and* succeed on tests by (a) not abandoning pedagogy that we know will excite, entice, broaden, and, as Eisner (2006) writes, "tickle the intellect" (p. 44), while (b) teaching students to transfer knowledge from more thoughtful contexts into the testing genre. We can further support that ability by involving students in critical analysis of tests and the testing industry through inquiries into the goals of test makers and the strategies that successful test takers use (Mills et al., 2004). In this way, testing does not drive curriculum, but its realities can be addressed without selling out. It doesn't take much to learn (or teach) how to turn what you know into answers on standardized tests, but it can take a lifetime to undo damage caused to students' abilities to think critically when school experiences are dominated by teach-to-the-test practices.

Know that you do have a voice. Use it to take responsibility for your life as a teacher.

During our first year, it was easy to feel that we weren't making a difference in the profession at large. Most of us were uncomfortable voicing our views about teaching if they were different from views reflected in the practices around us. At the end of her second year, Erin wrote, "Last year I would never have dreamed of standing up for what I believed in a team meeting or in front of my principal. I was too busy pleasing everyone else even though it was making me miserable."

But we learned that sharing our views can happen in subtle and not so subtle ways. Paraphrasing Erin's words from Chapter 7, every time you speak your mind, it doesn't have to be a big deal. You have a voice and you can say what you believe without disastrous results.

Know that you do have a voice. Use it to take responsibility for your life as a teacher. Initiate conversations with administrators and colleagues when things don't feel right. You can question in kind and respectful ways. Don't just sit by and let things happen to you.

Know your stuff and keep learning.

Keep your knowledge base up to date. It does you little good to know how to implement a handful of practices if you don't continue to read, pay close attention to children, talk to other teachers, and build further practice from what you learn. Not only will you be a better teacher but you will also be able to justify your teaching to others. At the end of her second year, Robbie wrote:

> I know I am getting better as a teacher all the time. I feel so much more confident in my abilities. When someone asks me why I do something the way I do, I can reply with confidence because there is a real reason for everything I do in my classroom. I think things out a great deal and try to have some sort of research to back it up.

For this to happen, it's critical to create space in your life for reading professional literature regularly, even if it's just thirty minutes twice a week or an hour on weekend mornings. Take further course work. Join national professional organizations and listservs. Form a study group. Ongoing learning in the company of enthusiastic colleagues can be the biggest energizer of all. Feed their intellectual curiosity and let them feed yours. Regularly attending national professional conferences can have the same energizing effect. After attending her first NCTE annual convention, Robbie wrote, "I remarked to someone that a conference is a totally different experience once you have experience in your own classroom. The topics become so much more relevant and you can make so many more connections with what people are saying."

Defining yourself as a teacher who can't stop learning adds excitement to your career that you could not otherwise enjoy. At the end of her second year, Erin wrote, "What keeps me in the profession now? Knowing that I am growing as a teacher and my students are benefiting from that growth."

Leave situations that do not feed you as a professional.

One of the most important lessons we learned was that not all places embrace the beliefs we hold dear. This doesn't mean you cannot teach next door to someone with a very different style, but if there is no room for sharing and valuing one another's knowledge and continuing to grow together, it will be easier than you think to become stagnant, to feel progressively lonelier as a professional, and to slide into the status quo you set out to change.

If it becomes clear that you have landed in a situation that is not a good professional fit, cut your losses and leave. To recognize indications that it is time to go, reflect carefully on day-to-day life in your class-room and your school. Are you nurtured intellectually? Is the environment one to which you feel you can contribute? Do you feel good about the teaching beliefs reflected in your practice? Do you find yourself becoming a teacher you don't like? Is the environment a caring one? Is it a joyful place to be for teachers and children?

Enjoy.

Above all, enjoy the kids. They are why you went into this business to begin with. Notice the profound and wonderful things they say and do every day. Keep a clipboard or a diary for jotting down their astute observations of the world. Revel in their brilliance. Relax. Don't be afraid to show emotion with your children. Laugh, cry, hug. Smile often.

Every One of Us Can Give a New Teacher Hope

Nieto (2003) writes that "hope is at the very essence of teaching" (p. 53). We left our preservice experience full of hope. Through the next seven years, some of us lost hope to the point of nearly leaving the profession. Others lost and regained hope in temporary setbacks. Every educator who entered our lives played a role in helping us sustain, lose, and/or rediscover hope for ourselves as teachers. Teaching well is not something we can do alone. We need you. All of you. And we need to look to ourselves. Each of us has the power to perpetuate the cycle of despair that causes some teachers to leave teaching and others to lose the drive to move the profession forward. Together, we can work to put real changes in place that will make a difference.

Critical Insights from Chapter 8

For Administrators

- Encourage new teachers every day with a smile and a bit of conversation. Show genuine interest in us, our lives, and our ideas.

- Spend time in classrooms to enjoy and be fascinated by the kids, to learn, and to teach with us.

- Know that scripted programs constrain the heights we can reach. They rob us of opportunities to build knowledge and confidence and to contribute in dynamic ways to your school and to the field of education.

- While working to change systems governed by high-stakes tests, stand up with us to ensure that delight and fascination in teaching and learning are never suffocated by them.

- Make time for regular professional study and conversation a priority; join us as co-learners.

- Create an atmosphere in which it is safe to take risks; let us know that it's a good thing to try new ideas, reflect, regroup, and try again.

- Celebrate our excitement about innovation; help us see our successes.

- Build an environment defined by positive talk; recognize teachers' lounge negativity and turn it around.

- Give colleagues and mentors time to mentor.

- Simplify our lives.

- Make a caring community foundational to everything else.

For Colleagues and Mentors

- Stop by our rooms to ask how things are going.

- Offer to include us in field studies and special days.

- Invite us for coffee after school now and then.

- Reassure us that we're doing okay, that we're not alone.

- Offer assistance that builds on what we are doing well; we will need you to help us see our successes.

- Protect our time.

- If our teaching styles and philosophies are different from yours, respect our views while helping us learn to respect yours.

- Be sensitive to comments that might unintentionally degrade or make fun of ideas we are trying.

- Help us see the positive in our students and their families; steer us away from negativity.

- Allow mentorships to evolve as we get to know each other.

For Universities

- Make the process and the challenges of teaching visible.

- Encourage us to take things one idea at a time and to let go of the guilt.

- Help us begin to think about how to pin down the whirling ideas with which we leave our preservice programs.

- Support us in valuing worlds beyond our own while exploring the complexities of building rich classroom communities.

- Help us use our knowledge to articulate support for the practices we hope to employ.
- Guide us to know how to work within and beyond existing programs without compromising our beliefs; give us strategies to evaluate their effectiveness and to articulate our findings to colleagues and administrators.
- Help us understand how to support children in doing well on tests without compromising great teaching (when we did not know how to do this, it was easy to fall into the trap of teaching to the test).
- Don't abandon us at graduation; figure out ways to continue your support.
- Place us in internship classrooms where we can learn from and with teachers who:
    - ◆ Teach based on knowledge of theory, practice, and knowing children well.
    - ◆ Are excited about working with interns; will take time to talk and study with us.
    - ◆ Are excited about their own continued professional growth.
    - ◆ Know how to address mandates without selling their soul.
    - ◆ Look at children and families with a positive spirit, not from a deficit perspective.
    - ◆ Are kind to children; love teaching and learning.

For Job Seekers

- Practice articulating—out loud—what you believe and why.
- Be prepared to describe how you will use your knowledge to work within and beyond mandated programs without compromising your beliefs.
- Prepare questions to ask of both teachers and administrators. Pay attention to interactions between members of the interview committee.
- Get beneath the rhetoric. Ask for clarification and deeper explanations.
- Look for warmth, openness, and evidence of teacher knowledge, autonomy, and responsiveness to children.
- Think long and hard before taking the job. Go with your gut feelings; trust your instincts.

For New Teachers

- Have a life.
- Take things slowly; look for your successes.

- Don't be afraid to show emotion with your students: smile, cry, hug. Laugh every day.
- Find like-minded colleagues.
- Keep learning.
- Use distant teachers for inspiration, not recipes.
- Stay away from negativity.
- While working to change it, learn to work within the test-driven culture without compromising your beliefs.
- Refuse to buy into a deficit perspective; look for what children and families know and can do and build from there.
- Don't try to be someone else; be true to your beliefs but respect colleagues' right to teach as they feel most comfortable.
- Know that you do have a voice; use it to take responsibility for your life as a teacher.
- Leave situations that do not feed you as a professional.

9 Our Visions Today

I guess I was worried about our writing—about presenting the world of teaching as totally hopeless, that it's just too hard. But it is hard and there are a ton of things out there making it hard. You guys have been trying to tell me that all along but, in the back of my mind, I was thinking, "Soon we'll get to the happy ending for everybody." But that's just not the case. Endings are only new beginnings anyway.

Susi began this journey wanting to know what happened to new teachers during their early years of teaching. Secretly, she harbored a wish for a happy ending; we would face challenges, overcome them, and all would be well. Looking back at the first September evening at Erin's house, we see a group of new teachers who also expected a happy ending—a finite, tangible, textbook outcome. After examining seven years of data, we all agree that such notions trivialize the complexity of our lives as teachers. Erin explained, "To say that we went from inexperienced teachers to experienced, happy ones who sing through our days doesn't do justice to the complex task of growing as educators." As we wrote this book, Carly said, "I am adamant about not telling just a feel-good story. We don't have a happy ending if that means that we went out there and conquered all," and Carmen wrote, "We didn't stop the tape for the perfect story. We opened ourselves up to say why certain perfect situations did not exist for us."

But there is definitely happiness. We have exhilarating moments of great joy with children, parents, colleagues, and administrators every day. Most of us feel that we can teach with our doors wide open with no hesitations about being observed, not because we are that good but, as Erin says, "because we can explain why we do what we do." At the same time, we have deep concerns about situations in which teachers feel constrained because of mandates or perceived mandates and wonder how we can encourage more professional conversations that build on the intellectual foundations of teaching. Eight years ago Erin's experiences with programmatic mandates were an anomaly in our worlds. Today, we see them more frequently. We want to work with colleagues and administrators to better appreciate and address these and other issues—recognizing the problems, we hope to be a part of the solutions.

And so, while we are, in many ways, very happy, we know that a part of our joy and energy has to come from getting involved in ways that have the potential to make a difference. As such, we have come to believe that learning to teach is not a full-circle experience. We don't, as Carmen wrote, "leave despair hanging," but we recognize that significant issues remain. As eight educators who are more confident than we were seven years ago but who still face challenges, we describe the teaching experience using Robbie's metaphor: it's all about "the excitement as well as the struggle to climb the mountain, only to realize that it's a false summit because teaching is all about reaching summit after summit."

What Did We Find?

The answers are as complex as the process of learning to teach itself.

Seven years ago, we asked: What happens to the enthusiasm, confidence, knowledge, and energy of new teachers as they enter the profession eager to make a difference? What barriers do they find? What support sustains them? Dudley-Marling (1997) writes that even the most systematic, theoretically grounded, intentional reflection cannot lead to absolute truths. We agree. There is no once-and-for-all answer to explain how we can sustain and build from the energy of new teachers and why we lose them to other professions or to a disappointing status quo. The answers are as complex as the process of learning to teach itself. We can, however, make some educated speculations.

Nurturing new teachers' enthusiasm, confidence, knowledge, energy, and drive to make a difference is about many things. We are nurtured when we work with kind and supportive colleagues and administrators in a culture in which ongoing professional learning—the insatiable desire to know more—is the norm. We are supported when we work within systems that value teaching as the process of getting to know children well and using that knowledge to create dynamic learning environments. We can tackle challenges better when a strong preservice experience allows us to develop a knowledgeably critical eye. We are nurtured when we find a school home that is a good pedagogical fit, a place where we can give as well as grow. We are supported when we work with educators who care for and nurture one another, and who are committed to building and sustaining an educational environment in which responsible autonomy, mutual trust, and respect are fundamental, and in which "tests do not define worthiness and numbers do not measure or create identities" (Kozol, 2005b, p. 287).

In the end, however, it all seems to boil down to talk. Reflecting across experiences that left us unhappy and disillusioned or full of confidence and hope, we see the greatest support in schools and districts defined by opportunities for genuine dialogue as teachers and administrators build knowledge together. Such opportunities allow us to hear one another's perspectives and begin to work toward common ground —or agree to respectfully disagree. With that in mind, we hope our stories will provide a basis for other educators to share and reflect with one another as they work to make a difference for the new teachers in their lives.

Where Are We Today?

Today, we are less judgmental, but that doesn't mean we believe in everyone just freewheeling.

When we graduated from the university, Susi wondered if our beliefs were really *our* beliefs or if we were toeing a party line. The fact that we hold similar convictions today speaks to the depth of our beliefs as beginning teachers. If anything, our convictions have strengthened through further study, our interactions with children, and our attempts to address controversial issues in our schools. But that doesn't mean we don't sometimes lose our direction. Even with experience, it can be very difficult to stay strong when we are alone. We need collaboration with others to maintain that strength.

Recognizing the importance of collaborating with colleagues and administrators to build knowledge, work through conflicts, and better understand one another, we also see the importance of being less judgmental. We no longer see differences as rights and wrongs, but as perspectives based on different experiences and knowledge. Carly wrote:

> I think what comes across strongly in our conversations today is that we have learned to respect other teachers more. I think it shows a maturity on our part and a greater appreciation of diverse views. We were kind of judgmental in the beginning, particularly about anyone who taught differently from us. It doesn't mean that we have to give up our views, but we are better at respecting others' rights to believe and teach differently.

We also realize that most teachers go into teaching for the right reasons. Ami said, "I used to believe that many people go into education because they think it will be easy, but I have come to believe that the vast majority of educators want to make a difference no matter how they teach."

Today we are better able to appreciate that the path taken by one teacher may be totally different from the path taken by another. That is not to say, however, that we believe in "anything goes." As Carmen wrote, "Being open to other views doesn't mean I believe everyone should be able to teach any way they feel is best. Sometimes it just isn't good practice and it's damaging to children. Just because we are less judgmental doesn't mean we believe in everyone freewheeling."

Today, we realize that teachers need respites now and then. It doesn't mean you've given up. It just means that you need to renew and recharge.

Working to live up to your beliefs can, over time, wear you down and wear you out. Teachers need respites now and then. Taking time to step back may, in fact, be critical to staying in the profession long term. Carly explained, "When you feel like your back is against the wall and you're struggling to make a difference, you get tired. So you have to step back for a while." Stepping back might mean going underground temporarily—closing the classroom door to teach well while gathering energy for renewed efforts that are more visible. It might mean deciding to focus more on family than on profession for a period of time. It could mean changing jobs and looking for fresh faces and perspectives. It might mean saying "no" to a committee, a project, an opportunity, or an evening meeting no matter how enticing they might be. Stepping back doesn't mean you've given up. It just means that you need to take a deep breath to renew and recharge. Carmen said it well:

> The reality is that we wanted to stop and have a glass of wine, go to the mountains with our husbands, and show love to our babies. So we had to make choices sometimes, and people need to know that reality of teaching. It doesn't mean that you have lost your zest for the profession. You just realize that it is OK to give in to self-indulgences sometimes. Because we didn't read or hear about that when we were in graduate school, we didn't realize it was a reality and so, initially, we felt guilty about stepping back. We don't feel that way anymore.

Today, perfect has taken on a whole new meaning.

One of our biggest struggles, and a barrier that is particularly difficult to overcome, is the feeling that we should look, sound, act, and react in a particular way. We now believe that, as Robbie wrote, "ideal teachers realize that there is no such thing as perfection. They realize that you never stop growing." Robbie went on to describe ideal teachers as defined not by programs or practices, but by a commitment to keeping a sense of intellectual curiosity alive for themselves and for their students within caring classrooms:

Ideal teachers use children's needs to inform curriculum. They use curricula as guides, not dictates. They listen to others' feedback and reflect. They teach all children. They create warm, caring learning environments where it is safe to take risks, environments that welcome all children and parents. They do what they know is best for children and fight for those practices. They know when to stand up and when it is time to lay low.

Rather than perfect teachers, we think about perfect conditions that nurture teachers as thoughtful, intelligent professionals. Erin explained:

> Perfect conditions include teachers being treated with respect and, in turn, behaving with utmost respect for the profession. This means reading professionally, collaborating, getting to know students, planning, assessing, reflecting. Perfect conditions don't isolate teachers. Perfect conditions don't allow teachers' work to be dominated by test scores and a teacher-on-the-bottom-of-the-hierarchy mentality. Perfect conditions empower teachers to make changes that affect their day-to-day lives.

Eight Teacher Researchers Today

In the following pages, we return to individual narratives to write about our lives today. We consider how we feel now about the visions we embraced as we left graduate school, the visions we continue to hold dear, and concerns that remain.

Ami

My profession fits me like a favorite pair of jeans.

My profession fits me like a favorite pair of jeans. My classroom is an extension of me and an environment that makes me feel invigorated and energized every day. Today, I teach first grade in the school where I began teaching eight years ago. I still get to school before seven each morning, but I no longer stay until the sun goes down. I am much more balanced than I was in my early years. I was heading toward burnout being a grade-level chair, spearheading a district multiage program, serving on multiple school and district committees, representing faculty on the School Improvement Council and in the Parent-Teacher Organization, and tutoring children every afternoon after school. I am happier and healthier because I am learning to give myself boundaries. I know my students are lucky to have me as their teacher. I am very blessed to be a part of their lives. They make me smile and laugh every day, and I continue to learn from them as they share themselves and we grow together.

I still believe that children learn best when they are supported as inquirers. I believe in using real literature to teach children to become lifelong readers and writers; creating warm, nurturing communities; building bridges between homes and schools; having an open-door classroom; using authentic assessments; and continuing my own professional growth. I still strongly oppose scripted programs. I believe they mock professional judgment and undermine teachers' abilities to make curricular choices. They make it difficult to drive the curriculum through children's inquiries.

I think teachers can blossom when they are respected and encouraged to collaborate, read professionally, attend conferences, take professional classes, and teach responsively. I think teachers need to act professionally to earn the respect of other professionals. This includes how we speak, dress, and act as we put our best foot forward as a professional group. I believe all teachers need to continue taking courses throughout their careers. We need to stop whining and empower ourselves to make changes and decisions that affect our day-to-day lives and the students we touch every day. At times I feel exhausted and frustrated with the bureaucracy of education, especially the crazy testing mentality, but the kids keep me energized. I realize that I can't change the world, but the power of teaching is profound.

April

I am never satisfied with myself as a teacher, but that is what being a great teacher is all about.

After seven years of teaching kindergarten, I moved this year to teaching four-year-olds. I still love teaching kindergarten, but when this opportunity arose I thought it would be exciting to begin with children at age four and loop with them through kindergarten. It is an exciting experience watching them come in, some of them just having turned four. I can't wait to see what the year will bring.

Even though I still love teaching, I don't love everything about my job right now. It seems that we just get used to one set of directives and then minds change at the district level, and a completely different set of directives comes down the line—new evaluation programs and then new components to old evaluation programs. There is a heightened sense of being closely watched that I didn't experience as much when I started teaching. Today, I feel more confident as a teacher thanks to the support I receive from peers, parents, children, and administrators. To be voted Teacher of the Year by my colleagues was certainly an honor and a boost to my confidence.

I still have the same feelings and beliefs I had in my first year. My desire to find the best strategies for teaching is still there. I am still never satisfied with myself as a teacher, but I think that's what being a great teacher is all about—always trying to grow and seek the best possible ways to reach each child. Even though, in my first years, I said that teachers should be learners for a lifetime, I was never really comfortable when things didn't go as well as I expected. I am more comfortable with that now.

I still believe that all children can learn; you just have to find where they are and move them forward from there. I believe that children should be loved, cared for, disciplined, read to, talked to, listened to, and befriended. I believe that the classroom environment should be welcoming, organized, child centered, and full of literacy. I believe that all children do not learn the same way. I need to pay close attention to them and then develop and redevelop different strategies to guide them to become independent learners. Learning to know every child, we can't help but seek to grow as teachers as each year passes.

I cannot think of any other job I would rather do. Though it is stressful at times, I feel that I am good at it and I see rewards every day. Spending the day with children who laugh with you, smile with you, sing with you, dance with you, learn with you, read with you, and just plain have fun with you is well worth it. There are days when I think, "Is there something that I would rather do?" But the answer always comes back to teaching.

Carly

It's awesome to know that I can find comfort in our book. Our words immediately put me at ease and let me know that I'm not alone.

I'm now teaching kindergarten for the first time since I interned with Donna Jarvis's five-year-olds. I love it! A friend of mine said that she has never seen me this happy. I love going back to so many of the ideas I learned in graduate school. I also love how diverse our school is now. We have such a wonderful variety of languages represented. Many of them are new to me. It will be fun to learn more as the year goes on.

A year ago at this time, I went back to the classroom after three years at home with my children. I eased back in with a part-time job-sharing position in a fourth grade. After being gone for so long, I felt much like a first-year teacher again. Reading our manuscript, I realized that I was making some of the same mistakes that plagued me then. But it's awesome to know that I can find comfort in our book. Our words immediately put me at ease and let me know that I'm not alone. They give me real advice.

Returning to teaching after only three years, I was amazed at the swift changes in education that had taken place. The No Child Left Behind tornado has taken its toll even in our small corner of the world. It's so sad that, in a school district I once revered because it looked beyond the face value of test scores, I now see panic building as educators jump on the bandwagon of the testing frenzy. The vision statement for the entire school system has changed since I taught here before. Now it is filled with directives like: "We will be in the top 10 percent of the nation's schools in all areas of academic achievement on or before 2014." This pressure trickles down to frantic teachers trying to shove as much content as possible into the heads of students in hopes that it will stick for the big tests at the end of the year.

I still believe everything as passionately as I did when I graduated from the MAT program, maybe even more so because I see the horrifying path that education is going down. It scares me on behalf of my own children. Being a mom has made me a more compassionate teacher and much more aware of political issues that affect the lives of children in and out of school. I also have more confidence to voice my opinions about policies and ideas.

Today I am better at recognizing that it's okay to say enough is enough. Teachers can only internalize so many new ideas before going into overload. Sometimes I feel as though I've done so much reading that all the ideas just end up swimming around in my head. At that point, I get overwhelmed and totally shut down. It's been important for me to learn when to slow down, stop reading for a while, put ideas into practice, and allow plenty of time for reflection.

Carmen

I listen to those around me, but I stand firm in my beliefs.

As I look back on how far I have come, I find myself much more confident about what I know about teaching. I listen to those around me and respect what they believe, but I stand firm in my beliefs. I don't mind doing my own thing. It is a good feeling, and I smile as I write these thoughts. I have come so far from the teacher who kept her door closed because of insecurities. I now teach with my door wide open. You can hear the noisy buzz of children learning in cooperative groups or classical music playing in the background during writing or reading time. I believe even more strongly in the importance of creating opportunities for children to write and read for enjoyment or interest, and I see the difference it makes for my students to choose what they write and read. I know that my practices are based on sound theory, and I feel good about it. I no longer wish that my students had someone else to teach them because I fear I am not good enough. I am constantly seeking knowledge to be a better educator. This is what good teachers do, and that is what children need.

I focus on teaching, but I also focus on my personal life. I enjoy my husband and choose to take things a week at a time, sometimes a day at a time. This does not mean that my desire to make a difference has waned. I am still going to fight the good fight when I see an injustice being done. I just know that every battle is not a reason to exhaust every ounce of energy.

As far as what plagues me—in some ways, I feel as though I am a new teacher all over again. Having moved to a new state, there is much to learn. It is as though I am peering through a small scope again, and I am unable to see beyond my classroom. I don't want it to be that way, because there is so much work to be done. I want to be an agent for change for all children, not just my students. Sometimes I think we get so hell-bent on test scores that we forget what's really important. I want to educate children to know that it is just as important to help Hurricane Katrina victims as it is to make an A.

I believe children are meant to be loved unconditionally. The children are my priority; they come before putting things on the classroom wall or taking care of housekeeping duties that consume so much time. I know some people don't think learning should be fun. I beg to differ. My students should laugh and they should see me laugh. This creates a community that feels good about learning. Too many times I hear parents tell stories about children who are so fearful of their teachers that they don't want to go to school. It breaks my heart. I *know* it is not meant to be this way.

Erin

I love every hour of my working life now, every single one.

I love every hour of my working life now, every single one. What I do—working as a university-school liaison, planning professional development, supervising student teachers, and teaching undergraduate literacy methods courses—allows me to stay in a field about which I am passionate while still being able to spend time with my own children. Although I always thought I would be best as a working parent, when I was a classroom teacher I never felt that I was both a good teacher and a good parent. I guess I needed to find the right work and the right amount of it. I definitely have that now, which is a blessing I am thankful for each and every day.

As a classroom teacher, there were struggles I couldn't seem to overcome. For instance, I never knew how to work with a team that didn't share my views on teaching. I felt constrained and didn't learn to cope with that constraint. And, even though I knew that high test scores were not lofty educational goals and that we can teach children to be thoughtful learners while helping them do well on tests, I never learned how to explain that adequately to colleagues who felt otherwise.

I hold myself responsible for much of what happened to me my first year of teaching. It's not that our data aren't real, or that my struggles were in my imagination, or that rigid systems don't make life miserable for energetic new teachers. Real barriers definitely existed for me. But I'm at a place in my life where I ask about most everything, "What could I have done differently?" In my first year, I allowed myself to become intimidated beyond belief. I was so afraid of doing something wrong. I fell into the victim role in a way that is embarrassing to me now. In that sense, I've changed *within* more than anything. Now I know that I could have stood up for my beliefs and the world wouldn't have come to an end. The worst (or best) thing that would have happened is what *did* happen—when I stood up for my beliefs, it became clear that I needed to change schools. The sad thing is that I still see teachers afraid of doing *the wrong thing*. I want administrators to know how that takes away from teachers' belief in themselves.

The preservice teachers I work with now ask how they will be able to stay passionate in the field they will soon enter. I give them words of encouragement, but deep down I worry because I know how easy it is to lose passion without a chance to grow as a thoughtful professional. I worry that they will face the contradiction of one-shot workshops that ridicule the idea of thoughtful, long-term growth and change. My concerns compel me to take action by joining efforts at the local and national levels. So, while I am concerned, I am also energized. The preservice teachers give me hope. Seeing their passion has refueled my own.

Julie

I want to play a role in making positive changes happen.

My convictions today are much the same as those I held leaving the MAT program. I want my students to be enthusiastic lifelong learners who love to read and write. I still believe that children learn when they have authentic reasons for doing so. I still believe that teachers need to create a community in which children feel safe taking risks to work and learn together. I've learned that teachers need to communicate consistently with parents in a positive way to establish respectful relationships. I strongly believe that teachers need to seek out like-minded colleagues as a support network. My belief in the importance of a supportive administration has definitely been confirmed. The attitude of a school's administration can make or break the morale of first-year teachers, as well as the morale of experienced teachers. Today, even in the midst of other frustrations, I stay excited about teaching because I really enjoy the enthusiasm that children bring to my life as they learn new things and make connections.

A major change for me in the past few years is that I'm much more likely to speak up to explain my practices and give the theoretical background for my beliefs. I take on added projects, requests, and tasks with much less trepidation than I did seven years ago. Participating in groups like our district's Kindergarten Advisory Board gives me hope that, seeing changes that need to be made, I can play a role in making them happen.

I still struggle with the frustration of not being a master of many things at once, but I fight this urge and refocus on what I am doing successfully. I've learned that becoming a great teacher is a process that takes time, reflection, and dedicated persistence. Someone told me recently that I am a calm teacher. I take that as quite a compliment. Looking back on myself as a first-year teacher, I would describe myself as panicked, overwhelmed, and frustrated.

Writing this book has pushed me to live as a writer. I've had to fight the "I can't write" feelings and make myself put words on paper. As a result, I've come away with a great appreciation for writers. The process has made me so much more reflective about myself; my practice; collaboration; relationships with students, their families, and administration; and my role as a positive influence in the field of education.

Robbie

I believe in the decisions I make for my classroom and my students.

I am currently teaching two-year-olds in a small preschool. I love my job. I left my public school job for two reasons. One reason is that our first child was soon to be born and I always wanted to be able to take time off to raise my children. I am fortunate to have the opportunity to do that. The other reason is that I am fed up with the problems I see in public education, and I don't see many people working toward solutions for the near future. I am tired of administrators compromising their own beliefs to please those higher up. I want administrators to stand up for teachers and for what they know is right for their school and for children. It saddens me to see teachers who are forced to follow scripted programs because administrators do not trust that their teachers are knowledgeable and dynamic *or* they don't provide opportunities for ongoing study so that teachers can become more knowledgeable. I am also exasperated by the ways that teachers are held accountable. I believe wholeheartedly that teachers need to be held to very high standards, but I don't want test scores to be used to tell me how well I am teaching. Come into my room and observe me. Watch me document students' growth from the beginning of the year to the end. Watch me use that documentation to inform instruction. I needed to take a break from issues like these. By taking a deep breath, I might be able to return someday and meet these problems with a fresh outlook.

I have grown to understand that whatever a child's background, support system, or attitude, he or she will learn given a supportive environment. We need to stop making excuses. As teachers we cannot expect others—parents, administrators, or other teachers—to find or make those conditions for our students. We have to accept the strengths and weaknesses the child brings to school and help him or her grow from that point.

Things that would have bothered me in my first year or two of teaching are much easier to understand and deal with now. I think this is because I believe in the decisions I make for my classroom and for my students, and I am not afraid to admit mistakes. I know that people may fault me now and then, and that is okay. With experience, you realize that people are not scrutinizing every move you make, which is how I felt when I was a brand-new teacher.

Susi

This group has taught me so much that helps me now.

Since this project began, I've gone from being a second-year assistant professor through the "interesting" process of tenure and promotion into my tenth year at the university. Like the other group members, I love many things about my job. University professors are fortunate to be in positions that give us flexibility to build relationships with teachers and children who bring us great joy and cause us to question what we think we know. Also, like other members of our group, I feel the need to take a step back more often—to be careful not to miss the rich part of my life that is family and friends. It doesn't mean that my convictions are less strong, but it does mean that I need to do a better job of recognizing when it's time to rejuvenate and recharge.

The beliefs I held when the teachers in this book were my students have deepened in many ways and changed in others. One of the biggest changes is recognition of the lip service I gave to helping teachers value difference. I thought we were exploring issues of cultural and linguistic diversity. In reality, we only scratched the surface. We read about and discussed culture, race, and bias, but those discussions were never *really* connected to day-to-day life in classrooms, and we didn't deeply examine our own perspectives in relation to those of others. These days, I work with colleagues to experiment with assignments that take preservice teachers into homes and communities as learners, positioning family and community members as those from whom *we* have much to learn. The work of others who have headed in the same direction helps me tremendously (Cochran-Smith, 2004; Fine & Weis, 2003; Nieto, 2004; and others cited throughout this text). But there is still much for me to learn.

I continue to learn from our group's research as it guides my teaching every day. I cringe to think about how I sent them off to change the world without helping them see the struggles that new teachers experience, particularly when confronted with conflicting educational realities. In some ways, I set them up for disappointment when I read the picture book *Miss Rumphius* and urged them to go out, like she did, and make the world a more beautiful place. Of *course* they wanted to change the world tomorrow. I still believe in the sentiment wholeheartedly, but I've learned that, when it is not accompanied by acknowledgment of the challenges they may face *and* strategies to help them address challenges, it's an unfair and naive charge. I don't present a gloom-and-doom version of teaching but, thanks to our research, I can share hard stories and happy ones as part and parcel of the fascinating complexity that is life as a teacher. I also recognize that simply altering engagements and assignments in my classes is not enough. I need to spend more time working with schools and communities. Staying away for too long makes my teaching stale, lifeless, and irrelevant—disconnected from issues that matter.

I really did go into this study expecting to find a happy ending. Even though I articulated the complexity of teaching, learning, and research in previous work, I needed to relearn the lesson. Answers don't come in tidy packages. I didn't find a traditional happy ending, but I found much more. Shortly before mailing an early draft of this manuscript to our editor, our group met for dinner at a local restaurant. We didn't talk about the book or much about school. We just enjoyed one another's company, telling stories about how we spent Valentine's Day, holding Robbie's two-month-old Josie, being enchanted by Carmen's three-year-old stepdaughter Ari, and giving love to members of our group going through difficult times. We now talk about the direction our group will take next. Our tensions and triumphs work together to create a newly defined happy ending. It *is* merely another beginning.

We *Can* Disrupt the Pattern

> We need teachers who bring their heart, soul, and intellect to teaching, and we need to keep them in the profession.

Barriers to becoming the educator you envision yourself to be can seem impenetrable when you are a new teacher. Our stories describe the kind of support that helped some of us thrive and barriers that nearly drove others out of the profession. Our experiences do not exist in isolation from those of thousands of other new teachers. We share them because we believe that if we want to retain new teachers, people who have the power to make a difference need to understand the issues from new teachers' perspectives. Preventing new teachers from disappearing within an unacceptable status quo or from leaving the profession altogether *is* possible. Schools, districts, and universities have the responsibility to create opportunities for new teachers not merely to survive, but to thrive. Inspired by Sonia Nieto's (2003, 2005) work, our group recently asked why we continue to teach: what pushes us to care so deeply that we won't settle for merely surviving, even when thriving means figuring out how to face tough issues *and* sometimes stepping back for a while? Excerpts from our responses are embedded throughout this chapter, but we also share Carmen's response in its entirety. It helps us articulate why teaching can be an incredible way to spend a career.

> I still teach because I still love it. I love the kids. I love being around them, and I am fulfilled. I look for the best in them and it makes my heart smile when I do it. I know I am still where I want to be when I hear my husband tell me to "Let it go and *go to sleep!*" If I really reach into my soul and ask what keeps me here, I know that the answer lies in my godbrother's story. His parents were told, after just six weeks of first grade, that he wouldn't make it to second grade. They refused to believe it. They worked and worked with him at home. They instilled in him a perseverance that I had never seen before. They stayed up many nights just to help him "get it." Some would label him a slow learner, but *he was a learner*. He wanted what all children want. He wanted to be smart, do well, and make his parents proud. He was passed to second grade. His parents lit the fire, and today he is in school to become a veterinarian. I want to be that person for children who don't have what he had. I want to be the person who convinces parents that it's not too late, that they *can* make a difference with their children. It does not matter that you have a ninth-grade education. We can learn together. I want to put the spark back in a child's eyes that a teacher before me may have blown out. Sometimes when I really feel like I want to get out of teaching, that's what keeps me in. My heart won't let me leave.

We need teachers who bring their heart and soul and intellect to teaching, and we need to keep them in the profession. We all have the power to do that—to disrupt the pattern that we see across the country as new teachers become disillusioned, disappointed, frightened, and fed up. Just as easily, we can perpetuate conditions that destroy new teachers' hope, vision, confidence, and conviction. In a world full of quick fixes, we urge colleagues of new teachers, mentors and directors of induction programs, school and district administrators, and university faculty to take time to carefully consider the roles you might play in supporting new teachers in real and lasting ways. This requires an honest evaluation of people and programs and a commitment to separating rhetoric from reality. And new teachers—believe that you are wonderful for children. Seek a place where you find support for what you know as well as opportunities that feed your desire to continue learning. There is hope. You will succeed.

Epilogue

Husbands, children, parents, friends, colleagues—it's time to celebrate. Yes, we really *were* working on a book all those mornings, afternoons, evenings, and weekends we left you to meet with the infamous research group. To those who asked so many times, "Haven't you finished that book yet?," all we can do is try to communicate the complexity of the task undertaken when eight educators sift through seven years of data to make sense of such an important part of their lives. It has been a joyous, enlightening, frustrating, exhausting, energizing, and life-changing experience. As tired as we are at this point and as ready as we are to turn our work over to those who might read it, it's been a part of us for so long that we know we will feel a bit lost without it. We will, of course, relish the return of our weekends and sleep-filled nights. We look forward to getting up early for something other than dashing straight to our computers, but the process has become an integral and almost sacred part of our lives.

We will continue as a group. We are anxious to be even more involved in one another's teaching lives and, in the process, work together to effect change beyond our group. First, however, we will allow ourselves the luxury of time together to talk, drink, eat, and catch up on one another's lives. There is talk of a midyear weekend at the beach. Or maybe we'll spend some weeks reading and talking about a bestseller. A few years ago we read *The Secret Life of Bees*, a wonderful novel written by a South Carolinian. We went to hear the author, Sue Monk Kidd, and then to dinner to talk about the book and our lives. More of that kind of activity is very appealing.

As we type the last lines of this, our final draft, we are reminded of a book that Carmen gave Susi and from which Susi read aloud at the end of a summer writing retreat. The book is *Life Is So Good* (Dawson & Glaubman, 2000) and the words are George Dawson's, a man who learned to read at age 98. At 101, with elementary school teacher Richard Glaubman, George Dawson wrote the story of his life. In the last pages, they share a conversation about the completion of their book and its potential to make a difference in the lives of others. George says, "I will be happy if the only man who changes is the man that wrote it. If you needed to write a whole book to do that, fine." Richard gives George a hug and says, "The book is done then. I guess we're finished" and George replies:

No, son, we're not finished. We just don't need us a book anymore. You can just come and visit anyway. I might go to see your family like we said we would. We did our best. I don't care if nothing else happens with it or if somebody was to print a hundred copies. I have my own copy and I can read it now.

We also began writing with the hope that our book might help to change things—so that new teachers could grow with confidence and joy, so they would stay on another day to make a difference. At this moment, however, George's words and Richard's feelings resonate with our own. The process has been the important part. If books are written to change the men and women who write them, then our book is indeed finished. But *we* are not finished. We just don't need us a book anymore.

Beach retreat, 2005: Ami, Carly, April, Julie, Carmen, Susi, Robbie, Erin.

A Selection of Books That Help Us Understand More About . . .

The importance of regular conversation and collaboration between colleagues as we take on the role of teacher as intellectual

Darling-Hammond, L. (1997). *The right to learn: A blueprint for creating schools that work.* San Francisco: Jossey-Bass.

Fletcher, R. (1991). *Walking trees: Portraits of teachers and children in the culture of schools.* Portsmouth, NH: Heinemann.

Mills, H., & Donnelly, A. (Eds.). (2001). *From the ground up: Creating a culture of inquiry.* Portsmouth, NH: Heinemann.

Nieto, S. (2003). *What keeps teachers going?* New York: Teachers College Press.

Nieto, S. (Ed.). (2005). *Why we teach.* New York: Teachers College Press.

The process and challenges of becoming a teacher

Dudley-Marling, C. (1997). *Living with uncertainty: The messy reality of classroom practice.* Portstmouth, NH: Heinemann.

Hayes, I. (Ed.). (1998). *Great beginnings: Reflections and advice for new English language arts teachers and the people who mentor them.* Urbana, IL: National Council of Teachers of English.

Palmer, P. J. (1998). *The courage to teach: Exploring the inner landscape of a teacher's life.* San Francisco: Jossey-Bass.

Power, B. M., & Hubbard, R. S. (Eds.). (1996). *Oops: What we learn when our teaching fails.* York, ME: Stenhouse.

Salas, K. D., Tenorio, R., Walters, S., & Weiss, D. (Eds.). (2004). *The new teacher book: Finding purpose, balance, and hope during your first years in the classroom.* Milwaukee, WI: Rethinking Schools.

The importance of learning to understand and value difference

Fassler, R. (2003). *Room for talk: Teaching and learning in a multilingual kindergarten.* New York: Teachers College Press.

Gregory, E., Long, S., & Volk, D. (Eds.). (2004). *Many pathways to literacy: Young children learning with siblings, grandparents, peers, and communities*. New York: RoutledgeFalmer.

Hankins, K. H. (2003). *Teaching through the storm: A journal of hope*. New York: Teachers College Press.

Irvine, J. J. (2003). *Educating teachers for diversity: Seeing with a cultural eye*. New York: Teachers College Press.

Ladson-Billings, G. (2001). *Crossing over to Canaan: The journey of new teachers in diverse classrooms*. San Francisco: Jossey-Bass.

Long, S., & Sibberson, F. (2006). Broadening visions of what counts: Home and community literacies. *School Talk 11*(4).

Nieto, S. (2004). *Affirming diversity: The sociopolitical context of multicultural education* (4th ed.). Boston: Allyn and Bacon.

Schultz, K. (2003). *Listening: A framework for teaching across differences*. New York: Teachers College Press.

Ways to take it slowly, be kind to ourselves, balance work and life

Codell, E. R. (1999). *Educating Esmé: Diary of a teacher's first year*. Chapel Hill, NC: Algonquin Books.

Fisher, B. (2000). *The teacher book: Finding personal and professional balance*. Portsmouth, NH: Heinemann.

Goodnough, A. (2004). *Ms. Moffett's first year: Becoming a teacher in America*. New York: Public Affairs.

Graves, D. H. (2001). *The energy to teach*. Portsmouth, NH: Heinemann.

Using our voices; being political

Berliner, D. C., & Biddle, B. J. (1995). *The manufactured crisis: Myths, fraud, and the attack on America's public schools*. Reading, MA: Addison-Wesley.

Coles, G. (2003). *Reading the naked truth: Literacy, legislation, and lies*. Portsmouth, NH: Heinemann.

Garan, E. M. (2004). *In defense of our children: When politics, profit, and education collide*. Portsmouth, NH: Heinemann.

Meier, D. (2002). *In schools we trust: Creating communities of learning in an era of testing and standardization*. Boston: Beacon Press.

Sacks, P. (1999). *Standardized minds: The high price of America's testing culture and what we can do to change it*. Cambridge, MA: Perseus Books.

Smith, F. (2003). *Unspeakable acts, unnatural practices: Flaws and fallacies in "scientific" reading instruction*. Portsmouth, NH: Heinemann.

References

Alliance for Excellence in Education. (2004). *Tapping the potential: Retaining and developing high-quality new teachers.* Retrieved August 6, 2006, from http://www.all4ed.org/publications/TappingthePotential/TappingthePotential.pdf

Atkinson, P., & Hammersley, M. (1998). Ethnography and participant observation. In N. K. Denzin & Y. S. Lincoln (Eds.), *Strategies of qualitative inquiry* (pp. 110–36). Thousand Oaks, CA: Sage.

Auton, S., Berry, D., Mullen, S., & Cochran, R. (2002). Induction program for beginners benefits veteran teachers, too. *Journal of Staff Development, 23*(4). Retrieved August 19, 2006, from http://www.nsdc.org/library/publications/jsd/auton234.cfm

Ayers, W. (1993). *To teach: The journey of a teacher.* New York: Teachers College Press.

Beck-Frazier, S. (2005). To stay or not to stay: That's the dilemma. *Delta Kappa Gamma Bulletin, 71*(2), 28–33.

Birchak, B., et al. (1998). *Teacher study groups: Building community through dialogue and reflection.* Urbana, IL: National Council of Teachers of English.

Botelho, M. J., Turner, V., & Wright, M. (2006). We have stories to tell: Gathering and publishing stories in a Puerto Rican community. *School Talk, 11*(4), 2–3.

Boutte, G. S. (1998). *Multicultural education: Raising consciousness.* Belmont, CA: Wadsworth.

Boutte, G. S. (2001). *Resounding voices: School experiences of people from diverse ethnic backgrounds.* Boston: Allyn and Bacon.

Boutte, G. S., & Hill, E. L. (2006). African American barbershops: If schools were like barbershops. *School Talk, 11*(4), 5.

Brown, M., & Khazei, A. (2004). *City year: Founding stories.* Retrieved June 6, 2006, from http://www.cityyear.org/about/who/foundingstories.cfm

Bullough, R. V., Jr. (1989). *First-year teacher: A case study.* New York: Teachers College Press.

Cambourne, B. (1988). *The whole story: Natural learning and the acquisition of literacy in the classroom.* Auckland, NZ: Ashton Scholastic.

Carter, B. (1996). Hold the applause! Do Accelerated Reader & Electronic Bookshelf send the right message? *School Library Journal, 42*(10), 22–25.

Cochran-Smith, M. (2004). *Walking the road: Race, diversity, and social justice in teacher education.* New York: Teachers College Press.

Cochran-Smith, M., & Lytle, S. L. (Eds.). (1993). *Inside/outside: Teacher research and knowledge*. New York: Teachers College Press.

Codell, E. R. (1999). *Educating Esmé: Diary of a teacher's first year*. Chapel Hill, NC: Algonquin Books.

Coles, G. (2003). *Reading the naked truth: Literacy, legislation, and lies*. Portsmouth, NH: Heinemann.

Compton-Lilly, C. (2004). *Confronting racism, poverty, and power: Classroom strategies to change the world*. Portsmouth, NH: Heinemann.

Cooney, B. (1982). *Miss Rumphius*. New York: Viking.

Darling-Hammond, L. (1997). *The right to learn: A blueprint for creating schools that work*. San Francisco: Jossey-Bass.

Darling-Hammond, L. (2003). Keeping good teachers: Why it matters, what leaders can do. *Educational Leadership, 60*(8), 6–13.

Darling-Hammond, L. (2004). From "Separate but equal" to "No child left behind": The collision of new standards and old inequalities. In D. Meier & G. Wood (Eds.), *Many children left behind* (pp. 3–32). Boston: Beacon Press.

Dawson, G., & Glaubman, R. (2000). *Life is so good*. New York: Random House.

Delpit, L. (2002). No kinda sense. In L. Delpit & J. K. Dowdy (Eds.), *The skin that we speak: Thoughts on language and culture in the classroom* (pp. 31–48). New York: New Press.

Dewey, J. (1916). *Democracy and education: An introduction to the philosophy of education*. New York: Free Press.

Dewey, J. (1938). *Experience and education*. New York: Macmillan.

Doake, D. B. (1985). Reading-like behavior: Its role in learning to read. In A. Jaggar & M. T. Smith-Burke (Eds.), *Observing the language learner* (pp. 82–98). Newark, DE: International Reading Association/Urbana, IL: National Council of Teachers of English.

Donnelly, A., et al. (2005). Transformative professional development: Negotiating knowledge with an inquiry stance. *Language Arts, 82*(5), 336–46.

Dudley-Marling, C. (1997). *Living with uncertainty: The messy reality of classroom practice*. Portsmouth, NH: Heinemann.

Dyson, A. H., & Genishi, C. (2005). *On the case: Approaches to language and literacy research*. New York: Teachers College Press.

Eisner, E. (2006). The satisfactions of teaching: An educator reflects on why he teaches. *Educational Leadership, 63*(6), 44–46.

Fine, M., & Weis, L. (2003). *Silenced voices and extraordinary conversations: Reimagining schools*. New York: Teachers College Press.

Fisher, B. (1995). *Thinking and learning together: Curriculum and community in a primary classroom*. Portsmouth, NH: Heinemann.

Fisher, B. (1998). *Joyful learning in kindergarten*. Portsmouth, NH: Heinemann.

Fletcher, R. (1993). *What a writer needs*. Portsmouth, NH: Heinemann.

Fletcher, R. (1996). *Writer's notebook: Unlocking the writer within you*. New York: Avon.

Foss, A. (1999). Leaving my thumbprint: The journey of a first-year teacher. In J. W. Lindfors & J. S. Townsend (Eds.), *Teaching language arts: Learning through dialogue* (pp. 295–302). Urbana, IL: National Council of Teachers of English.

Fox, M. (1993). *Radical reflections: Passionate opinions on teaching, learning, and living*. San Diego: Harcourt Brace.

Fox, M. (2001). *Reading magic: Why reading aloud to our children will change their lives forever*. New York: Harcourt.

Freire, P. (1973). *Education for critical consciousness*. New York: Continuum.

Garan, E. M. (2002). *Resisting reading mandates: How to triumph with the truth*. Portsmouth, NH: Heinemann.

Garan, E. M. (2004). *In defense of our children: When politics, profit, and education collide*. Portsmouth, NH: Heinemann.

Gilbert, L. (2005). What helps beginning teachers? *Educational Leadership, 62*(8), 36–39.

González, N., Moll, L., & Amanti, C. (Eds.). (2005). *Funds of knowledge: Theorizing practice in households, communities, and classrooms*. Mahwah, NJ: Lawrence Erlbaum.

Goodman, Y. M. (1978). Kid watching: An alternative to testing. *National Elementary Principal, 57*(4), 41–45.

Goodman, Y. M., Watson, D. J., & Burke, C. L. (1987). *Reading miscue inventory: Alternative procedures*. New York: Richard Owen.

Goodnough, A. (2004). *Ms. Moffet's first year: Becoming a teacher in America* New York: Public Affairs.

Graves, D. H. (2001). *The energy to teach*. Portsmouth, NH: Heinemann.

Gregory, E., Long, S., & Volk, D. (Eds.). (2004). *Many pathways to literacy: Young children learning with siblings, grandparents, peers, and communities*. New York: RoutledgeFalmer.

Hankins, K. H. (2003). *Teaching through the storm: A journal of hope*. New York: Teachers College Press.

Harste, J. C., Leland, C., Schmidt, K., Vasquez, V., & Ociepka, A. (2004). Practice makes perfect, or does it? The relationship between theory and practice in teacher education [Electronic Version]. *Reading Online, 7*(4). Retrieved October 18, 2005, from http://www.readingonline.org/articles/art_index.asp?HREF=harste/index.html

Hayes, I. (Ed.). (1998). *Great beginnings: Reflections and advice for new English language arts teachers and the people who mentor them*. Urbana, IL: National Council of Teachers of English.

Heard, G. (1999). *Awakening the heart: Exploring poetry in elementary and middle school*. Portsmouth, NH: Heinemann.

Hindley, J. (1996). *In the company of children*. York, ME: Stenhouse.

hooks, b. (2003). *Teaching community: A pedagogy of hope*. New York: Routledge.

Hubbard, R. S., & Power, B. M. (1999). *Living the questions: A guide for teacher-researchers*. York, ME: Stenhouse.

Ingersoll, R. M. (2002). High turnover plagues schools. *USA Today.* Retrieved February 2, 2006, from http://www.usatoday.com/usatonline/20020815/4362653s.htm

Irvine, J. J. (2003). *Educating teachers for diversity: Seeing with a cultural eye*. New York: Teachers College Press.

Jacobson, T. (2003). *Confronting our discomfort: Clearing the way for anti-bias in early childhood*. Portsmouth, NH: Heinemann.

Johnson, S. M. (2004). *Finders and keepers: Helping new teachers survive and thrive in our schools*. San Francisco: Jossey-Bass.

Kane, P. R. (Ed.). (1991). *My first year as a teacher*. New York: Signet.

Karp, S. (2004). NCLB's selective vision of equality: Some gaps count more than others. In D. Meier & G. Wood (Eds.), *Many children left behind* (pp. 53–65). Boston: Beacon Press.

Kelley, L. M. (2004). Why induction matters. *Journal of Teacher Education, 55*(5), 438–48.

Kohn, A. (1999). *Punished by rewards: The trouble with gold stars, incentive plans, A's, praise, and other bribes*. Boston: Houghton Mifflin.

Kohn, A. (2000). *The case against standardized testing: Raising the scores, ruining the schools*. Portsmouth, NH: Heinemann.

Kozol, J. (2005a). Confections of Apartheid: A stick-and-carrot pedagogy for the children of our inner-city poor. *Phi Delta Kappan, 87*(4), 264–75.

Kozol, J. (2005b). *The shame of the nation: The restoration of apartheid schooling in America*. New York: Crown.

Krashen, S. (2003). *The power of reading: Insights from the research*. Englewood, CO: Libraries Unlimited.

Ladson-Billings, G. (1994). *The dreamkeepers: Successful teachers of African American children*. San Francisco: Jossey-Bass.

Ladson-Billings, G. (2001). *Crossing over to Canaan: The journey of new teachers in diverse classrooms*. San Francisco: Jossey-Bass.

McCann, T. M., Johannessen, L. R., & Ricca, B. P. (2005). *Supporting beginning English teachers: Research and implications for teacher induction*. Urbana, IL: National Council of Teachers of English.

Meier, D. (1995). *The power of their ideas: Lessons for America from a small school in Harlem*. Boston: Beacon Press.

Meier, D. (2002). *In schools we trust: Creating communities of learning in an era of testing and standardization.* Boston: Beacon Press.

Meier, D. (2004). NCLB and democracy. In D. Meier & G. Wood (Eds.), *Many children left behind* (pp. 66–78). Boston: Beacon Press.

Mills, H., & Donnelly, A. (Eds.). (2001). *From the ground up: Creating a culture of inquiry.* Portsmouth, NH: Heinemann.

Mills, H., with Jennings, L. B., Donnelly, A., & Mueller, L. Z. (2001). When teachers have time to talk: The value of curricular conversations. *Language Arts, 79,* 20–28.

Mills, H., O'Keefe, T., & Jennings, L. B. (2004). *Looking closely and listening carefully: Learning literacy through inquiry.* Urbana, IL: National Council of Teachers of English.

Morgan, D., Saylor-Crowder, K., Stephens, D., Donnelly, A., DeFord, D., & Hamel, E. (2003). Managing the complexities of a statewide reading initiative. *Phi Delta Kappan, 85*(2), 139–45.

Moustafa, M. (1997). *Beyond traditional phonics: Research discoveries and reading instruction.* Portsmouth, NH: Heinemann.

Moustafa, M., & Land, R. E. (2002). The reading achievement of economically-disadvantaged children in urban schools using *Open Court* vs. comparably disadvantaged children in urban schools using non-scripted reading programs. Retrieved February 2, 2006, from http://instructional1/calstatela.edu/mmoustafa/the reading achievement of economically-disadvantaged children in urban schools

National Commission on Teaching and America's Future. (2002). Unraveling the "teacher shortage" problem: Teacher retention is the key. Retrieved February 2, 2006, from http://www.nctaf.org/documents/nctaf/Unraveling_Shortage_Problem.doc

Newkirk, T. (Ed.). (1992). *Workshop 4, by and for teachers: The teacher as researcher.* Portsmouth, NH: Heinemann.

Nieto, S. (2003). *What keeps teachers going?* New York: Teachers College Press.

Nieto, S. (2004). *Affirming diversity: The sociopolitical context of multicultural education* (4th ed.). Boston: Allyn and Bacon.

Nieto, S. (Ed.). (2005). *Why we teach.* New York: Teachers College Press.

O'Keefe, T. (1997). The habit of kidwatching. *School Talk, 3*(2), 4–5.

Ostrow, J. (1995). *A room with a different view: First through third graders build community and create curriculum.* York, ME: Stenhouse.

Peterson, R. (1992). *Life in a crowded place: Making a learning community.* Portsmouth, NH: Heinemann.

Peterson, R., & Eeds, M. (1990). *Grand conversations: Literature groups in action.* New York: Scholastic.

Ray, K. W. (1999). *Wondrous words: Writers and writing in the elementary classroom.* Urbana, IL: National Council of Teachers of English.

Ray, K. W., with Laminack, L. L. (2001). *The writing workshop: Working through the hard parts (and they're all hard parts)*. Urbana, IL: National Council of Teaching of English.

Rosenblatt, L. M. (1994). *The reader, the text, the poem: The transactional theory of the literary work*. Carbondale: Southern Illinois University Press.

Routman, R. (1996). *Literacy at the crossroads: Crucial talk about reading, writing, and other teaching dilemmas*. Portsmouth, NH: Heinemann.

Routman, R. (2000). *Conversations: Strategies for teaching, learning, and evaluating*. Portsmouth, NH: Heinemann.

Sacks, P. (1999). *Standardized minds: The high price of America's testing culture and what we can do to change it*. Cambridge, MA: Perseus Books.

Sacks, J. (2002). *The dignity of difference: How to avoid the clash of civilizations*. New York: Continuum.

Salas, K. D., Tenorio, R., Walters, S., & Weiss, D. (2004). *The new teacher book: Finding purpose, balance, and hope during your first years in the classroom*. Milwaukee, WI: Rethinking Schools.

Schultz, K. (2003). *Listening: A framework for teaching across differences*. New York: Teachers College Press.

Short, K. G., Harste, J. C., & Burke, C. (1996). *Creating classrooms for authors and inquirers* (2nd ed.). Portsmouth, NH: Heinemann.

Short, K. G., & Pierce, K. M. (Eds.). (1998). *Talking about books: Literature discussion groups in K–8 classrooms*. Portsmouth, NH: Heinemann.

Short, K. G., et al. (1996). *Learning together through inquiry: From Columbus to integrated curriculum*. York, ME: Stenhouse.

Sleeter, C. E. (2001). Preparing teachers for culturally diverse schools: Research and the overwhelming presence of whiteness. *Journal of Teacher Education, 52*(2), 94–106.

Smith, F. (1995). *Between hope and havoc: Essays into human learning and education*. Portsmouth, NH: Heinemann.

Smith, F. (1997). *Reading without nonsense*. New York: Teachers College Press.

Smith, F. (2003). *Unspeakable acts, unnatural practices: Flaws and fallacies in "scientific" reading instruction*. Portsmouth, NH: Heinemann.

Smith, K., & Hudelson, S. (2001). The NCTE Reading Initiative: Politics, pedagogy, and possibilities. *Language Arts, 79*(1), 29–37.

Villegas, A. M., & Lucas, T. (2002). Preparing culturally responsive teachers: Rethinking the curriculum. *Journal of Teacher Education, 53*(1), 20–32.

Volk, D., & Long, S. (2005). Challenging myths of the deficit perspective: Honoring children's literacy resources. *Young Children, 60*(6), 12–19.

Vygotsky, L. (1978). *Mind in society: The development of higher psychological processes*. Cambridge, MA: Harvard University Press.

Weaver, C. (1994). *Reading process and practice: From socio-psycholinguistics to whole language* (2nd ed.). Portsmouth, NH: Heinemann.

Weaver, C. (2002). *Reading process and practice: From socio-psycholinguistics to whole language* (3rd ed.). Portsmouth, NH: Heinemann.

Whitin, D. J., & Wilde, S.(1992). *Read any good math lately? Children's books for mathematical learning, K–6.* Portsmouth, NH: Heinemann.

Wolcott, H. F. (1994). *Transforming qualitative data: Description, analysis, and interpretation.* Thousand Oaks, CA: Sage.

Wood, G. (2004). A view from the field: NCLB's effects on classrooms and schools. In D. Meier & G. Wood (Eds.), *Many children left behind.* Boston: Beacon Press.

Zentella, A.C. (Ed.). (2005). *Building on strength: Language and literacy in Latino families and communities.* New York: Teachers College Press.

☙

This book was typeset in Palatino and Helvetica by Electronic Imaging.
Typefaces used on the cover included Helvetica Compressed, Trajan,
and Shannon Book and Bold.
The book was printed on 50-lb. Williamsburg Offset paper by Versa Press, Inc.